CONTENTS

WHAT IS A KIT INTERIOR?

As an auto trim specialist, I began my career by making my own seat covers and door panels because there were only a few seat cover sets available, and they were not made very well. If you ask anyone who has purchased and installed a prefabricated interior what they thought of the fit and finish, most would say that they would never buy one again. Why? It's because the individual components of a reproduction kit do not fit as well as the original covers and panels that came from the original manufacturer.

The seat covers have many issues with the materials that are used and the actual tailoring of the seat cover. Patterns used in manufacturing vary greatly among manufacturers, and the fitment is not standard for the different models that are offered. Another problem with so many of the upholstery products offered is the poor quality of the materials.

Not all of these reproductions are as accurate as they could be. Some seat covers fit better than others, as with door panels and other interior pieces. There are also issues with the embossed patterns on the panels. Some are sharp and clear, while others have been known to lift from the backing material. A few manufacturers use their own version of the original-style patterns, and what they produce does not fit as well as it could. Some of the material choices used in

the manufacturing process are not the correct factory grain or color and are not as durable as they should be.

Until now, it was the opinion of others that swayed the buyer on what to purchase and where to purchase the new materials for their project. These opinions were often harsh and unjustified for many reasons. What I have found is that a majority of the aftermarket products were just poorly installed, which is no fault of the maker. Problems encountered with a product should be discussed with the manufacturer without making a disparaging post online.

So, what are the best products to use and where do you get them? Well, I just do not have a good answer for that. There are too many variables, and there are no guarantees on the results you will get upon installation of a premanufactured interior component. I have installed many different products supplied to me by my customers and have made them work. I know firsthand that there can be problems with mail-order items.

There are many reasons why a car owner would buy a reproduction interior product. One reason is because they are much easier for restoring a car and less costly to obtain than to have an interior made from scratch by a professional auto upholsterer. Another reason is because many interiors have complex embossed

patterns in the vinyl panels that cannot be replicated by sewing the design into the upholstery. The biggest factor is that many restorations are performed because of the love of the car, and the owner wants to do as much hands-on work as possible. Unfortunately, most restorers do not have all the skills or knowledge that they wish they had.

Installer Error

A lot of misinformation has been dumped on prefabricated kit interiors and their manufacturers for many years, which gave them a bad reputation.

The common problem with prefabricated interior kits is that most people do not know how to install them correctly. There are a lot of little tricks to get the cover to fit well and look good. As a trimmer, it has always been my job to install interior components wrinkle-free and have them look as if they were originally installed at the factory. I will show you how to get the best fit and finish on a kit interior with the least amount of trouble.

My aim is to provide you with the confidence to install a prefabricated interior, tips to overcome some of the most basic installation problems, and knowledge to help you complete your project with exceptional results.

HOW TO INSTALL
AUTOMOTIVE
INTERIOR KITS

Fred Mattson

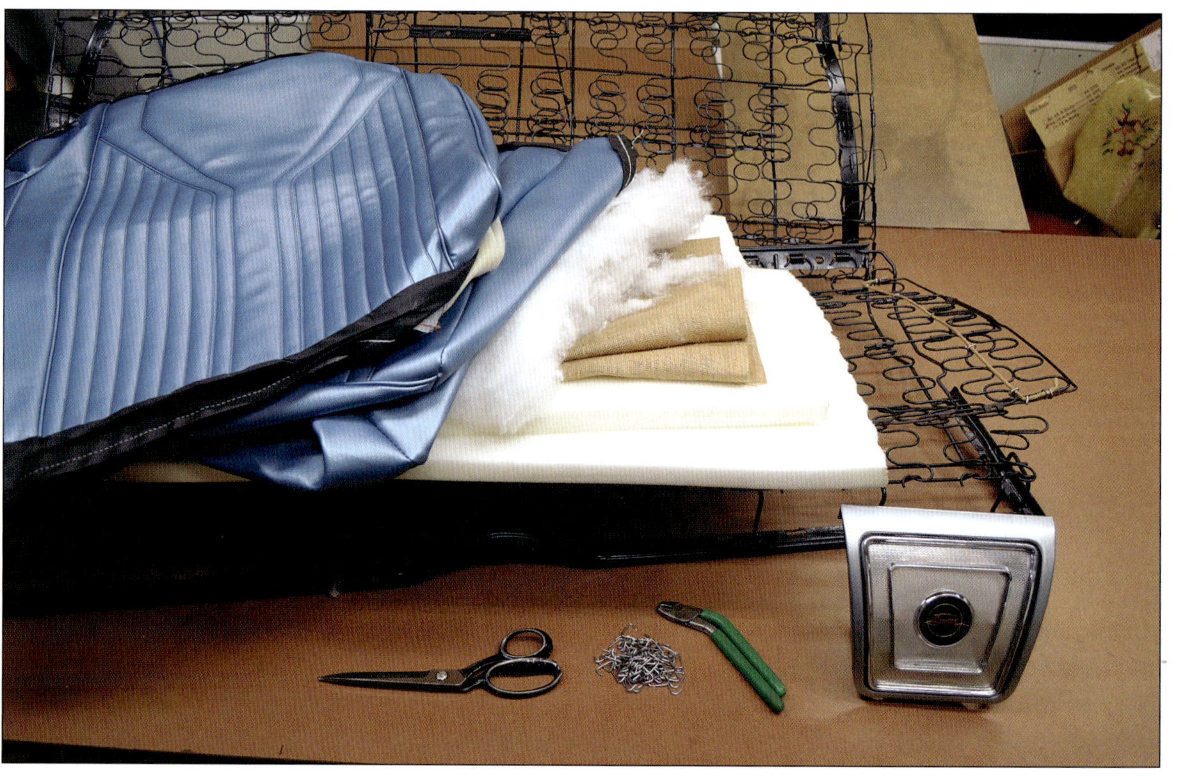

CarTech®

CarTech®

CarTech® Inc.
838 Lake Street South
Forest Lake, MN 55025
Phone: 651-277-1200 or 800-551-4754
Fax: 651-277-1203
www.cartechbooks.com

Edit by Wes Eisenschenk
Layout by Monica Seiberlich

ISBN 978-1-61325-526-1
Item No. SA475

Library of Congress Cataloging-in-Publication Data

Names: Mattson, Fred, 1960- author.
Title: Installing automotive interior kits / Fred Mattson.
Description: Forest Lake, MN : CarTech, Inc., [2021] | "Item no. SA475."
Identifiers: LCCN 2021058704 | ISBN 9781613255261 (paperback)
Subjects: LCSH: Automobiles–Interiors. | Automobiles–Upholstery. | Automobiles–Parts–Installation.
Classification: LCC TL256 .M385 2021 | DDC 629.2/6–dc23
LC record available at https://lccn.loc.gov/2021058704

Written, edited, and designed in the U.S.A.
Printed in China
10 9 8 7 6 5 4 3 2 1

DISTRIBUTION BY:

Europe
PGUK
63 Hatton Garden
London EC1N 8LE, England
Phone: 020 7061 1980 • Fax: 020 7242 3725
www.pguk.co.uk

Australia
Renniks Publications Ltd.
3/37-39 Green Street
Banksmeadow, NSW 2109, Australia
Phone: 2 9695 7055 • Fax: 2 9695 7355
www.renniks.com

Canada
Login Canada
300 Saulteaux Crescent
Winnipeg, MB, R3J 3T2 Canada
Phone: 800 665 1148 • Fax: 800 665 0103
www.lb.ca

MANUFACTURERS

Many independent manufacturers of restoration interiors and classic car parts go into the business because of their personal love of the automobile. Most of these individuals found that there just were too few new old stock (NOS) parts available to repair their prize car. This gave them the initiative to create new parts that were missing from the marketplace.

These innovators grew businesses that have made the automobile restoration hobby stronger, better, and safer. Over the years, the premade and restoration market has improved its capabilities and is now capable of making exact replicas of the factory original components. The seat covers and door panels are tailored to fit and look as good as or better than the originals. Hard-to-find pieces are also available due to the demand for high-quality parts that would otherwise not be obtainable.

Auto Custom Carpet

When looking for automotive floor coverings, Auto Custom Carpet (ACC) is by far the leading provider of OEM-style carpet. It has a rich history and has grown by acquiring other companies from 1977 to the company that it is today. It employs over 150 workers in Alabama and Georgia.

Carpet sets can be made from seven of the original carpet materials used by the manufacturer in many color choices with different padding options. ACC also produces custom floor mats that can be embroidered with more than 230 licensed logos. Vinyl flooring and trunk liners are also offered in different patterns to fit your car.

All of these labels were removed from premade seat covers that had manufacturing or fitment issues. When I custom tailor the seat cover to fit correctly, I remove the identification tag because it is no longer an original reproduction from that manufacturer.

A true leader in automotive flooring, Auto Custom Carpets offers over 40,000 flooring applications for vehicles built from the 1940s to present day. Original-style carpet and accessories are made to order in hundreds of color options and embroidered logos to complement your project. (Photo Courtesy Auto Custom Carpet)

Cars Inc.

Some of the most popular cars being restored today are the Tri-Five Chevys. One source for authentic parts and reproduction interior pieces is Cars Inc. The company's facility is located in Rochester Hills, Michigan, which is a northern suburb of Detroit.

From its beginning in 1976, the business evolved by collecting NOS parts from local Chevy dealership shelves, taking the rare parts to auto swap meets, and reselling them to other car enthusiasts who were desperate to get their hands on these much-needed pieces. As requests for replacement panels grew, Cars Inc. began making its own replacement panels and interiors to sell.

Over the years, Cars Inc. has grown into an over-65,000-square-foot facility that produces and sells more than 30,000 different restoration parts for the classic Chevy market.

Ciadella Interiors

Who knew that a man with a love for old Chevys would become the innovator of premade interiors for some of the most sought-after cars in the world? When you hear someone needing an interior for a Tri-Five Chevy you must automatically think of Pete Ciadella.

After re-establishing itself in 2009, Ciadella Interiors now operates in a facility in Tempe, Arizona. Some of his original craftsmen have over 25 years of dedicated service in making original and custom interiors for your classic Chevy. Seat covers, door panels, and trim pieces are all made from original patterns with exact reproductions of the original fabrics and vinyl to bring your interior back to life.

Distinctive Industries

One of the oldest manufacturers of prefabricated interiors for American muscle cars emerged out of Santa Monica, California, in 1969. Distinctive Industries began as a trim shop that made OEM seat covers and door panels for many of the favorite models at that time.

Distinctive Industries started making replacement interior components in 1969 from a small auto upholstery shop in Santa Monica. Today, it has expanded to create OEM seat covers and door panels for some of the most popular collector cars in the country. (Photo Courtesy Distinctive Industries)

Cars Inc. has been providing performance and high-quality restoration parts for Tri-Five and classic Chevys for more than 43 years. Authentic handcrafted seat covers, door panels, and full interiors components are made by skilled craftsmen in house at the facility in Rochester Hills, Michigan. (Photo Courtesy Cars Inc.)

Pete Ciadella was best known for his passion with the Tri-Five Chevys. As one of the first in the industry to produce ready-made restoration seat covers and door panels, Pete worked with original patterns and grew his business by making some of the finest handcrafted original and custom Chevy interior pieces available. (Photo Courtesy Ciadella Interiors)

Continued growth and expansion led to innovations that are used today. These replica interiors are produced with digital cutting machines, and they are sewn to equal the originals in detail by matching techniques and materials that satisfy the needs of today's hobbyists. Additional patterns and products are being developed all the time to meet the needs of the auto enthusiast.

You can see all of the products available by visiting the online catalog located on the Distinctive Industries website. To obtain authentic Ford and GM interior components for your project, you will need to purchase them through one of Distinctive Industries' many distributors.

Legendary Auto Interiors is based in New York and has grown to be the premier maker of classic Chrysler and Dodge interior upholstery in the industry. It also offers a wide selection of GM and AMC interior pieces and produces a line of custom rubber floor mats. (Photo Courtesy Legendary Auto Interiors)

Legendary Auto Interiors

From a modest beginning in 1979, the vision to fill the needs of auto enthusiasts has evolved and grown from producing Mustang, Chevelle, and Camaro interiors to an empire that produces some of the most sought-after restoration interiors in America.

The primary focus of the business changed to creating Mopar soft trim products in 1984. By recognizing the demand for Chrysler, Dodge, and Plymouth interiors, Legendary added more full-time employees to meet the requests of customers.

By the early 1990s, a new facility was constructed, and Legendary Interiors expanded its product line to include more models and options. The television and movie industries began to use Legendary Interiors in their productions because they recognized a need for authentic restoration interiors.

Metro Moulded Parts Inc.

For more than 100 years, Metro Moulded Parts Inc. has made some of the best automotive rubber products you can get from its manufacturing facility in Minnesota. Its Metro SuperSoft brand keeps the weather out and will last years longer than other foreign-made hard rubber products. (Photo Courtesy Metro Moulded Parts Inc.)

The Hutchinson Rubber Company began as an auto innertube manufacturer in 1918. At the beginning of World War II, founder John Hajicek began to make rubber parts for the military. When the war ended, the company moved to Minneapolis

Since 1977, Parts Unlimited Inc. has supplied quality interior pieces at the fairest cost to the consumer. Seat covers and foam, door panels, headliners, sun visors, and window sweeps are all made available from its facility in Kentucky for you to restore your classic car or truck. (Photo Courtesy Parts Unlimited)

to make custom-molded intricate industrial parts.

John's son, Donald Hajicek, started the restoration of an L29 Cord in 1962, only to discover that restoration parts for classic cars other than Fords were hard to come by. Donald took it upon himself to make molds and create the parts he needed for his restoration and began advertising the parts in *Hemmings Motor News*. The response from customers was overwhelming with requests for more items. Accepting the challenge, the company grew into the modern manufacturing facility it is today.

Most people do not think about all those rubber bumpers used to cushion glove box doors or seat backrests. Being able to keep the weather out is why a quality convertible top roof rail set is a reason to visit Metro Moulded Parts Inc.

PUI Interiors

A leader in the automotive restoration parts industry, Parts Unlimited Inc. Interiors (PUI) began producing interior components in 1977. Located in La Grange, Kentucky, PUI Interiors creates an extensive collection of authentic reproduction seat covers, door panels, and headliners.

With in-house manufacturing capabilities and vast experience, PUI Interiors has been able to offer restoration products to the automotive hobbyist at modest prices, while maintaining quality control. Because PUI Interiors is committed to the industry, it stands behind its products, and that is what makes it a great company.

Trim Parts

When it comes to obtaining the highest quality restoration parts for your project, consider the items available from Trim Parts. What makes the products from Trim Parts better is that the company is licensed to manufacture authentic reproductions of GM and Mopar parts. This means you are getting a new part that meets or exceeds the original manufacturers specifications.

All the detail of cast emblems, door handles, and other interior pieces are going to fit and perform just like the originals. These parts are made with pride in America and usually cost less than the Chinese knockoffs that do not perform like you would like them to.

Putting your car back together with parts that look nice and perform well is the key to a great restoration. Trim Parts has been reproducing authentic emblems, sill plates, lenses, and more for over 40 years. Everyone knows that when it comes to quality, it's all in the fine details. (Photo Courtesy Trim Parts)

PARTS AND **A**CCESSORIES

Many car enthusiasts begin their search for replacement parts and accessories by combing the local swap meets and junkyards. These sources are not very convenient and do not always have the pieces you need. If and when you find that rare gem that you desperately need, it is usually not in the best condition to install on your car. And so, the search continues.

Box Houses

Before the internet dominated the marketplace, there were the go-to catalog sources to order parts. Fingerhut and JC Whitney pioneered and once ruled the mail-order business for automotive products. These companies sent out catalogues that offered auto parts and accessories that you just could not get at your local auto parts store. Innovation and customer feedback helped propel the mail-order business into the industry it is today.

Searching for parts at a swap meet is not only a challenge but it is also a great way to enjoy an afternoon. You can pick up some real bargains, but you need a lot of patience and must be willing to devote a lot of time to find the parts you really need.

Protective seat covers are stylish and very practical. Fingerhut started its business by providing these low-cost seat covers to motorists to preserve the upholstery in their new cars. The slip-on design made the cover an easy-to-install project for the consumer.

Fingerhut

The Fingerhut empire got its start in 1948 by selling automobile seat covers out of a Minneapolis garage run by William Fingerhut. William's family's sewing business produced the slip-over seat covers that were, in turn, sold to his brother, Manny, who was the manager at a used car lot. The seat covers were designed for the protection and preservation of the upholstery in the car. The Fingerhut brothers and their employees had annual gross sales of nearly $100,000 in their first few years in business.

After working the local car dealer market, they sold thousands of their seat covers all over the country. This eventually led to the expansion of Fingerhut into a major mail-order catalog company that sells everything from household goods to power tools.

JC Whitney

For a company that started business as a scrap metal yard, JC Whitney grew a catalog business built on hard parts. Founded by Israel Warshawsky, the car parts mogul began with small advertisements in the classified sections of *Popular Mechanics* and *Popular Science* magazines. The 1950s and 1960s showed great expansion of the company as the JC Whitney catalog provided low-cost parts to budget-minded enthusiasts to keep their hot rods on the road.

As the parts industry changed, companies like eBay and Amazon began to dominate the marketplace. Roy, Israel's son who took over the company from his father, retired from JC Whitney in 1991 and died in 1997. The business was sold to Riverside Company in 2002. Eventually the name of JC Whitney was used as a storefront for the new owner, US Auto Parts.

Modern Box Houses

Today, anyone with an internet connection or cell phone can order just about any part necessary to complement his or her project. The unfortunate reality of this scenario is that box houses do not always have what you need, and they do not always speak the same language as you.

By this, I mean that you are a dedicated car enthusiast, and they are just there to take an order. They do not always have the time to get all the facts, and some vendors do not care if the parts you order will be compatible with the car you are restoring. It is your responsibility to know as much as you can about the car you are working on. To avoid lost time and aggravation from returning parts that are wrong for your car, you must know exactly what you need and how the part will work with the car you have.

Unfortunately, the box houses do not have everything necessary to complete your project. Every project will require some necessary parts and items that are not available through an online supplier, but they can often be obtained from an upholstery supplier.

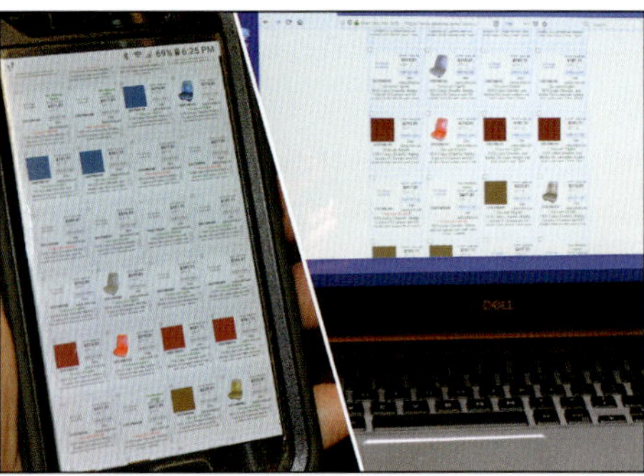

In the old days, if you needed parts or accessories, you would visit the local auto parts store or place an order from a mail-order catalog. Today all you need is a computer or smart phone to browse and order the items you need for your project.

Setting Up an Account

Before you place an order for any restoration parts, you need to know the year, make, model, and bodystyle of the vehicle. To gain an advantage with any vendor, create an account with them. The benefits of establishing an account will help you check out faster and track the status of your orders. Other perks that vendors extend to registered buyers are discounts and special email offers.

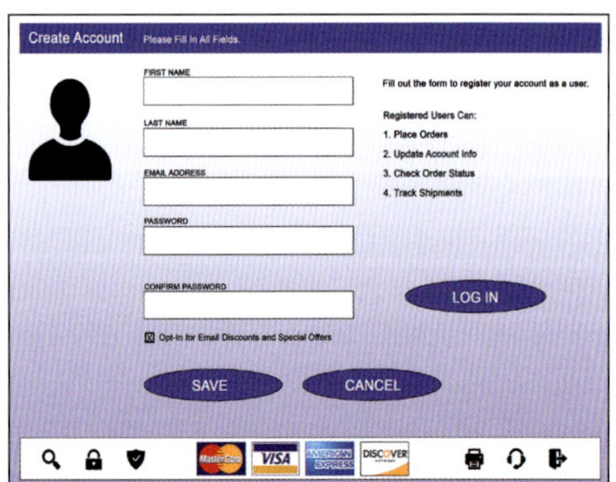

Ordering parts online is much easier when you have an account with the vendor. The application process takes only a few minutes and can save you time and money when you opt in for email specials. Always verify that you are on a secure page when entering your personal information.

For many years, JC Whitney has published catalogs filled with thousands of parts and accessories for the repair and restoration of motor vehicles. Although the printed catalogs are no longer being distributed, you can still view and order from its online catalog.

    INSTALLING AUTOMOTIVE INTERIOR KITS

The registration process typically consists of submitting your name, address, email, and the make and model of the car on which you are working. This information helps the vendor process your order and flags mis-ordered items by verifying that the products you ordered will fit your project.

Placing an Order

To save time, make a list of the items you need by searching the pages of the vendor catalog and browsing the website. With your list in hand, there are a few ways to order the parts. Many customers feel comfortable filling out the online form and submitting an order. This may be the simplest way to get a part or two, but if you have questions or any special requests, it may be to your benefit to call the vendor. If you are not sure if a piece will fit or you need to know if it is in stock, the operator will be able to assist you. You can also ask if the vendor has parts you need that may not be listed.

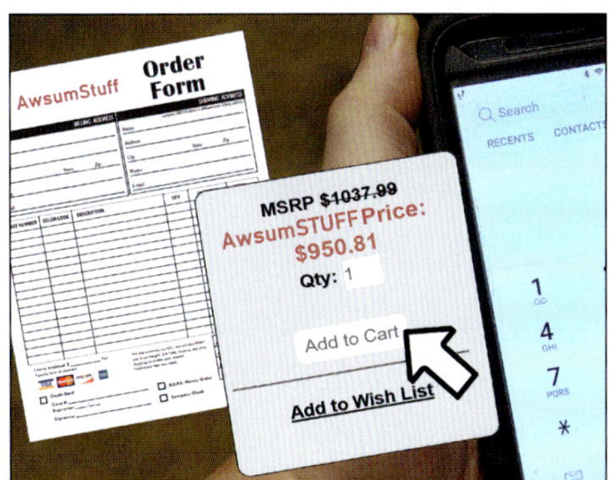

Placing an order can be as simple as making a phone call. If you are internet savvy, just click the "Add to Cart" button, and your parts are on their way. If you are old school, use the order form from the back of the vendor catalog. Just fill in the blanks, put a stamp on the envelope, and mail it in.

There are three major shipping services available to deliver your parts: United Parcel Service (UPS), Federal Express (FedEx), and the United States Postal Service (USPS). The cost will vary among them, but any one of these carriers will deliver a package to your front door.

Shipping Charges

One of the necessary evils of ordering items is shipping charges. Some vendors may offer free shipping on orders, which can save you a lot of money, so do not be alarmed to find out that shipping can get expensive.

Shipping is calculated by the size of the package and not necessarily by weight. Large items, such as seat foam, can weigh almost nothing. However, the cost to get it to your door can be almost as much as the item itself. Determining the actual cost of shipping can only be done after the item is packaged for delivery. Be aware that some box houses will assess shipping costs based on the price of an item. This can result in you overpaying to have the product shipped.

The best way to get your items shipped for less is for the seller to combine items together and send them in one box. This can save you a lot of money, but you have to ask them to do it. Also ask for the cost of United States Postal Service (USPS) over UPS and FedEx.

Other Charges

You can expect additional costs on a shipped package for handling, insurance, COD (cash on demand), and drop shipments. These charges are not standard and can be added to an order at the vendor's discretion for preparing a package. It is always a good practice to ask the vendor what the actual shipping costs will be before you finalize your order.

How to Pay

When shopping online, the items are placed in a virtual shopping cart. The cart will allow you to make changes by adding or deleting items. You can also enter any discount codes you may have and make corrections to your shipping information.

To complete the purchase, the vendor will ask you for a major credit card or PayPal account to pay for the products you ordered. Check your browser to make sure that it is on a

All your parts will need to be prepaid with a major credit card before the vendor will fill the order. Some vendors also accept other types of payment, such as personal checks or cash on delivery (COD). These orders may have restrictions or additional charges depending on the payment method.

secure page before you enter any personal or financial information. If you are not comfortable with entering your card information online, you can place your order by calling the vendor over the phone.

Returns or Exchanges

No one enjoys the process of returning an unwanted or defective part. The best way to avoid a return is to order the correct parts the first time. Although this is not always going to happen, knowing how to return or exchange a product will make the experience go smoother.

To correct a problem transaction, you must first understand the vendor's return policies. Do not assume that the vendor will just give you your money back; it is your responsibility to read and understand these procedures before you make an order for parts. It may also be your responsibility to pay the return shipping charges on an item.

When you need to return a part for any reason, it is best to contact the customer service department and ask for a return merchandise autho-

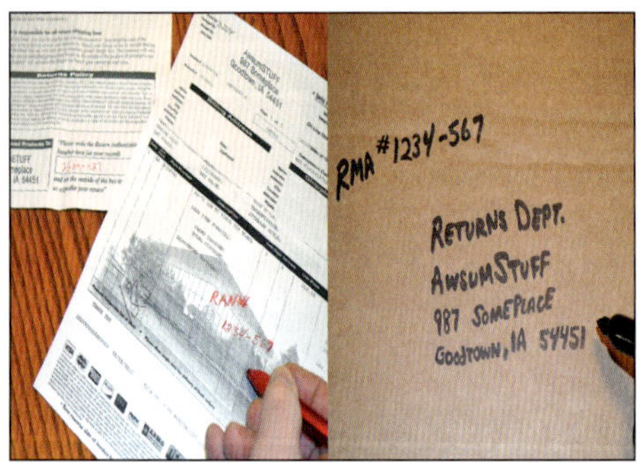

After you have given your order number and reason for a return to customer service, the representative will assign a return merchandise authorization number (RMA) to your account. This number should be written on the outside of the box and on a copy of the invoice placed inside the box.

Be Polite

The old saying of "You can catch more flies with honey than with vinegar" applies when requesting a return. Your attitude alone will make the process easier.

Speak calmly and respectfully when talking to the customer service representative, and above all, refrain from cussing and using bad language. I cannot express this point strongly enough. Be nice to the person on the other end of the phone. The customer service representative is just doing his or her job and wants to help you. You are not the only customer with which the customer service representative has dealt, and if you become upset and act rude toward him or her, you may not get the results you are looking for. Say thank you to the customer service representative for helping you, and be sincere. It will help the customer service representative, and you will also feel better.

rization (RMA) number and instructions on how to package and ship the part to them for a credit. Most vendors will not accept a package without prior authorization. Also when returning a package, request a tracking number to be assigned to the parcel. This number will allow you to follow the package's shipment and know when it arrives at the vendor.

Restocking Fees

Some vendors may offer a full refund, credit, or exchange if the product is returned within a specific period of time. After the grace period, be prepared to pay a restocking fee. These fees are typically 25 percent of the purchase price. The fee is assessed to cover some of the costs incurred by the vendor associated with handling and repackaging parts.

Damaged in Shipping

If a product arrives damaged, the vendor will most likely replace the item without any additional costs to you. Filing a damage claim is just part of doing business by mail order. You will need to contact the vendor immediately and provide as much

Not every package arrives in pristine condition, and it can be very upsetting to see a box in this condition laying on your doorstep. Always take photos of the damaged package before opening the box and before you contact the vendor with a claim to see how it wants you to proceed with any return.

information as you can by taking pictures of the item and filling out a damage claim form.

If the item is to be returned, the vendor will provide an RMA number and a return shipping tag to place on the box. Once the package is received, a replacement will be sent out. This process can take a few extra days to get the new item packaged and shipped. However, be patient. The vendor is trying to serve you the best that it can.

Original Parts Group Inc. (OPGI) is one of California's largest suppliers of classic General Motors parts. It has a great variety of catalogs that can be ordered. Each catalog contains many colorful pictures of parts, descriptions, and prices for each specific make and model of car. (Photo Courtesy Original Parts Group Inc.)

The Parts Place Inc. has a warehouse and showroom located in Dekalb, Illinois, that is stocked with thousands of parts you need for your car. The company employs car enthusiasts and hosts an open house and annual car show for its customers. (Photo Courtesy the Parts Place)

Original Parts Group Inc.

For more than 35 years, Original Parts Group Inc. (OPGI) has been manufacturing restoration parts and accessories for GM cars. The company originated in Santa Ana, California, in November 1982 and operated under the name "Chevelle Classics." The goal was to provide Chevelle and El Camino parts to collectors and repair centers.

Chevelle Classics changed its name to Original Parts Group Inc. in June 1990 and has a wide range of body and engine parts along with trim and upholstery products. You can see its vast selection of parts by going online and browsing the website. While you are there, order a catalog to view at home and sign up for special offers.

The Parts Place

A great source for restoration and replacement parts for cars and trucks can be found at The Parts Place. When you need something for your GM muscle car or a late-model car or truck, it will most likely be in stock and ready to ship from its 70,000-square-foot warehouse in Dekalb, Illinois.

Since its start in 1990, The Parts Place is now one of the largest suppliers of NOS, used, and reproduction parts in the country. Many of the parts it sells are made in-house, which allows the company to sell better-fitting parts for less.

The Parts Place stocks upholstery for many models and can ship it to you right away. Check its catalog or website for the parts that you need. You can also call and talk to a sales representative if you have questions or are unsure about any of its products.

Year One Inc.

With more than 30 years of supplying top-quality parts and supplies for the collector and restoration car industry, Year One Inc. has a catalog filled with great items for your project. You can check out its website or visit the Braselton, Georgia, parts counter to order the parts and accessories that you need to finish your muscle car.

If you have a question about a part, contact customer service by calling Monday through Friday from 9 a.m. to 6 p.m., or stop in the showroom between 10 a.m. and 5 p.m.

If you can't find what you need by searching the website, order one of the Year One Inc. catalogs and browse the pages to get what you want. Customer service is only a phone call away, and they are ready to take your order. (Photo Courtesy Year One)

MATERIALS

The interior components of a car are covered with many different materials to protect the passengers from the sharp underlying metal of the seat frames and inner structure of the cab. Each component of the interior must withstand the use and abuse that a car owner can inflict upon it. Selecting the right materials will not only add beauty but also enhance the comfort of the car.

Vinyl

Vinyl products are too often referred to as pleather, faux-leather, or Naugahyde, which is a brand of vinyl invented by U.S. Rubber in Naugatuck, Connecticut. All of these names (and others) refer to artificial leather. One of the most common materials that you will find in a car interior is vinyl. Automotive vinyl is often confused with real leather. The embossed grain on the surface of the vinyl is intended to mimic the look of genuine leather, but vinyl is used to cut the cost associated with real leather products.

The truth is that automotive vinyl is made from PVC (Poly Vinyl Chloride). Upholstery vinyl is manufactured with a knit backing that provides support and stretch to the material. The common width of vinyl goods is 54 inches and is available on 40-yard rolls. Cut yardage is available from most manufacturers

Not to be confused with natural leather, automotive vinyl was developed as a cost saver for auto manufacturers. The grain detail is intended to look like leather, but the colors and weather-repellent nature, along with the ability to be embossed with very detailed patterns, is what sets vinyl apart.

to make seat covers and door panels.

One notable feature of vinyl is the ability to repel water. This makes it a great choice for convertible interiors. Another advantage of vinyl is that it can be embossed with pleats and patterns. Embossing gives the seat cover and door panels a unique appearance that adds to the styling effect of the interior.

Genuine Leather

Nothing screams *luxury* more that genuine leather. The soft and supple

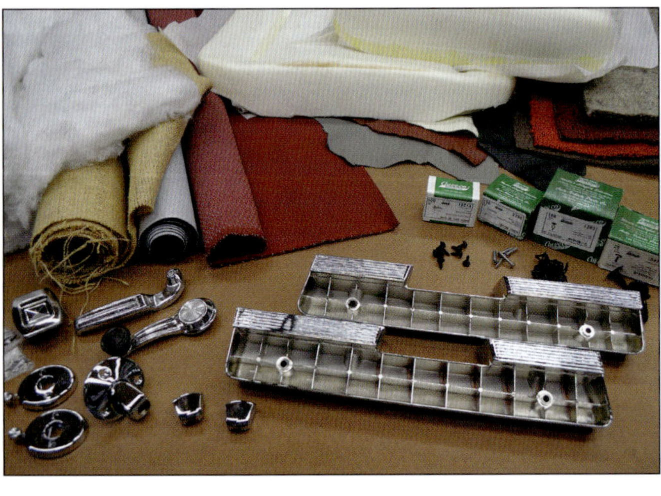

A variety of materials are used to make the interior components of a car attractive and comfortable. Some materials hold up better than others, and knowing what to look for is an advantage that will help you make better choices that will save you time and money.

Leather used in modern manufacturing is much softer and more luxurious than it used to be. More colors and textures are available to meet the demands of custom interior designers. The average size of a modern hide is about 50 square feet.

nature of the natural leather gives the interior of a car that premium look and feel, making it a perfect choice for use in many luxury cars. Before vinyl was perfected, leather was the most commonly used material for the interior of a car. The abundance of leather also made it a cost-effective choice over man-made materials. Leather was also an extremely durable material that comes from the hide of horses and cows. The natural ability of leather to repel moisture made it a natural choice for the early open cars.

In today's market, leather comes with a much higher price point than other interior upholstery choices due to the process of treating and dyeing the hides. With modern technology and production methods, the cost of producing textiles and vinyl-coated material has become much less than natural leather. Hides are also often plagued with flaws from natural hazards. Insects bites and barbed wire leave behind scars that mar the surface of the leather, and these blemishes can make working with leather difficult and drive up the cost of manufacturing.

Hides vary greatly in size but usually yield around 50 square feet of usable leather, which is the equivalent of 3½ yards of vinyl. The exact amount of useable leather on a hide cannot be determined due to cutting around the natural flaws that may be in the hide.

Body Cloth

Every era of manufacturing has had its distinct advantages for the interior coverings used on seat covers and side panels. Early-model cars used the natural fiber of wool as an upholstery material due to its durability. Wool is made from the fleece of sheep and goats. After the animal has been sheered, the fleece is cleaned, dyed, and can then be woven into many different patterns and textures.

As technology evolved, synthetic fibers were developed, bringing more color and design to interior fabrics. Nylon and polyester are great choices for automotive body cloth because of the durability and colorfast nature of the materials.

Body cloths used for auto interiors have changed over the years from the natural woven fibers made from animal fleece to intricately designed man-made synthetic hard cloth. Modern seat covers use soft plush fabrics in vibrant colors to enhance the comfort of the car's interior.

The width of woven goods produced range from the standard 54 inches and can be as wide as 65 inches or more, depending on the manufacturer. The stylish finished interiors were not only attractive but also more comfortable to sit on, which was in part due to the natural ability of the cloth material to breath.

Headliner Materials

The overhead fabric used to make a headliner needs to be strong and lightweight. Since gravity is a factor, heavy materials tend to sag and cause problems as they age. Brushed cotton fabric was a common choice for headliners for many of the pre–World War II cars until the early 1960s when a lighter-weight vinyl material was adapted for use as a headlining material.

Suspended headliners are supported by wire bows that hang the material from side to side as it is stretched from the windshield to rear window over the length of the roofline. Glue, staples, and metal

Over the years, the fabric used for head linings has changed from a brushed cotton to a knit synthetic fiber. One thing that has not changed about headliners is that the material remains lightweight as it complements the interior of the car without detracting from the beauty of the overall design.

retainers help hold the headliner to the outer edges of the cab.

In the mid-1970s, carmakers changed the design of headliners and began to use a solid shell-style liner to cover the inner roof. These shells were made of a thin polystyrene or compressed fiberglass material that was contoured to give a unique shape to the inner roof of the car. The material used to cover these seamless headliners was made of a knit polyester fabric that was bonded to a 1/4-inch foam backing material. The seamless design gave the cab a modern futuristic look and feel that is smooth and flowing.

Floor Coverings

Over the evolution of the automobile, a variety of materials have been used as automotive floor coverings. Manufacturing and technology played big rolls in the development of textiles from natural to synthetic fibers to protect and beautify the car floor.

Several options are available when it comes to dressing up the floor of a car. Early cars had little more than the wooden floor on which to rest one's feet. To quiet the cab, a parlor rug would be cut to fit and then tacked in place to keep it from sliding about. As the car evolved, so did the floor coverings.

Rubber Mats

Floor boards in an open car could only withstand so much exposure before they rotted away. Protecting the wood meant that a utilitarian non-slip surface was needed. Flat rubber matting was utilized as a surface that could repel the elements, and it was easy to clean. Eventually

Modern floor coverings available in a wide range of colors and textures can be obtained in custom-molded kits. These premolded carpet sets make great sense for the DIYer to get factory results when replacing the carpet in a car.

It was common for prewar cars to have a rubber mat covering the front section of the floor. This material choice, which was made by manufacturers, was due in part to the cost of the material. It was more practical, and woven carpet was reserved for the rear of the car.

form-fitted rubber mats were developed, but car owners wanted more comfort, and the rubber mat soon fell out of favor.

Carpet

Before synthetic fibers were created, natural fibers (such as wool) were used for auto carpet. The coarse woven material proved to be luxurious and durable. As the modern car evolved, so did textiles and manufacturing techniques. Modern carpet mills began to produce colorful and inexpensive carpet that could be formed to fit the contours of the stamped-metal floor of vehicles.

Many colors and styles of carpet are now available to blend with the modern interiors of today's cars.

Panels

Hard surfaces are covered by many different types of panels. These panels are not only decorative but they also conceal mechanical and electrical components, keeping them out of reach of fingers and harm. Over the years, the composition of these panels has changed, but their purpose has not.

Door Panels

The earliest door panels were simply cover plates made of steel, and they were held in place by sheet-metal screws. As interiors evolved, cardboard was used as a base material and wrapped in the matching upholstery fabric.

As cover material choices improved, so did the base materials and attachment methods. Cardboard was replaced with Masonite, which is a high-density waterproof panel board. Modern sculpted panels are now made from ABS plastic.

Kick Panels

Just as the name states, these are the forward panels that take the abuse of the front passenger's feet. Often, the kick panels will house the lower vent covers and controls. The paper versions of these panels often failed due to the abuse they received, and manufacturers began to mold them from ABS plastic to improve longevity.

Package Tray

This often-forgotten trim panel was originally made from a color-matched panel board. Since the package tray was located under the rear window, it was prone to water and sun damage due to failed window seals and UV rays.

Many package trays also suffered damage from the installation of additional speakers. Large holes were cut into the surface of the panel to accommodate speaker grilles.

Hardware

You couldn't build a car interior without an assortment of screws, clips, and staples. These special metal fasteners keep trim moldings and panels in place. The size and head type of screw fasteners can vary greatly, and they can be chrome

New original-style interior trim panels are available for many makes and models of American classic cars. Authentic reproductions of these door panels are offered as well as new molded kick panels. Rear package trays are also available to replace missing or damaged components.

Corrosion and temperature changes can cause damage to interior trim and fasteners. Chrome plating will wear from use, and pitting happens from high humidity and damp conditions. Left unchecked, moisture can ruin the appearance of the interior.

Chinese knockoff restoration parts do not always fit the way you want. Always look for a restoration part that carries a licensed and authorized certification seal issued by the original manufacturer to make sure the part looks right and fits correctly.

plated, painted, or phosphor coated to prevent corrosion.

Rusty, broken, and missing trim screws can now be easily replaced with original preplacement hardware, which are available from several sources. Some suppliers can also provide prepackaged master kits that include every fastener necessary to restore your car.

Many fasteners used in newer cars are made of plastic, and they are prone to breaking when they are removed. If a fastener breaks, it should be replaced with the correct size and type of fastener. Many of these original fasteners can be obtained from an upholstery supplier.

Hard Parts

Many interior handles and parts become pitted and damaged over time. The reconditioning and re-plating of these original parts can be done by many specialty shops, but this can be costly. A lower-cost alternative to restoration for many cars is done by obtaining new reproduction window cranks and trim moldings.

Many resources are available for these replacement and restoration parts, but not all of them measure up. Some reproduction parts are not made to the same specification as the originals, and these can be very frustrating to install. You really want to seek out the original-quality parts that are made by an authorized and licensed manufacturer. Factory-authorized dealers reproduce the new parts to meet or exceed the specifications of the original part. These parts fit better and match the worn pieces exactly. Surprisingly, they do not always cost more than the poor-quality knockoffs.

Rubber Seals

Keeping the water out requires rubber seals. These are the pieces found around door and trunk openings. Many older cars used a thick molded rubber piece around the window glass to hold it securely in place. As time passes by, these rubber seals dry out and fail, allowing water to get by, which leads to damaged upholstery and rusty metal.

Good rubber is soft, pliable, and does not crush or deform over time, allowing it to make a watertight seal. Poor-quality rubber is very hard, and it does not compress well. This prevents doors and lids from closing nicely, which leads to damage to the car by forcing the parts together. Always ask about the return policy on a rubber part if it is not correct or it does not perform as it should.

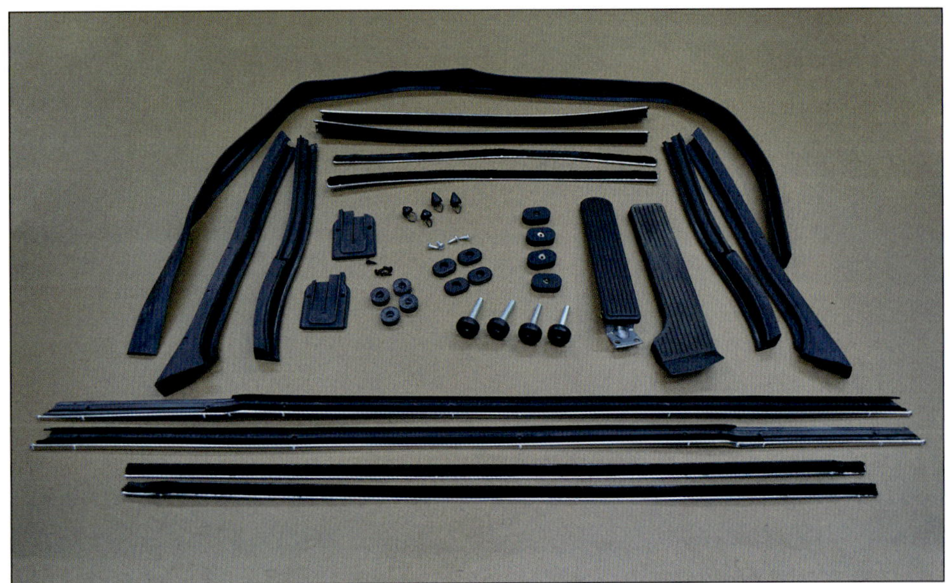

Reproduction rubber weather seals bring back the original look and feel of the car and restore the protection needed to keep water from entering the cab. High-quality rubber parts make a big difference in how a window or convertible top will perform.

TOOLS

Each and every upholstery project requires some hand tools to properly install the interior component. Many of these tools are most likely already in your tool box, but there are some specialty tools to acquire that will make the job easier and give you the finished result that will make your interior look like it was installed by a professional.

A simple socket set and ratchet is needed to remove the seats from the car. Standard SAE and metric sockets are available in 1/4-inch, 3/8-inch, and 1/2-inch drives. Six-point sockets are better for removing stubborn bolts because they will grip the head of a bolt better than a 12-point socket.

Wrenches

Combination wrenches are also helpful for installing and removing nuts and bolts. Having the option of an open-end or boxed-end wrench will allow you to get into tight places.

Screwdrivers

An assortment of screwdrivers is needed for the removal of hardware from the car. Various sizes and lengths of straight-blade screwdrivers along with multiple sizes of Phillips screwdrivers (#1, #2, and #3) will get you started.

Measuring Tools

Nothing beats a good a tape measure and an assortment of straightedge rulers to make accurate measurements of interior components. A basic carpenter's square is also a valuable tool for squaring up upholstery materials before it is cut.

Hog-Ring Pliers

If you are serious about installing a seat cover, obtain a good pair of hog-ring pliers. These are essential for securing a seat cover to the seat frame. However, be aware that not all hog-ring pliers are the same. They can vary greatly in performance.

Hog-ring pliers were created to cinch metal rings in the nose of pigs. The hog ring causes discomfort to the pig and discourages rooting. The

If you are working on your first project or plan to make a career out of auto trimming, choosing the right tools is a process that happens over time. It is not always a good idea to buy everything at once. You can gather tools as your experience and needs evolve.

Choosing the right hog-ring pliers is a personal choice on how they feel in your hand as you use them versus the results they yield. Here, you can see the difference in what a professional tool looks like compared to what the industry thinks passes for hog-ring pliers.

large size of agricultural pliers and composition of hog rings are not suited for upholstery purposes.

Many reproduction kits include a set of basic hog-ring pliers and some hog rings. The hog-ring pliers are usually made of 1/4-inch round stock joined by a rivet. They also tend to be smaller in size than a professional pair, which makes it difficult to use because the pliers do not provide enough handle length to adequately cinch the hog ring. The hog rings in these kits are also smaller in size and thickness and do not have the holding power needed to keep the seat cover in place.

Better-quality hog-ring pliers are made of stamped steel or cast iron. The stamped-steel pliers work well when they are new but tend to loosen up and get sloppy with a lot of use. Because of their bulky design, they eventually will not properly hold a hog ring, which makes the cinching process difficult.

Ultimately, a cast-iron or forged set of hog-ring pliers will last a lifetime. They are available with a vari-

ety of angled handles that will give you the ability to place a hog ring in a difficult place and then secure it without failing. The longer handles of the professional-grade tool make cinching a hog ring almost effortless. Better-quality pliers are made to last, although I have actually worn out a pair of C.S. Osborne hog-ring pliers after using them for more than 30 years. The investment in a quality tool has proven to be a good bet for me.

Scissors

There has been a lot of discussion about which brand of scissors is best for the auto upholstery trade. There is no simple answer because the end user must decide what works best for him or her. You can get by with a basic pair of scissors, but if you plan on doing any amount of trim work, you will want to consider obtaining a few different pairs.

Instead of stating a brand to purchase, I will explain the different types of scissors and their capabilities.

Household Scissors

These are lightweight scissors that are fitted with molded plastic handles. They work well if you want to clip coupons or an occasional recipe from a magazine, but the thin blades dull quickly and become uncomfortable to use when cutting heavy material or carpet. It is also difficult to have the scissors repaired or sharpened because the blades are riveted together.

Industrial Scissors

These are the heavy-duty cast scissors made for the upholstery trade. The forged-steel blades can hold an edge and are joined with a screw to allow the precision-ground

Cutting heavy material, such as carpet pad and panel board, requires a heavy-duty pair of scissors that can retain a cutting edge and also feel comfortable as it is used. Lightweight plastic-handled scissors are not designed to be used for auto upholstery fabrics and materials.

blades to be adjusted, which makes them a solid choice for auto upholstery. They come in different lengths with straight- or bent-handle models. The handles are designed to reduce fatigue on the user while cutting heavy materials. These scissors can cost $40 or more depending on the size and style of the blades.

Precision Shears

Hair dressers, manicurists, and surgeons use refined and balanced shears. They are called shears because they cut with great accuracy and without fatigue. They cost hundreds of dollars for a pair and can hold an edge for a long time. Their delicate composition is not suited for the upholstery trade.

Hammers

When it comes down to brute force, nothing beats a hammer to mash objects together. Every project requires a specific hammer to achieve a particular result. Having several different hammers will make the assembly process easier and provide better

Several types of hammers are used to aid in the installation and removal of interior trim. The most common hammer used in the trade is the magnetic tack hammer. Machinist hammers and dead-blow mallets are also used to help align and set fasteners on panels.

Fastening upholstery materials sometimes requires the use of a staple gun. These devices range in operation from a basic mechanical model to an electric or pneumatic model. Depending on your needs and budget, any one of them will accomplish the task they are required to do.

results when you use the right tool for the job.

Tack

Back in the day, upholstery was done with small blued tacks that were applied with a magnetic-tipped hammer. These hammers came in different styles to facilitate the different types of tacks used on a project.

Some tack hammers are magnetized to hold a tack. The ends of the hammer vary depending upon the function needed. Some hammer ends have split tips to set a tack, while the solid end is used to drive the tack fully into the work.

Other specialized hammers are designed for setting decorative tacks or stripping the old material from a frame to prep the project for a new covering.

Ball Peen

Generally, ball-peen hammers are known as a machinist hammer. The hardened surface of the rounded end of the hammer is designed not to leave marks on the surface of metal, which makes it perfect for metalwork. The hemispherical end of the

hammer is ideal for setting rivets and shaping metal. The ball-peen hammer is a great choice when working with a punch or chisel.

Machinist hammers are available in many sizes and weights. Whether you are working on lightweight materials or trying to free a stubborn part, they are a great tool for almost any project.

Dead Blow

For many years, I used a clenched fist to help set panel clips by striking the part with my hand. My doctor told me that this practice would eventually cause physical damage to my body. Well, he was right. I developed nerve damage, and now I use a dead-blow hammer for the assembly of car interiors.

Dead-blow hammers come in many different sizes to suit the work you need them for. A dead-blow hammer is made with a rubber or plastic outer casing and is uniquely designed with loose sand or steel shot encased inside the hammer head. When the hammer strikes an object, the loose internal material continues to drive forward, which adds additional force without exerting additional energy to swing the hammer. This makes working easier and less fatiguing without causing injury to your body or work surface.

Staple Guns

A staple gun is one of the must-have tools that every trimmer should own. There are many different types of staplers available, and choosing the correct one will depend on your budget and needs.

Purchase the best tool you can afford. With the amount of use that a stapler gets, a cheap staple gun

will most likely fail and leave you scrambling for another. A quality tool will perform well and last a very long time with the proper care and maintenance.

Manual

There is a wide variety of manual staple guns that range from light to heavy duty. They are spring-loaded, lever-action devices that are powered by squeezing a lever to eject a staple into the work. Some models have a tension option that gives the plunger of the stapler more push.

Manual staplers are good as an entry-level tool due to their lower cost. The biggest downside of a manual stapler is that they rely on physical effort to operate the lever, which tends to cause fatigue and limits the amount of work that can be done at one time.

Electric

An electric stapler is another option for assembling projects. Although these staplers are less fatiguing to the user, there are some things

---

to consider before purchasing one. The first thing is that it will cost a lot more money than any other type.

Light-duty electric staplers are not well suited for the upholstery trade. They are good for a hobbyist working on small projects, but the electromagnetic coil of the consumer-grade models is not built tough enough to endure the strain and prolonged use needed for larger projects.

Heavy-duty models are designed for the carpet and upholstery trades and can withstand continuous use without overheating and breaking down. They also have the power to drive staples deep into wood, plastic, and tack-strip materials.

One of the downsides of an electric stapler is the bulky size of the appliance. They tend to be heavy and awkward to operate, which makes them difficult to get into tight places. They also require a higher amperage outlet to operate properly without causing damage to the electromagnetic coil.

Pneumatic

Commonly referred to as an air stapler, these devices are real workhorses. They are typically slim in size and very lightweight. One great feature of the air stapler is the ability to adjust the amount of penetration of the staple by increasing or decreasing the air pressure.

The cost of a pneumatic stapler is generally about $150, but the big expense is the air compressor. Having an adequately sized air compressor is a good investment because it can be used to run a number of tools, as well as spraying glue.

Headliner Tuck Tools

It takes finesse to tension a suspended headliner, and having the right tool can make the job much easier. Many choices of tuck tools are available that can help you install a headliner, but the tool you use should be based on how it feels in your hand when working.

Curved-Blade Economy

One of the most basic tuck tools available is the curved-blade headliner tool. This tool is stamped from a single piece of metal. The blade's metal can be a little thick to get into tight places. The handle that is formed onto the tool may also be a bit too short for many users to hold onto, which makes the tool difficult to work with.

Premium

Most professionals prefer this type of tuck tool because of its blunt, square blade, which is much easier to use. Having a thinner blade makes manipulating headliner material a breeze. The wood handle of the tool also fits well in your hand, giving the user much more control and a better finished result.

This tool is available with a variety of blades for working on different projects. The standard tuck tool has a rigid blade for lifting thick

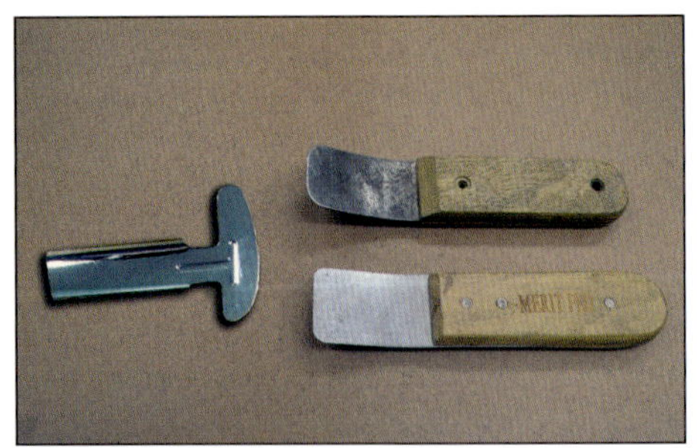

The small handle and curved blade on the economy tuck tool makes it hard to use. For a few more dollars, you can get a much better tool that will get the job done without hurting the headliner material or your hand.

rubber window seals. A thinner, flexible-blade version with rounded corners is used for tucking headliner material into tight places. The wide blade helps prevent material tear-out while allowing the material to be smoothed into position. Another version of this tool comes with a rounded, more triangular blade for finer detail work when building door panels.

Glue Guns

Many upholstery projects require glue to attach materials. Aerosol cans usually do not have the right type of glue needed for auto upholstery projects because the adhesive will not hold up to the high heat conditions associated with the interior of a car. Also, the application of glue is not thick enough to hold most materials in place. When sprayed from the can, a web pattern is created, which makes the glue dry out faster, spreads it very thin, and decreases its holding ability.

Different glues require specific application devices. Low-cost sprayers are available to apply adhesives in a controlled and even pattern. Hot glue guns require the appliance to be plugged into an electrical outlet, while cup guns need compressed air to function.

When working with auto interiors, glue can be applied with a brush or sprayed directly onto the surface of the piece that you are working on. Using a brush works well for small projects that require control over the amount of glue applied and the area that is covered.

Larger jobs, such as installing carpet, need a spray-gun delivery system to apply more volume when large areas need to be covered quickly and evenly. Many options are available for spraying glue, and each project dictates the best way to get the glue onto the materials.

Siphon Cup

When gluing foam or lightweight materials, a small siphon-cup sprayer works well. This type of spray gun has little in the way of spray-pattern adjustments. The simplicity of the device delivers adhesive by blowing compressed air across a pick-up tube that draws the glue from a screw-on refillable cup.

Spray Gun

Originally, spray guns were used to paint cars. This type of cup gun has fallen out of favor for painting, but they are great for spraying heavier vinyl top adhesives.

Many parts make up this type of sprayer. One of the most notable features of the spray gun is the air cap and needle valve. These components allow the spray pattern to be adjusted from a small spot to a wide fan. The amount of adhesive that is dispensed from the sprayer can also be adjusted depending on the size of the fluid needle and how much pressure is on the trigger. The 1-quart siphon cup is easy to detach and refill with glue.

Hot Glue

Anyone who has done craft work is familiar with hot glue. Solid glue sticks are inserted into the tool and heated until it is soft and fluid. When applied to the surface of the material to be glued, it creates an almost-instant bond.

Hot glue has many uses, but due to the nature of the adhesive, it is often too thick to use in the upholstery trade. Adding bulk to a seam can make a trim panel too big, which will rub on a mating surface and cause it to wear eventually, creating a hole in the panel.

Steamers

When it comes to fitting seat covers and removing wrinkles, a steamer is a go-to tool. There are many choices and types of steamers, but not all are designed for upholstery use. Low-cost units are not always a bargain. Some features you need to look for include a steam head that can get into any angle without spilling water on the upholstery. Small hand-held garment steamers do not have a very large water reservoir, and they may leak if turned sideways.

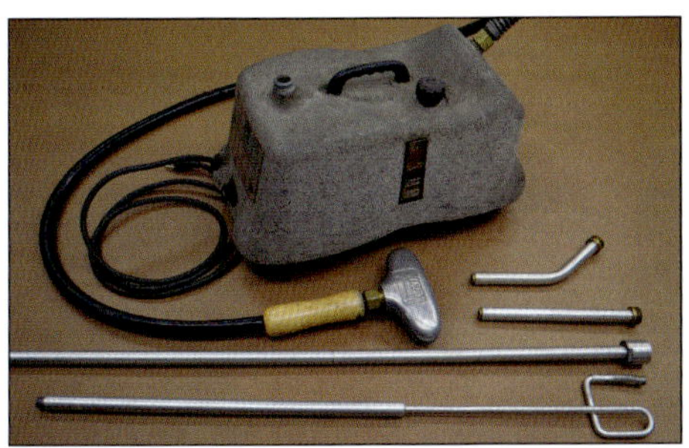

Obtaining a wrinkle-free finish can be simplified with a little steam. This professional-model steamer has interchangeable heads that allow it to be used for many different applications. Lower-cost units can give you good results but are more difficult to use.

Jiffy Steamers

Professional steamers cost a little more than light-duty steamers, but they perform better and can be repaired if a component fails. I have used the J4000A model made by Jiffy Steamer Company for many years. This model has a longer supply hose that has an interchangeable tool feature.

Professional tools are better suited for the upholstery trade. A flat iron steam head is used for removing wrinkles in seat covers and carpets. The pipe tool is handy for getting into the tight places of a convertible top frame to help remove wrinkles.

Heat Guns

There are many times when you need to warm up an interior component to soften the material so that it will fit better. This can be done with steam or a heat gun. Heat guns are powerful tools when they are used correctly. They can also cause a lot of damage if you are careless and overheat a part.

A heat gun is a very useful tool for removing small wrinkles or softening materials to make them conform. Small projects, such as heat shrinking or paint removal, can be accomplished with a simple heat gun. A professional model has variable heat settings and can be repaired if it wears out.

Not all heat guns are suitable for auto upholstery work. The best heat guns have replaceable heating elements and adjustable heat settings to allow the user to get the most out of the tool. Since most professional-grade tools are built better than light-duty tools, they can be serviced with new parts if they fail.

Light Duty

Upholstery materials can be warmed with a hair dryer, but they are not designed for the rugged use that an upholstery project can demand. Some heat guns have simple features that can get your material warm enough to work with but lack durability.

A basic heat gun may have one or two preset temperatures. These tools are good for small tasks, such as shrink-wrapping electrical connections or craft projects. Because they do not have a cooldown mode or a replaceable heating element, they are prone to failure when you need them most.

Professional

Better-quality tools are designed to withstand prolonged use without breaking down. These tools have an initial cost that is higher than a basic tool. However, they will save you money over the life of the tool.

A premium heat gun allows you to work larger areas with less effort. Because most professional-grade heat guns have variable heat controls, you can work more efficiently with less fatigue. One feature a heat gun should have is a fan-only mode to help the element cool down, which will prolong the life of the heating element.

Rivet Tools

Joining materials together is a big part of upholstery. Glue is often used

Pop rivets are an easy way to attach materials. Hand-operated setters are great for small jobs that only require a few squeezes to set a rivet. Tougher projects may require the use of a more versatile hydraulic tool that is capable of setting threaded inserts into worn or oversized anchor holes.

to assemble panels, but sometimes you need a stronger physical bond. Metals can be welded together, but you will often encounter dissimilar materials that cannot be welded or glued effectively. Joining these materials is best done by riveting them together.

Manual Pop Rivet

Using a hand-operated tool is often necessary for setting pop rivets. A simple squeezing action is used to pull on the pin part of the rivet to expand the base into the materials being joined. As tension increases, the head of the pin distorts the rivet, and the pin will break off, setting the rivet.

Most tools have a fixed lever action and are often difficult to use in tight places. A swivel-head rivet tool allows greater access and is easier to use to set a rivet. Squeezing the tool requires a lot of muscle and can cause fatigue.

Hydraulic

Working efficiently will allow you to get more done without becoming

fatigued. A hydraulic rivet tool takes less effort to set a pop rivet than a manual rivet tool. Interchangeable pieces allow for different sizes and types of fasteners to be set.

These devices are capable of setting more than rivets. Threaded inserts called riv-nuts can be set into panels to replace worn out or damaged threads. They are a great option to have when you are working on a convertible top and need to fix a blown-out anchor hole in the rear tack rail.

Curved Needles

It is inevitable that you will need to repair a popped stitch at some point. The best way to repair a loose seam is to remove the seat cover and place it under a sewing machine, but that is not always an option. Using a curved needle and thread is great for sewing when you want to make a repair without removing the seat cover.

Curved needles are available in many sizes and point types so that you can make a proper repair with ease. Curved needles are available at

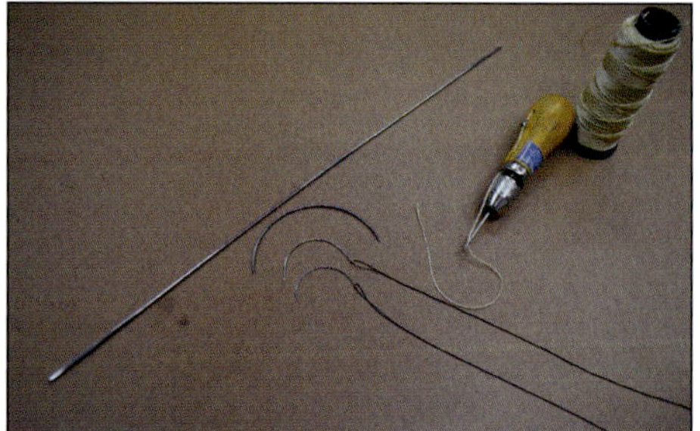

Having an assortment of hand-sewing needles can be very useful. Curved needles are great for repairing small splits in seams. For tougher tasks, a sewing awl can easily pierce leather and canvas, and a diamond-point needle makes attaching buttons a breeze.

most retail sewing centers and upholstery suppliers.

Quick Stitch Awl

Another great hand-sewing tool is the quick stitch awl. This tool helps join materials together when a sewing machine is not a practical option. Thread is dispensed from a bobbin located inside the handle of the tool. When the needle of the awl is pushed through the materials to be joined, the thread is locked in place by feeding the tail of the thread through the loop made by the inserted needle.

Regulator

Everyone has a go-to tool. My favorite upholstery tool is the regulator. This is a steel needle-like tool that can be used to tuck and fold material, align mismatched panels, or do anything else that requires an extra-long finger to get into tight places.

This tool was originally designed to help get stuffing into the places you couldn't reach as well as help smooth and even out (regulate) the padding under the fabric cover of an upholstered piece of furniture.

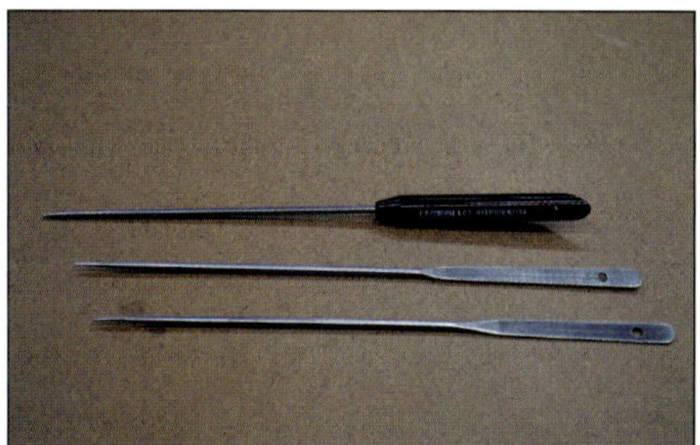

The upholsters' regulator can be used for many tasks. The pointed end helps locate and align screw holes in garnish molding installations, and the long, slim design makes tucking material into tight places a breeze. They are also available with a handle.

For the auto trimmer, it works well to precisely apply small amounts of glue and find hidden screw holes behind garnish moldings.

Panel Removal Tools

Many varieties of this tool are used in the auto upholstery trade. The composition and design of the tool can vary, but the main purpose of the tool is to get behind a panel fastener and lift it from the door without causing damage.

There are a lot of modern plastic panel-lifting tool sets available. They

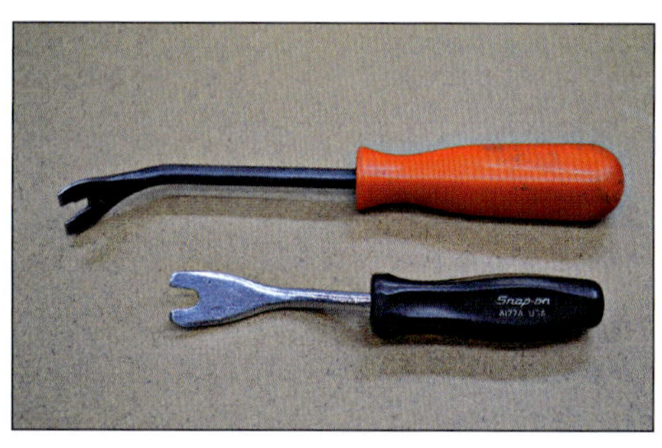

Removing a door or interior trim panel with the proper lifting tool will help prevent unnecessary damage by safely prying up on the panel fastener without harming the car or panel. Lifters are available in different lengths and can be made of steel or plastic.

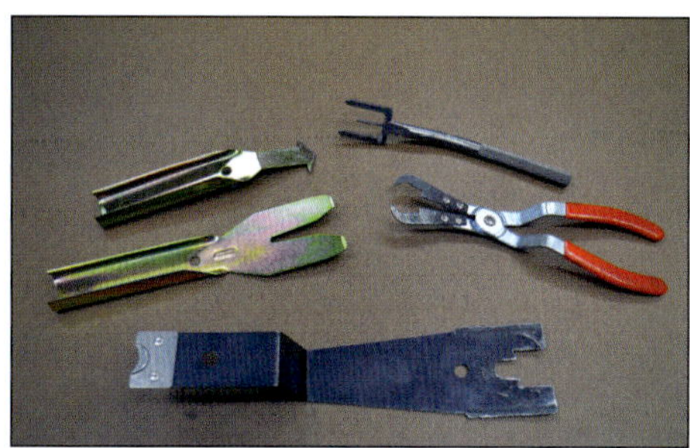

Special tools are needed to remove the hidden clips and pins that retain door handles and window cranks. Using the correct tool for the task will prevent damage to the panel and yourself. Accessing the hidden clip without the correct tool can be frustrating.

usually consist of a variety of tools that can be used to lift the panel from the underlying door. Since the tools are made of a heavy plastic, they are less likely to scratch the painted surface of the car.

A more traditional panel-lifting tool has a forked metal blade that extends from a rigid handle. The length of the blade helps with lifting and leverage to ease the fastener from the car. These tools vary in design depending on the manufacturer.

Window Crank Removal Tools

Choosing the correct tool to remove the interior handles can be a challenge. A variety of fasteners are used to keep the handles in place. Early-model cars use a pin to hold the crank to a square post. A special fork design tool is used to depress the escutcheon down the shaft as a center tine pushes the pin through the crank, releasing the handle.

As manufacturers developed more ornate cranks and handles, the fasteners evolved to small spring clips that hold the device onto a splined shaft. Removing the small spring clip requires a pliers-like tool that is capable of getting behind the crank to pull the clip from the shaft of the regulator.

Later-model cranks are fitted with larger clips that can be removed with a flat-blade tool that is slid under the handle to spring the clip from the retainer slot in the crank base.

Before a vinyl top can be installed, the exterior glass moldings are released with a thin arrow-shaped tool to help pull the spring clip away from the molding. This is done by inserting the tool under the molding and hooking the retainer so that no damage is done to the stainless steel.

SUPPLIES

A lot of what you do not see gives support to the cover materials. These support materials are often overlooked in a replacement or restoration of an interior. To get the final restoration result that you desire, the support materials must be upgraded or replaced before the new cover materials are installed.

Underneath the seat cover is a variety of additional items that are necessary for the proper installation of a replacement seat cover. Installing new upholstery over old foam and cotton will result in an uncomfortable seat that will show signs of premature wear.

You may need to address the springs. Broken springs should be replaced and properly tensioned so that they will support the weight of a passenger. It is also essential to use new foam and cotton to soften and fill the small voids in the seat cover.

When you understand the importance of the support materials, it will only make sense that you spend the extra money necessary to obtain and have them installed. Without the support materials, you are essentially wasting your money by doing half the job.

Reproduction Seat Covers

From the mid-1960s to the late 1970s, a lot of the seat covers had

Having the correct seat covers and door panels is only part of the restoration and installation process. What matters the most are the support materials that will give the installation the edge to make the finished product look perfect. You can obtain them from an upholstery supplier because most box houses do not offer these extra materials that are necessary to the success of your project.

Restoring the seats in your car is a lot easier today with the large selection of premade seat covers. There are a lot of companies that make original and custom seat covers for many of the popular car models. Not all models and styles are available, but several manufacturers are bringing more patterns to market every year.

intricately embossed patterns. It takes special equipment to do this dielectric embossing, and there are many companies that have the skill and tooling to make the reproduction pieces you need to restore your car. The one issue with these restoration pieces is that not all of the companies produce pieces that have the quality that you would expect to get for the money that you spend. Unless you are doing a concourse restoration, most of the available pieces will turn out just fine.

Burlap

Burlap is made from a natural fiber called jute. This inexpensive material is used to cover the metal springs in the seats of the car. The burlap tensions the springs and helps them work in unison to provide comfort and support for the passenger. Without the burlap, the springs would move independently, which would make sitting in the seat very uncomfortable.

Having a layer of burlap over the top of the springs also helps keep the springs from cutting into the foam padding. Cotton can be applied over the burlap to level the springs. This gives the foam a solid surface to rest upon, which also helps the upholstery to lay evenly over the foam cushioning.

As technology improved, so did textile manufacturing. Modern burlap is made from synthetic fibers. This new material is stronger than jute burlap and is naturally resistant to mold and mildew.

Cotton

Cotton is a natural plant fiber that is used in upholstery to soften the sharp edges of springs and frames. Prior to the use of foam and other man-made materials, prewar cars used a thin cotton sheeting called coach wadding to soften trim panels. Under the seat cover, you would find thick layers of cotton batting. This filler prevented the seating material from sagging and wrinkling, which aided in the longevity of the seat cover. The firm nature of the padding also gave comfort to the passenger.

Cotton batting is sold by the pound and rolled into small bales to make it easier to handle. New cotton is easy to work with, and it can be split and torn into workable pieces. The downside of using natural cotton is that mice love to get into this material and make nests. This type of damage can make the interior of a car smell bad. If the padding gets wet, it is prone to forming mold and mildew that can cause respiratory problems.

Modern cars no longer use cotton in seat manufacturing due to the high cost of production. Interior seat padding has been replaced by molded foam and synthetic fibers.

Foam

Springs and cotton provide a major portion of the padding and comfort to a car seat, but when you add a layer of high-density foam cushioning over them, you achieve a level of comfort that will make your driving experience much more enjoyable.

The foam used in pre-1960 bench seats was made of latex or soy. A slab of the foam was used on the lower seat cushion to help pad the springs.

Jute burlap is used to help tension the seat springs and provides a foundation for the foam and cotton padding. Burlap can be purchased by the roll, or you can get it in cut yardage. Typically, burlap has a natural tan color, but it can also be found in many widths and colors to suit your needs.

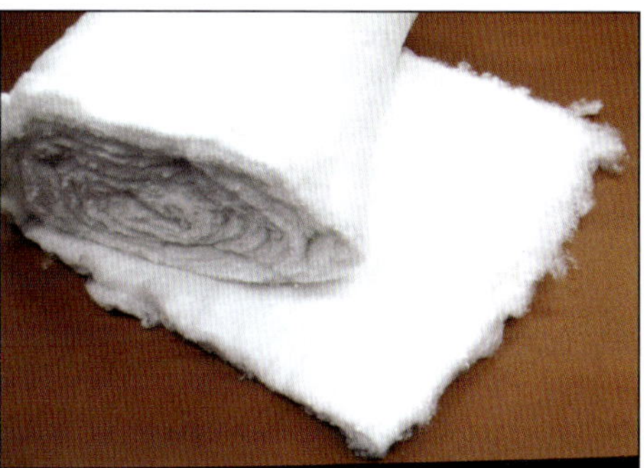

Cotton batting has been used for padding car seats for over 100 years. This soft white natural material is used to fill voids and make seat covers look smoother. High production costs have made the use of cotton in modern production prohibitive. Modern cotton is a synthetic blend that is made from 100-percent recycled post-industrial materials.

A variety of foam has been used to improve the comfort of the car seat. Slab foam worked well to cover the springs of bench seats for many years until it was replaced by molded foam buns that created a unique shape and style for the bucket seat.

This foam was very soft and made the seat quite comfortable for the passengers. As the latex foam aged, it would begin to break down from exposure to sunlight, turning it to a yellowish cornmeal-like powder that made the seat uncomfortable. Improvements in foam technology led to the development of synthetic foams that costed less and lasted much longer.

As technology improved and interior styles changed, bucket seats began to gain in popularity. Under a bucket seat cover, you will find a molded foam bun. The dense foam fit over the seat springs and could withstand a lot of compression, providing comfort to the passenger. Foam buns are sometimes made with an internal wire structure to which the seat cover is attached.

Springs

The car seat evolved by altering the wooden frame of furniture. Support for the passengers was provided from metal helical springs that were tied together, padded with straw, and covered in leather. As the car evolved, so did the construction techniques used to make seats. Metal stampings replaced the wooden frame, and the coil springs were later replaced by sinuous or zigzag-type springs.

In the early 1950s, auto makers began using zigzag springs in the manufacture of car seats. They provided support and comfort and were much easier to install, which lowered the overall production cost of assembling a car seat.

The problem with a spring is that it does not work well all by itself. When the springs are installed, they need to be tied, or tensioned, together to make the seat comfortable. Edge wire and clips hold the springs in shape, and a layer of burlap covers the springs, helping them work as a unit to provide a firm surface upon which the foam cushion can rest.

In the mid-1970s, car manufacturers decided to eliminate the use of springs and make the seat cushions completely of foam. This decision also cut costs and the weight of the car.

Hog Rings

Automotive hog rings evolved from industrial and agricultural hog rings. These devices are smaller in design and are made from mild steel, which is different than the composite copper and nickel materials used in agricultural hog rings.

The automotive hog ring is a little smaller in size and diameter, which allows it to hold tight to the seat frame and keep the seat cover securely in place. The ends of the hog ring are cut at an angle, and they are very sharp, which allows them to cut cleanly through foam and fabric when they are installed.

To secure the hog ring properly, a quality hog-ring pliers should be used. If the hog ring is not cinched correctly, it can pull out and create problems after the seat cover has been installed. It is important to use care when installing a hog ring to avoid getting hurt by the very sharp ends as they are set in place.

Listings

Before a seat cover can be attached to the seat frame, a retaining wire or

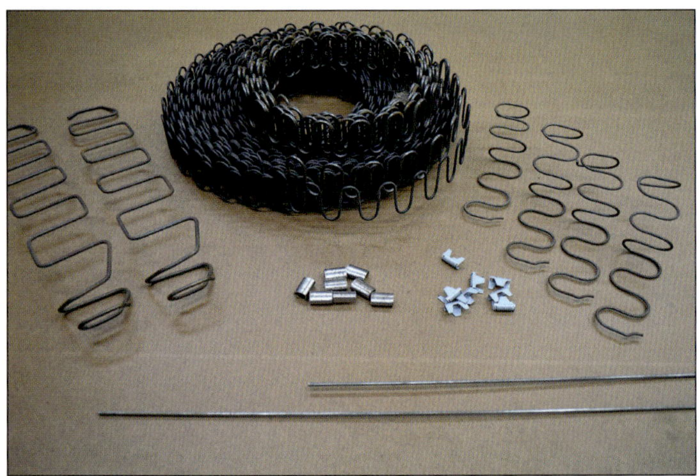

Seat springs come in many varieties and gauges to provide the proper support for the driver. Rolls of zigzag springs are available in 8, 9, and 11 gauges along with preformed seat and bolster support springs. Edge wire and spring clips are used to tie them together.

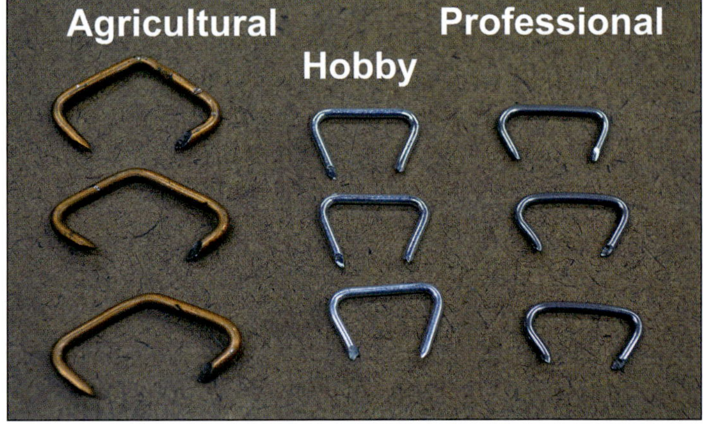

The composition of agricultural hog rings makes them too heavy and large to use in automotive applications. Professional-grade automotive hog rings are designed to hold a seat cover to a frame and are easy to install due to the very sharp ends. Non-standard hog rings are too small and do not crimp properly.

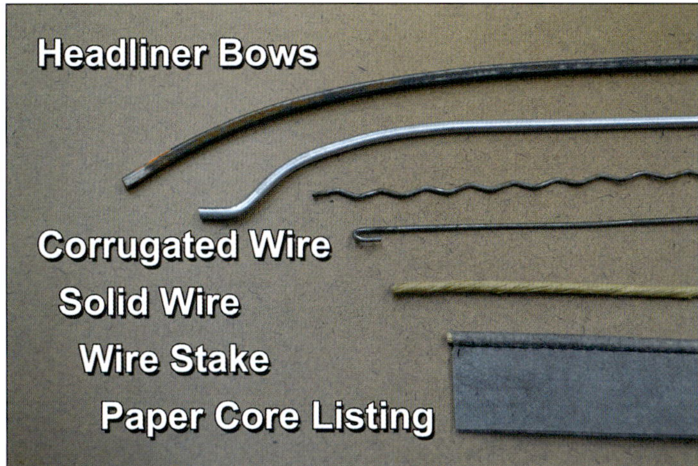

Listings hold a wire or cord that is used to attach uphol-stery to the car. When the listing is sewn to a seat cover, it helps define the shape of the seat as it keeps the cover in place without shifting. Headliner bows suspend the fabric and give definition to the inner roofline.

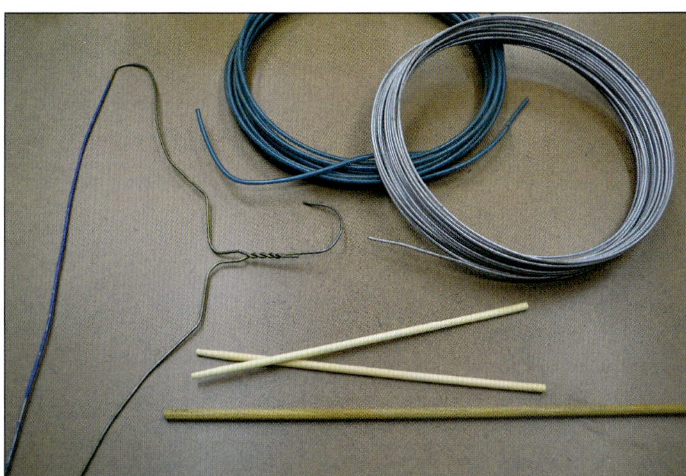

Listing wire should be rigid and strong enough to span a short distance without deflection. Coat hangers and clothesline wire are too soft and not suitable for seat cover installations. Chopsticks and wooden dowels are too brit-tle and will shatter when flexed.

cord is installed into a cloth pouch that runs along the outer perimeter of the cover and under the edges of the insert to secure the upholstery in place. A hog ring is then cinched through the listing, pinning it to the anchor listing wire attached to the springs.

The filler of the listing can be made of many things. Some list-ings have a heavy woven cord that is presewn into the outer edge of the listing. The cord can be hog-ringed directly to the seat without adding any additional materials, making the installation of a seat cover faster.

Most commonly, the listing wire is a paper-covered, heavy 16-gauge wire called wire-stake. Wire-stake is flexible yet rigid enough to retain a seat cover. Another material often used in a listing is corrugated wire. This rippled wire is very stiff and, because of its shape, can hold a hog ring extremely well. Other list-ing wires are nothing more than a heavy-gauge straight wire that has a loop formed in the end to make insertion into the listing sleeve eas-

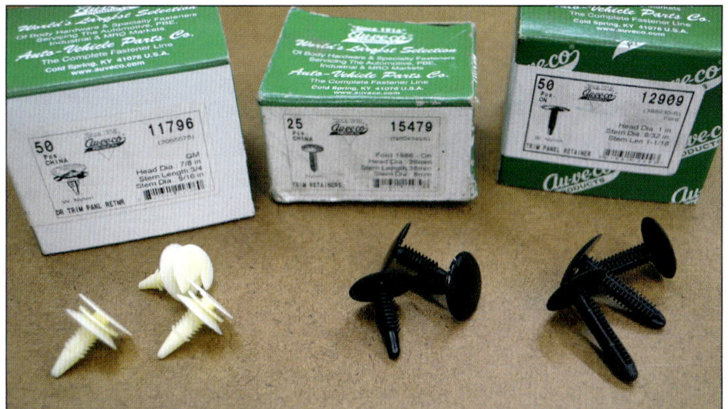

Panel fasteners come in many styles. Cars from the 1980s and newer have been using the push-in-style fasteners com-monly known to the industry as Christmas trees.

The name is derived from their bristle shafts that hold the panel securely when it is inserted into the car.

ier by allowing the wire to glide through the pocket without tearing the material.

Suspended headliners also use listings along their seams to retain the bows that the headliner is hung from. These pouches are a little deeper to allow the formed end of the thicker headliner bow to pass through.

Non-Listings

A poor choice for seat listings is aluminum wire, metal coat hangers, or wooden dowels. These materi-als are too soft and flexible to hold the proper tension on the seat cover when hog-ringed in place. A good rule of thumb to determine if a list-ing is strong enough to use can be determined by bending it between your fingers. If it bends easily, do not use it. If it is wood, well, build a bird-house with it.

Door Panel Hardware

Many types of fasteners have been used to attach the interior panels to the car. Each fastener is

---

designed to do a specific job even though they all do the same job of holding a panel in place.

Panel Clips

These fasteners are made of bent metal, and they slip into a slot on the backside of the door panel. The tips that extend outward have small extended tabs that flex and hold the panel secure when they are inserted into the clip socket located in the door of the car. You will find these clips on many cars made from the late 1960s to the early 1980s.

Spring Fasteners

There are many versions of door panel spring clips. These are the older versions of panel fasteners used from the mid-1960s until the early 1970s. The real difference is the length of the clip tip; it varies depending on the thickness of the material the clip will need to penetrate. Each tip is designed to collapse enough to allow the clip to pass through a retainer hole in the sheet metal on the car body and then spring back into shape to permit the fastener to hold the panel in place.

Nail Fasteners

Many people find this fastener difficult to use due to the fragile nature of the fastener. The head of a small ribbed nail is spot welded to a metal retaining tab, and they tend to break off with little effort. They did a great job of holding a door panel to the metal or plastic retainer in the inner door but were hard to remove and difficult to line up during installation.

Christmas Trees

It's a fitting name for a fastener that looks like a Christmas (Xmas) tree.

Nail fasteners were used to secure door and trim panels until 1966. The nail portion of the fastener was inserted into a nylon cup that had been inserted into the door of the car. Plastic inserts were used from the late 1960s until the early 1970s to help retain the metal spring clips attached to interior panels.

There is no need to reuse rusty or damaged hardware when you can purchase replacement screws and retainers from the Au-ve-co Products Company. A great selection of styles and sizes of automotive hardware are available from most supply houses.

Typically, these fasteners are made of nylon or plastic and are available in a wide variety of shapes, lengths, and diameters. The holding power of these clips come from the flexible ribs, or branches, when pressed into a retainer hole in the body.

Retainers

To make the fasteners effective, they need a place to be anchored. Some retaining points are nothing more than a small hole made in the surface metal of a panel. Some holes are larger and require an additional metal or plastic liner to give the clip something to grab.

Having the proper anchor for a fastener will also prevent unwanted noises from occurring while holding the panel securely to the inner surface of the car.

Trim Screws

Direct fastening of hard items, such as garnish moldings, require the use of decorative screws. Because these fasteners are visible and practical, they need to blend in with the interior. To achieve this, the screw is finished with a simple oval head. The size of the head is often smaller than the screw size to make it less obvious and intrusive. To further enhance the disappearance of the screw head, the hole in the garnish molding is dimpled inward to keep the oval head from protruding, making the finish almost smooth without drawing attention to itself.

Other upholstered and hard surfaces cannot be recessed, such as rear armrest panels and seat aprons. These rely on the use of an oval-head screw with an attached recessed washer. Although these screws are larger, they are necessary to hold trim panels in place and keep the screw from protruding into the cab which can cause a passenger to snag their clothing on the screw head.

Headliner Clips

Many carmakers relied on friction to keep the headliner bows in a vertical position. By the late 1960s, car bodies changed and manufacturers began using small plastic clips to position the headliner bows. These small fasteners attached to the rigid roof braces inside the cab and the bows snapped into the clips to give the headliner a crisp finish.

The clips are prone to damage from age and temperature changes and should be replaced if they

These headliner bow clips are used to stabilize and center the headliner bows along the inner roof of the car. Installation of a headliner without using the correct clip will make the bow rotate out of position and cause the headliner material to sag.

become cracked or can no longer hold the headliner bow securely.

Insulation

Precut headliner insulation is available for many applications. Rolls of Dacron batting can be purchased from any upholstery supplier and cut to fit your needs.

Installation is achieved by gluing the Dacron to the inner roofline of the car. After the insulation has been installed, the headliner can be fitted in place and finished as normal. Another benefit of using this synthetic fiber is that mice do not like it.

Carpet Pad

Before any floor covering is installed, a protective layer of padding should be used. The metal floor of the car has many sharp edges and deep ridges that will cause damage to the new floor covering. Without the padding, the carpet will appear wavy and uneven, making it uncomfortable to step on.

The main type of carpet pad used in the automotive industry is made of jute fibers. This product will not only help the carpet to lay smoother (as its name implies) but it will also keep the carpet from being damaged by wearing against the metal floor. Unlike the foam padding that is used in home carpet installations, jute breathes and will not hold water and rot your floorboards.

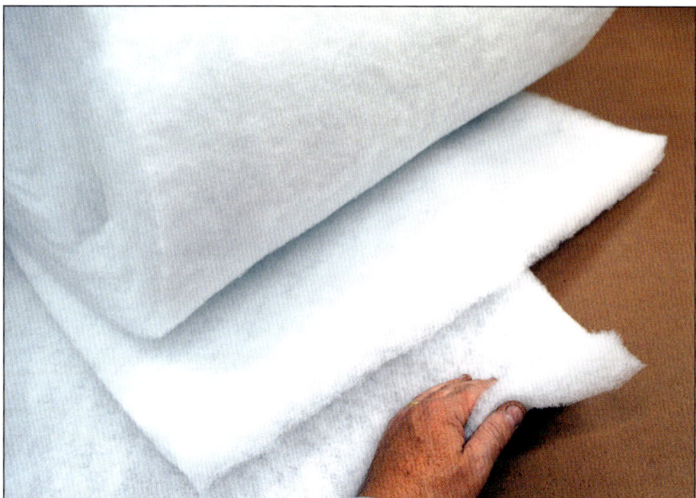

Modern spun Dacron is a replacement for the original fiberglass and asphalt insulation that was used to dampen noise and block extreme heat or cold from the cab. Dacron fibers are lightweight and have the same insulating and sound-deadening properties as the old fiberglass batting.

Automotive carpet pad is available in rolls and cut yardage. This is installed under the carpet to help with sound and heat transfer. Depending on your specific application, 1/2-inch and 3/8-inch thicknesses of jute carpet pad are available to protect your carpet from the metal floor.

Seat Covers

Many car enthusiasts choose to use a premade seat cover because of the skill and time required to cut and sew new covers. These reproduction seat covers can vary in quality and detail depending on the manufacturer. Most consumers are not aware of these differences and are generally satisfied with the products that they purchase. These differences tend to show up during the installation process. Getting the upholstery to fit and look proper is commonly a matter of installation skill and experience and not so much about the manufacturer.

Support Materials

Getting the most from your purchase requires that the proper support materials need to be in place to protect and fill the upholstery before the seat cover can be attached to the seat frame. Without the proper support, the seat cover will become wrinkled when a passenger sits in the seat. The wrinkles will eventually cause holes to form at the creases. If the seat springs are broken and not properly tensioned when a new seat cover is installed, they can puncture the seat cover. If you invest the money to refresh your interior, it makes sense to also spend the extra money to obtain the correct support materials necessary to preserve the integrity of the new seat cover.

To ensure that your new seat cover will last and look nice, fresh burlap along with new foam and a layer of cotton should be installed before the new upholstery is fitted. The downside of the old seat foam is its ability to lose its shape and become flat from age and constant compression. The lack of resilience causes the seat cover to bag and become loose. This deteriorated condition also makes the seat uncomfortable and will lead to holes developing in the seat cover.

Seat Frame

Whether the seat has a power option to make it go back and forth or a lever to make the backrest recline, each seat is constructed with the same basic components. A car seat has a metal foundation called a

Purchasing new, premade seat covers can save you a lot of time and money if you install them yourself. Inspect your new seat covers for flaws as soon as you take them out of the box and before they are installed.

frame. Springs, foam, and the upholstery are attached to the frame to define the shape and comfort for the passenger. There are two basic types of seat frames: the bench and bucket.

Bench Seats

Passenger seating on all cars came standard with a front and rear bench-style seat. Bucket seats were not offered as an option on most cars until the early 1960s. The two-door models were equipped with a split back that was divided in the center and would fold forward to allow the passengers to enter into the rear seating area of the car. There was a slight difference in construction of the four-door models, as they did not have a backrest with a folding option but utilized a solid or rigid backrest. The rear door provided ample access for passengers to enter and exit without disturbing the front seat passengers by folding the seat forward.

Some of these bench seats had a power option that allowed the frame to be adjusted forward and backward to accommodate the comfort of the driver. Deluxe features that were also available included a tilt feature and a center fold-down armrest.

Early Bucket Seats

When the Corvette was introduced in 1953, it was designed as a two-seater sports car, and bucket seats were standard equipment. Bucket seats were not offered as an option in GM cars until 1961. These seats were somewhat square in shape with a low-back design. The backrest on the 1961 to 1964 B-Body bucket seats tilted inward at an angle to allow easy passage into the rear seat area. The 1964 to 1965 A-Body models looked very similar, but the backrests tilted straight forward.

Strato Bucket

Designing a seat that moved in one specific direction proved to be a costly production error because the seats could not be exchanged from one side of the car to the other. A redesign proved to be the answer, and the frames became generic and could be configured for adding other features, such as head rests.

A whole new concept of the bucket seat was imagined with the redesign of the muscle car. The sleek curves of this low-back seat not only provided comfort to the passenger but also was stylish. The basic seat

Seat frames on mid-1960s bucket seats varied by body size. GM A-Body cars were fitted with bucket seats that had backrests that folded straight forward, and the B-Body seat back tilted inward. Eventually all the seats tilted forward to save on production costs.

frame of the Strato design was used by General Motors from 1966 until 1972. Each division of GM had its own seat cover designs that changed with each new year and model.

Small variations occurred to the function of the seat frame as it evolved. The 1966 model sported metal skirts without a locking mechanism. A locking device was added with a release button located on the upper outer side of the seat back on the 1967 to 1968 models. The difference in these seats was in the outside back and skirt material. Metal was used on the 1967 model and changed to plastic in 1968.

Another change was made to the locking mechanism in the 1969 to 1972 models. A push button was added to the center backrest along with headrests, which were mandatory standard equipment due to a change in national safety laws. The design of the 1969 headrests and locks

Here is something you do not see every day: a unique combination of the Strato bucket in a bench seat. GM offered this seat style for its full and midsize cars from 1966 to 1972. This 1967 Caprice seat is adorned with fabric inserts and buttons. Other options were head rests and power assist.

are one year only, but 1970 to 1972 headrests and locks are all the same.

Bucket Seat Tracks

Mounting and adjusting the bucket seat require tracks. The metal seat tracks are comprised of two separate runners that use a bearing and nylon guides to allow the two pieces of the formed track to slide back and forth. These pieces work together to provide a stable mounting base for the seat. The outside track is equipped with an adjustment lever that is designed to allow the seat to move in small increments to suit the driver. A passive track runs parallel to the adjuster track to help keep the seat in a straight line of motion.

Generally, all A-Body GM bucket seat tracks are interchangeable with each other by how the tracks mount to the seat bottom and the car floor. Some variations occur among model years with adjustment knob styles and levers.

Bench seat tracks usually have an interlocking adjuster on each track that is connected with an actuator wire. When the adjuster knob is pulled on the driver's side, a locking palm disengages with the passenger-side track to allow movement of the seat. When the adjuster is released, the palm reengages with the passenger-side track, locking it in position, which prevents the seat from shifting while the car is in motion. Seat tracks designed for use with a bench seat are not interchangeable with bucket seats.

Seat Removal

Before a new seat cover can be installed, the seat will need to be unbolted from the car and set up on

To remove the seat for the recovery process, it must be unbolted from the car. Adjust the seat position to allow better access to the attaching nuts or bolts that hold the seat tracks to the floor. The fasteners can now be easily removed with a wrench or socket.

the workbench for disassembly. To unbolt the seat, locate the retaining bolts holding the seat tracks to the floor of the car.

First, adjust the seat all the way to the rear to expose the front track bolts. Use a 1/2-inch socket or the appropriate-sized wrench to remove the bolts from the floor. Next, move the seat forward to access the rear track bolts and remove them. If the seat has a power option or seat belt alarm, the electrical coupler can now be disconnected. There will be a tab on one side of the connector that will need to be lifted to allow the connection to be pulled apart.

After disconnecting the coupler, the seat should be free and can be lifted carefully from the car. The seat may be heavy and bulky, so make sure you do not damage the door panel or scratch the paint when removing the seat from the car. After removal, the seat can be placed on the workbench for further disassembly.

Disassembly

Depending on the model and manufacturer of the seat you are working on, stripping down the

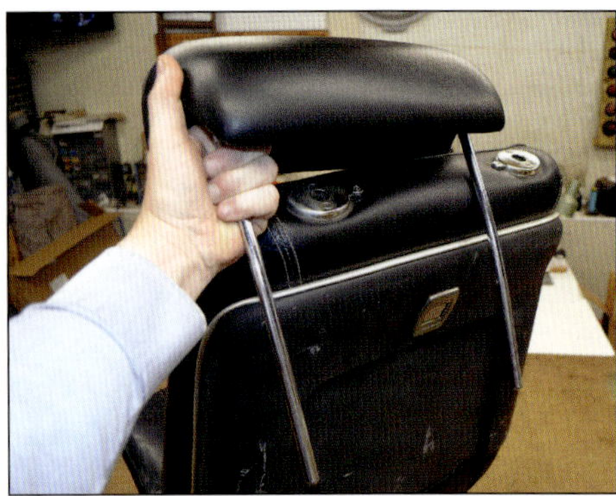

Removal of a headrest from the seat back usually involves nothing more than lifting it straight up and off the seat back. Some headrests have a locking retainer latch button that must be squeezed before the headrest can be raised and then removed.

Small screws are removed from the chrome cover on the lock bezel. Age has not been good to the plastic cover, so a new set of covers will be ordered to replace the damaged chrome. The new lock bezels will look and perform just like the originals.

seat is pretty basic. If your seat has a headrest, it will need to be removed. Depress the release buttons on the headrest locks and pull the headrest up to remove it. Check the condition of the headrest. If it is made from a molded vinyl and does not have any cracks or other damage, it may be reused after a good cleaning and reconditioning. Severely damaged headrests will need to be replaced or recovered.

Headrests with a sewn cover are most likely in need of a teardown to replace damaged foam. A new cover can then be fitted over the new foam to restore the headrest to like-new condition.

With the headrest out of the way, you can see the lock bezels located on the top of the seat back. Use the appropriate screwdriver to remove the attaching screws. Lock bezels without screws either unscrew from the base or they are snap-fit into the seat back and can be removed with a panel-lifting tool.

Inspect this hardware for damage. Worn chrome and cracked or rusted pieces should be replaced with a new reproduction part. If new parts are not available, the old pieces will need to be reconditioned before they are reinstalled.

Remove the headrest lock from the top of the backrest by taking out the retaining screws holding the lock cover in place. Under the lock cover is a guide plate, which is secured by two screws. Remove these screws and set the hardware aside to be used later.

Latches

Seats that have plastic or metal trim covers attached must come off prior to the seat cover being removed. Most trim covers are attached to the seat frame with screws. Before the trim can be taken off, release buttons and latches will need to be removed first.

On the seat back, you may find a large release button that operates the latch mechanism. The button is held in place by a spring clip and can be removed by inserting a flat-blade screwdriver from the side of the button and under the bezel. Apply pressure to the spring clip to help release it from the seat back. Use slight pres-

A flat-blade screwdriver is being used to depress the retainer spring on the latch release button. When the spring clip is compressed, the button can be lifted from the seat back. The chrome finish on this button is cracked and peeling, so it will be replaced with a new part.

sure to lift the button as you push in on the spring clip.

If the release latch lever has a small knob attached, look for a set screw on the underside of the knob. The set screw may require an Allen or hex-type tool to loosen the set screw. Back the set screw off until the knob can be removed. If the set screw comes out of the knob, be careful that you do not lose it.

Another latch variation will have a release lever located on the side of the seat back. These are attached with a small trim screw that holds the lever to the locking release shaft. Removal of the screw will permit the lever to be detached from the splined shaft. When all the latch hardware has been removed, a screwdriver will be needed to remove the retainer screws from the seat panels.

Trim Panels

Check the condition of the cover material to verify that it can be reused. Rust can destroy the integrity of a cover and it may not be suitable for restoration. Plastic covers can sus-

A simple scratch test has determined that the plastic seat back on this Strato bucket has sustained a lot of environmental damage. The surface has become chalky and has deteriorated to the point that it can no longer be restored. A new set of covers will be needed for this project.

tain sun damage and the surface can become chalky and scratch easily. This condition cannot be repaired, so the part should be replaced.

Trim screws are used to hold the rear panel to the seat back. Use a Phillips screwdriver to remove the screws. If the screws are in good condition, they can be set aside and reused to reattach the cover. Seats with lower skirts are also attached with trim screws. These skirts conceal

Early bucket seats used a decorative chrome cap to dress up the pivot post. A diagonal cutter is used to cut the cap away from the post. This action prevents unnecessary damage to the polished stainless-steel trim attached to the side of the seat. A new cap will be installed during reassembly.

---

the pivot points and hardware of the backrest.

Other models may have a small plastic cover over the backrest pivot arm that hides the pivot stud and retainer clip. Removal of these smaller covers can be accomplished by using a panel release tool to lift the retainer fastener from the cover. Slip the tool under the head of the fastener and pry the fastener away from the inner side of the pivot arm. The cover should now be loose and can be pulled down and away from the seat back arm.

Another pivot point cover variation is a decorative chrome cap that is applied directly over the pivot post. Under the cap is a spring clip that retains the backrest to the seat bottom. Removal of the chrome trim cap can be difficult without causing damage to the delicate seat trim or destroying the cap. To prevent damage to the stainless trim, cut into the cap with diagonal cutters to remove it from the pivot post. New caps are readily available from suppliers and will look better than the old, scuffed caps. Replacing the cap will cost less than repairing the trim molding.

Hardware

Seats have other external components that are used to support and retain the seat back. Small rubber bumpers are used to set the backrest pitch and cushion the seat frame when it is tilted. Other devices that are attached to the seat are back lock assemblies and latch hooks. These items are removed by taking out the retaining bolts that hold them in place.

Removing the backrest from the bottom cushion frame depends on how it is attached. Bolts holding the hinges of the backrest are removed

Small bumpers attached to the seat cushion help with tilt and backrest position. These devices are often damaged or missing and are easily replaced with the new seat cover. A screwdriver is needed to remove the sheet-metal screw that keeps the bumper in place.

with a socket wrench. Some backrests are retained by spring clips or E-type clips that are pressed onto a pivot post that extends from the side of the lower seat frame. Removing these clips requires a panel-lifting tool or flat-blade screwdriver to lift the clip from the post. Broken or missing clips are easily replaced with new hardware.

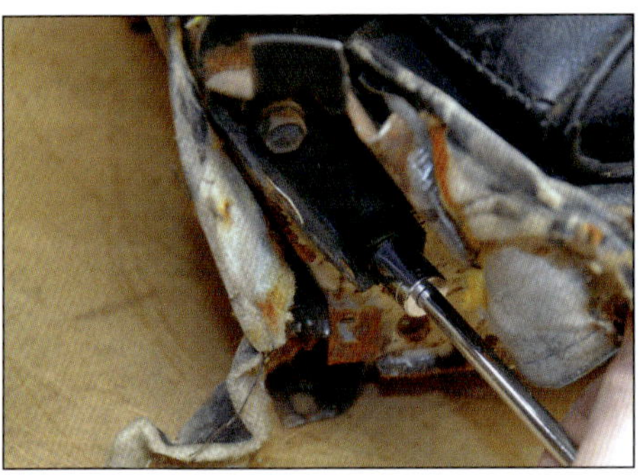

The seat back on the Strato bucket is attached with two bolts on each side of the seat cushion. The bolts also retain a small metal bracket that supports the lower side skirt. The seat cover is also attached to this bracket with hog rings. The bolts are revealed and can be removed when the hog rings are removed.

Bolts are removed from the base of the seat back lock mechanism, which is located in the rear center section of the seat cushion. A spring-steel connecting bar slides inside the lock mechanism and prevents the seat from unexpectedly flopping forward. The bar is riveted to the anchor plate.

After the backrest has been separated from the bottom frame, the seat tracks can be removed. Begin by turning the bottom cushion upside down to access the tracks. On each end of the track is a retainer bolt that needs to be removed before the track will come off. Use a socket and ratchet wrench to remove the track bolts.

A diagonal cutter was used to remove this spring clip from the pivot post on this 1965 Impala seat. Cutting the clip is the best way of removing the fastener from the pivot post without damaging the chrome trim that is attached to the sides of the seat backrest.

Bolts hold the seat tracks to the bottom of the seat cushion. When the cushion is inverted, use a socket wrench to loosen the bolts and free the seat tracks so they can be cleaned and painted. With the tracks out of way, the seat cover can be easily removed.

Adjustment knobs are either pressed on or retained by a small set screw. Remove the adjustment lever knob with a tack hammer to drive the knob off the end of the lever. A sharp blow will knock it right off.

Take a look at the release lever knob on the seat track. These are often missing or have severe wear and need to be replaced. If the chrome is pitted or damaged it should be replaced. Removing the knob is simple. It is either secured to the release lever by a set screw or just held on by friction. Removal of the knob can be done by striking the bottom of the knob with a tack hammer to drive it off the lever. Knobs with set screws will come off after you loosen the set screw.

Upholstery Removal

Taking off the old seat covers and support materials will most likely be smelly and definitely a dirty task. Protect yourself during the teardown process by wearing safety glasses and a dust mask. You will be surprised at how far and fast the pieces fly when cutting a hog ring, so do not risk being hurt. The rust, dust, and mouse dirt in the seat can cause other health issues when airborne.

Remove the old hog rings to release the cover, foam, and burlap from the frame. There are many tools that can be used to remove the fasteners. A long-handled diagonal cutter works well at gripping and twisting off the hog rings. You can cut the hog rings to remove the cover, but this action takes a lot of squeezing and can fatigue your hand when trying to cut through the crimped hog ring.

Hog Ring Removal

Place the bottom seat frame upside down on the workbench to get better access to the hog rings that are cinched around the perimeter of the seat cover. Firmly grip the hog ring with the cutter and begin twisting each hog ring off the seat frame. Be careful that you do not cut or twist off the anchor loop in the frame. These anchor points are needed to reattach the new seat cover. If the anchor loops are soft or weak, cut off the hog ring to prevent damage to the seat frame.

While you are working, keep your work area clean. Discard the old hog rings as they are removed to prevent them from building up on the floor. You definitely do not want to step on the bent and rusty metal.

When the cover is free from the frame, peel it back to reveal the

Someone used welding wire to secure the seat cover bolsters to the seat springs. As you can see, the wire was not strong enough to hold the seat cover in place and it failed. Hog rings should have been used to properly attach the listing to the anchor listing attached to the seat springs.

A diagonal cutter is great for getting into tight places to grip a hog ring and twist it out of the seat frame. If you squeeze too hard, the hog ring will be cut, and the pieces will fly all over the work area. Always think safety when working. Protect your eyes with safety goggles.

This spring liner is made of heavy chip board and was attached over the lower springs to act as a barrier and prevent the seat cushion springs from cutting into the seat cover when the springs flexed from being sat upon. Do not forget to reinstall a new spring liner with the new cover.

underlying foam cushion. Some seats may have a paper liner under the cover. This is used to protect the seat cover from becoming damaged by the seat springs. Remove the underliner and set it aside. If it is in good condition, it can be reused. Damaged underliners can be remade from new chipboard.

Bolster Listings

When the seat cover is lifted, you may find additional pieces of paper-covered wire hog ringed to the seat frame. These are anchor listings that help define the shape of the seat cover, and they restrict the foam cushion from moving, give it more support, and make it more comfortable to sit on.

The bolster listing is attached to the seat springs or an anchor wire. Remove the hog rings from deep inside the foam channel to release the listing. The seat cover should now be able to be completely removed to expose the foam.

If the seat cover has a decorative emblem or buttons attached, do not discard the old cover right away. The emblems may need to be removed from the old cover and reused on the new seat covers. Check with your interior supplier to acquire new emblems or buttons.

Emblem Removal

Seat emblems are specific to the year and model of car. These can be hard items to find because not all of them are available as a reproduction part, so saving the original is necessary to the restoration process. Removing the factory medallions from the old seat cover is easy. The first step is to measure for the location of the emblem. Take note of the reference points when you measure

Accurate measurements need to be taken prior to the removal of seat emblems. You will want to know where to install the emblems on the new seat cover. Placing the emblems in the wrong position will make your new seat cover look funny. Write down the measurement to avoid confusion later.

The emblem retainer is removed by snapping it off of the emblem studs. A flat-blade screwdriver is wedged under the retainer and quickly twisted to prevent the studs from breaking off. If the emblems are in good condition, they can be reused on the new seat covers.

to ensure that the emblems are correctly relocated to the new seat cover.

Most measuring begins from the welt line or a prominent seam in the seat cover down to the top of the emblem. Write this measurement down for installment accuracy. This works well for seats with sharp edges and medallions. If you have a round or irregular-shaped medallion, the reference point will be the center point. You may want to draw a picture to refer to when reinstalling the item.

Turn the seat cover over and locate the anchor plate on the backside of the insert. Most emblems have prongs or tabs that go through a baseplate. Tabs can be carefully bent upward to release the emblem from the anchor plate. A screwdriver blade can be used to snap the anchor off of the prong. When I say *snap*, that means to twist the blade quickly to

pop it free of the prong. Damage can happen if you pry slowly on this type of emblem. The anchor bases can always be straightened and reused, or new bases can be made if they are broken.

Bag and label all of the pieces and include the measurements and any drawings or pictures that you made to help with the reinstallation.

Seat Pad

Hog rings were used to secure the foam rubber cushion to the seat frame. A band of fabric is attached to the outer perimeter of the seat foam to provide a much more durable surface that prevents the hog rings from tearing up the foam.

The foam is wrapped over the spring edge wire and hog ringed to the seat springs from underneath. Remove the hog rings that are holding the foam to the seat springs. After

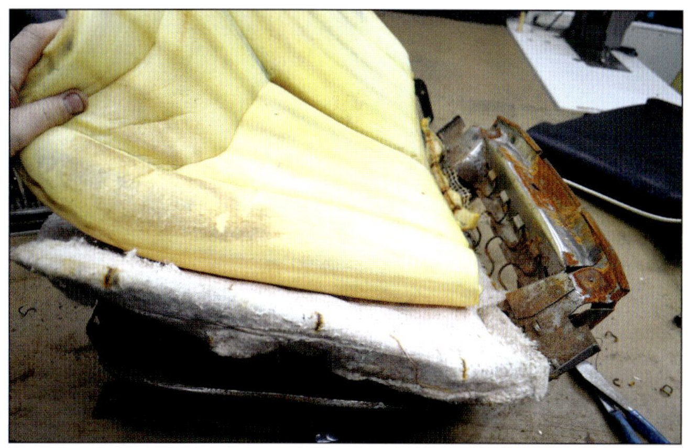

Old foam is dried out and does not have the ability to give the proper support to the seat cover. Properly discard the old cushion after it has been removed from the seat frame and use a new foam cushion to support the new seat cover.

A jute noise suppressor is attached to the bolster support spring. This might not look like much, but it helps prevent the spring from rubbing against the seat frame and other springs when the seat is flexed. It will be removed and used to create a pattern to make new pieces.

the hog rings have been removed, the old foam pad can be lifted off of the seat springs and discarded.

The foam is supported with a cotton pad that is attached along the spring edge wire with hog rings. To remove the cotton pad, the hog rings must be cut away. You may need to feel through the cotton to find the hog rings. The cotton padding is old and very dirty. It will need to be discarded and replaced with fresh new cotton.

Sitting over the seat springs is a piece of burlap with thin wires woven through the burlap. This assembly is the flexolator. The purpose of the flexolator is to provide tension to the individual rows of zigzag springs and make them work as a single unit. Age and wear cause the burlap to rot and the thin wires to break. When this happens, the flexolator does not function and is no longer useful.

Use a diagonal cutter to remove the hog rings that hold the burlap in place and lift the flexolator off the seat. Be careful that you do not poke yourself while discarding the burlap. The broken wires are sharp, and they may also be rusty. This type of material is no longer available for purchase, so new burlap will later be applied over the springs to tension the springs and give support to the new foam cushion.

Springs

You are now getting close to the core of a car seat: the springs. There are several parts that make up the spring unit. Bolster supports, filler spring, and edge wire are tied together to create a foundation that will provide a comfortable place for the driver to sit.

The last pieces to remove from the seat frame are the noise suppressors. These are thin jute pads attached to the springs. The suppressor helps with the squeaks and friction of the springs while the seat is compressed when sat upon. Remove the hog rings to release the old suppressor and set it aside to use as a pattern for new ones. The long, flat suppressor can be slid out from inside of the frame.

Repeat this process of disassembly for all the seat frames. When all the frames have been stripped to the bare springs, the restoration process can begin.

Frame Reconditioning

Your seat frame will need some attention before the new materials can be installed. Rarely will a seat frame and springs look shiny and new. The springs need to be inspected for weak or broken pieces. If you had any mouse infestations, the springs will show signs of rust and corrosion. The metal seat frame should be examined for stress cracks and damage from age or abuse.

The flexolator helped the seat springs work as a single unit. Small tempered wires gave rigidity to the spring surface along with support that prevented the cotton and foam cushion materials from being torn up by the springs. Removing the old, worn, and dirty material is necessary to prevent damage to the new materials.

A mouse nest is typically found inside an old car seat after the upholstery material has been removed. Wear a respirator mask and eye protection to prevent ingesting the dust and dirt while removing a mess like this. Do not forget to give your work area a good cleaning too.

A wire brush will quickly and safely knock the accumulated rust and scale off of the seat springs. This method will not harm the metal and takes less time than sandblasting. You will also be able to identify other issues such as broken springs and cracks in the frame this way.

Begin by giving the unit a thorough cleaning. Sandblasting is a quick and easy process. However, it can cause damage to the seat springs by drawing the temper in the springs, making them soft and weak. I recommend that you give the entire unit a good cleaning with a wire brush. This process will also reveal any previous unseen issues that may need attention and repair.

After cleaning, the dust on the metal can be blown off with compressed air and wiped down with metal prep to clean the springs for painting.

Broken Springs

Repairing a broken spring is not difficult, but it is necessary. Replacement spring units are available for many cars from your supply house. Stress cracks in the metal seat frame can be welded to strengthen the frame so that it can support the seat springs.

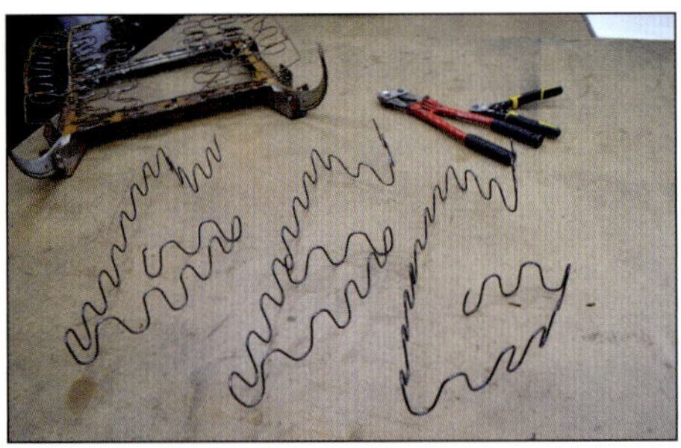

The old, damaged springs were removed from the backrest of this seat frame and new springs are ready to be installed. Welding the spring is not an option because the heat will draw the temper of the spring steel and the metal will become brittle and crack at the weld location.

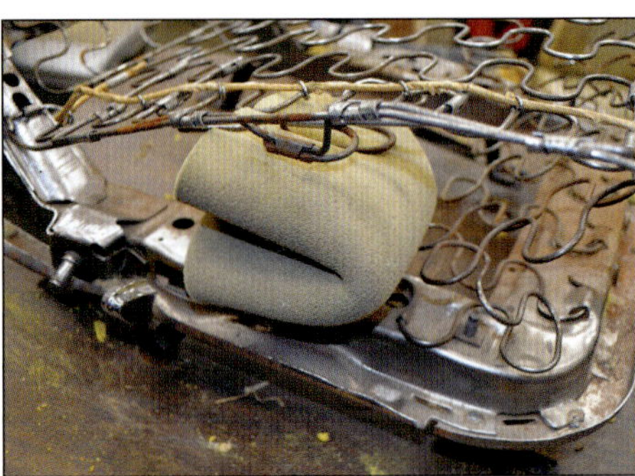

Do not do this! Placing a wad of foam under a broken spring is not the proper way to make a repair because it will only lead to more damage. It takes only a little more effort to do the job correctly, and you will have the satisfaction of doing it right instead of having to go back and make the repair again.

A broken spring cannot be welded, as the heat will draw the temper in the metal. When the spring flexes, it will break at the weld. Doubling up the spring and hog ringing it together will not hold. When the spring is shortened, it will no longer provide enough support. Stuffing the springs with foam to jack them up is also a waste of time and material. Proper replacement requires a new spring to replace the broken unit.

I find this type of repair all too often, and it always ends up with the seat being properly repaired. Bolster springs take a lot of abuse and need to be in top condition; otherwise, they will cause damage to the new upholstery. This broken spring will be removed and repaired correctly.

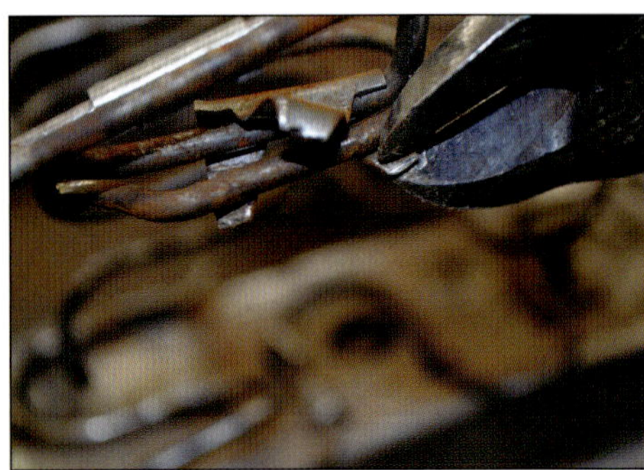

Automotive seat springs are bound together by small metal three-prong clips. The special clip is designed to grip around the springs and hold them in position without falling apart. Use a diagonal cutter to pry the fingers of the clip open to free it from the spring, and remove the clip.

To remove the broken spring, the first step is to remove the three-prong clips to release the broken spring from the edge wire. This involves a lot of twisting and awkward gripping to open up the prongs on the clip. The offset blades of a diagonal cutter will work well at getting into the tightly crimped clip. Sometimes a flat-blade screwdriver can be used to help get the tabs open enough so that you can use a pair of pliers to remove them.

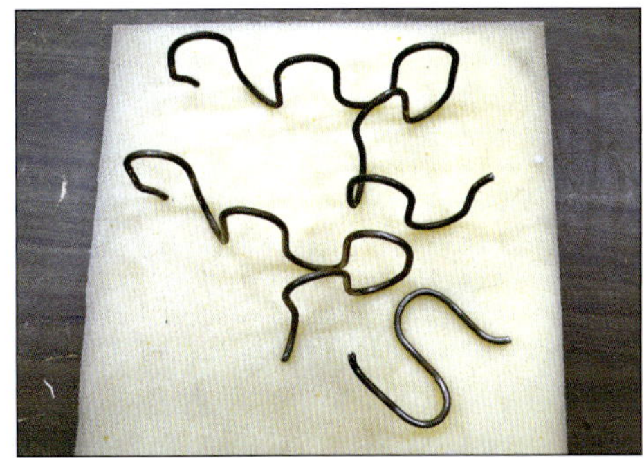

New bolster springs are available to replace broken or fatigued spring units. After the broken pieces have been removed from the seat frame, they can be compared to the new replacement unit to make sure they are the correct size and shape needed for the project.

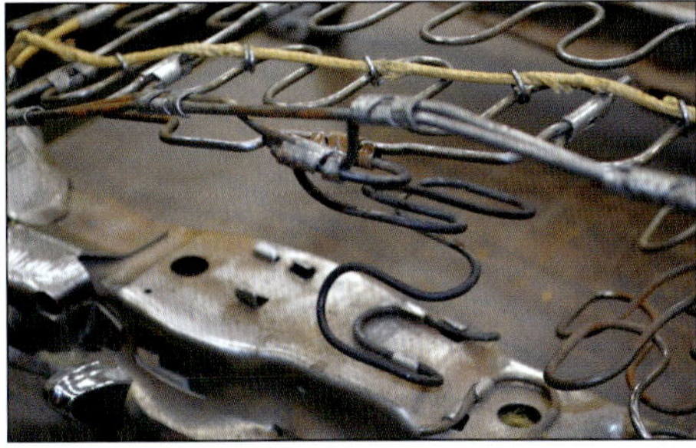

Installation of the bolster spring begins by twisting the spring into the clips on the seat frame. Three-prong clips are used to connect the springs to the other springs in the seat unit. A hog-ring pliers can be used to crimp the three-prong clip around the springs to secure it in position.

When the prong clips have been removed, the broken spring should be free and can then be removed from the seat frame. The loop ends of the spring can then be pulled from the retainers in the frame. A little twisting is also helpful to get the spring free.

Many spring sets are available from a supply house. Most are complete upper or lower unit sets that need to be attached to the seat frame. Side support or bolster springs are also available as a set and need to be inserted into the seat frame and connected to the rest of the seat springs with three-prong clips.

Hog rings are not strong enough to hold the springs in position, and they will loosen and cause damage to the new seat cover. If your new springs do not come with clips, the old ones can be straightened and reused. A special three-prong pliers is used to fasten the clips to the springs. These heavy cast devices are cumbersome and not always able to get into the tight places where a clip is needed. Although it will take a little longer to cinch the clips, a hog-ring pliers can be used and will work well to securely cinch the clip over the springs. Once the new spring material is inserted into the frame and the clips are replaced to secure the spring in their proper position, the frame can be painted before it is recovered.

Bolster Support

Strato bucket seat backrests have a support spring on each side of the spring unit. These are often broken or bent and need to be replaced. A three-prong clip holds the support to the outer side edge wire of the backrest, and the end is inserted into a small hole in the seat frame. If this hole is worn, it may need to be welded shut and redrilled to properly hold the support spring.

Check the condition of the GM Strato bucket seat back bolster support spring that is attached to the outer edge wire to see if it is broken or bent. The small spring helps give the backrest extra firmness and comfort. Compare the shape of the spring with the others and straighten or replace it if necessary.

One end of the bolster spring is attached to the outer side edge wire of the spring unit with a three-prong clip. The other end of the bolster support needs to be inserted into the small hole in the seat back frame. Worn-out anchor holes can be repaired by welding them solid and drilling a new hole.

Rusty or mouse-stained springs need a good coat of enamel paint to seal and protect them. The paint is flexible and will not chip off of the springs. Paint will also prevent any further corrosion from forming on the springs, and the smell of mouse urine will be sealed in the metal.

Painting

After the spring repairs have been made, the frame and springs can be painted to protect them from corrosion. Another benefit of painting the seat springs is that it will encapsulate the metal and lock in any smell that remains from mouse damage.

Powder coating the seat frame and springs is not a good practice. The hard surface produced by powder coating will most likely crack and flake off when the springs are flexed. Enamel is a durable paint and is a good choice to coat the seat frame and springs. Spraying the springs is a quick and easy task that can be done with a rattle can.

Be sure to cover the floor and surrounding area before spraying paint. Protect yourself by wearing a respirator to prevent breathing the paint and fumes. Follow the directions on the paint product to avoid other hazards.

Listing Anchors

Seats that have defined bolsters are usually attached to the seat springs by an anchor listing or a wire built into the foam cushion. The anchor listing does just what the name implies: it holds the seat insert or bolster listing in a fixed position to help define the profile of the seat cushion.

When the seat ages or it has had the upholstery replaced, the anchor listings get chewed up, and the paper covering on the core wire comes off. The inner wire does not have enough mass for a hog ring to effectively grab onto, and the result will be a loose or unevenly tensioned seat cover. The solution is to replace the worn or broken anchor with new material.

This anchor listing is damaged and no longer has its paper cover. There is not enough bulk on the wire to allow the correct tension when attaching a seat cover. Removing and replacing the old wire will give the seat cover a proper foundation.

Begin by removing the old anchor listing. The ends may be connected to the seat edge wire with three-prong clips or hog rings. Hog rings are used along the length of the anchor listing to prevent the wire from lifting away from the springs. Remove the fasteners to free the anchor listing.

New wire stake is used to replace the worn anchor listing. Start by forming the end of the anchor listing with a flat-blade pliers and make a 45-degree retainer bend about a 1/2 inch long. Move about 1½ inches up the wire and make a 90-degree bend. This part of the anchor listing will be secured to the rear section of the seat spring with either hog rings or a three-prong clip.

Now, straighten the wire and lay it along the surface of the seat springs until it flows past the front edge wire. Pull on the wire stake to make it taut, and then make a 90-degree bend in the wire with the pliers to make it parallel with the edge wire. Make another bend about 1½ inches from the last at 45 degrees. Cut off the wire stake a 1/2 inch from the last bend.

Secure the front of the anchor listing to the edge wire with hog rings or a three-prong clip. Add more hog rings along the length of the anchor listing, securing it to every other seat spring it passes over. Repeat the process for the other side of the seat bottom.

One variation of the anchor listing is having a curved insert or horizontal listings in the seat cover. The anchor listing is made with the same ends, but the shape and position will be attached to the springs in an arch to accommodate the insert design of the seat cover. The procedure for installing a curved anchor listing is the same as for the straight bolster listing.

Placing the Anchor Wire

1 *Shaping the new piece of wire stake is done with a pair of flat-blade pliers. A series of bends are made to form the new end of the anchor wire. This will prevent the anchor wire from shifting when it is attached to the seat springs.*

2 *Hog rings are used to secure the new anchor wire to the seat frame. A strong connection is made by cinching the hog ring diagonally over the wire stake and the seat spring below. The paper on the wire stake allows the hog ring to have a deeper hold on the wire inside.*

3 *There should be very little slack in the anchor wire to get the seat cover to fit correctly. The anchor wire must be stretched from the rear of the seat to the front edge wire where a sharp bend is made. This action will put the anchor wire at the correct length to be secured.*

4 *A hog-ring pliers is used to cinch a three-prong clip to secure the anchor wire to the front edge wire. Additional hog rings are used along the anchor wire to secure it to the seat springs. This prevents the anchor wire from rising up, which in turn causes the seat cover to bag.*

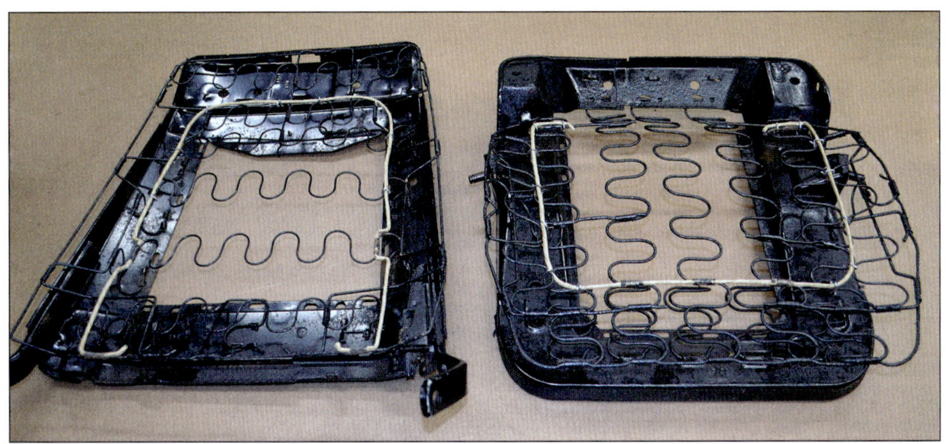

5 *A curved anchor listing is required to secure the seat cover to this deluxe Camaro seat frame. The arch in the anchor listing mimics the profile of the seat insert. Make sure the insert is evenly aligned to prevent any puckers from forming when the seat cover is installed.*

Another variation is to place the listing anchor on top of the burlap. This variation is done when you do not know the original position of the anchor. After the burlap has been installed, place the seat foam on top of the burlap to use as a reference guide. Lift the foam and mark the surface of the burlap with a Sharpie pen to indicate the location of the listing channel in the foam. Make the anchor listing from a wire stake

The foam cushion is temporarily fitted to the seat frame as a guide to locate the anchor listings. When the foam is lifted, the burlap is marked to indicate the position of the listing channels in the foam. New anchor listings will be installed over the markings.

Hog rings are used to secure the anchor listing to seat springs underneath the burlap. Additional hog rings are used along the length of the anchor listing to prevent it from lifting off of the seat. This will prevent the seat cover from being too loose or a condition called "bagging."

A pencil is used to trace the shape of the bolster spring silencer onto a piece of upholstery felt. The heavy material is well suited for this task because it is not only thin and will not disrupt the function of the spring, but it also is a strong and tough material that can withstand the flexing of the spring.

just as before and attach it to the face of the burlap with hog rings along the marker line.

Spring Silencers

Spring silencers are some of the many components that are forgotten or discarded and are deemed "not necessary" for the restoration of a car seat. It takes a little time to make and install these devices, but I add them back just the way the factory did.

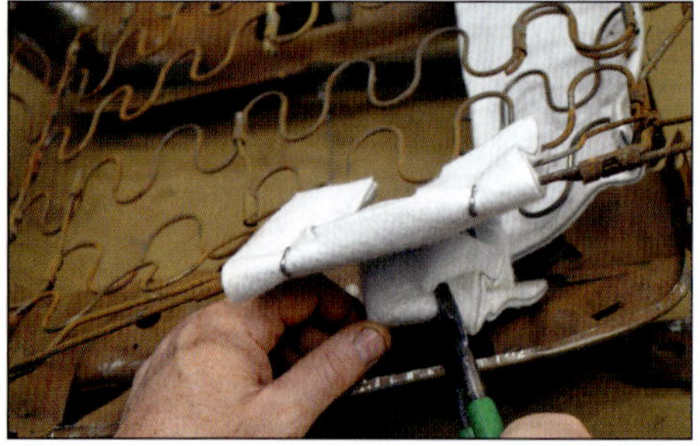

Hog rings are used to secure the spring silencer to the bolster spring after it has been wrapped. The springs still function as expected but without the squeaks and grinding sounds that emit from unwrapped springs. This extra effort makes a world of difference.

They make the seat quieter because they prevent the metal springs from rubbing on the frame and themselves, thus preventing premature wear that leads to broken springs.

Save the spring silencers from the teardown so that you have a pattern to cut new ones. If you didn't save them, you can improvise and achieve the same result. The new silencers can be made from upholstery underliner felt or 1/8-inch jute pad. The material has to be durable and thin enough that it will not interfere with the function of the springs.

Lay the old silencer on top of the new material and trace the shape.

Cut along the drawn line to make the new one. There may be two or three different pieces used in your seat frame, so make them all.

The easiest silencer to install is the front long and wide strip. This piece is slid along the frame and under the springs where they are anchored. It is then hog ringed to the springs on each end and once in the middle to keep it in place. The bolster springs are a bit more complicated to wrap with the silencer.

Take the flattened material and allow the slot in the silencer to go around the edge of the bolster spring so that the silencer can be folded in half, covering the front and back of the metal spring. Tuck the bottom of the silencer material under the bolster spring where it can rub on the seat frame and secure it with a hog ring. Next, wrap the top of the silencer over the outside of the edge wire and hog ring the ears of the silencer to the edge wire. This may take a couple of tries to get it right. Be patient and careful that you do not hog ring your fingers when securing the silencer.

Tension the Springs

Adding burlap to the top of the springs to restrict their movement will make them work together as a

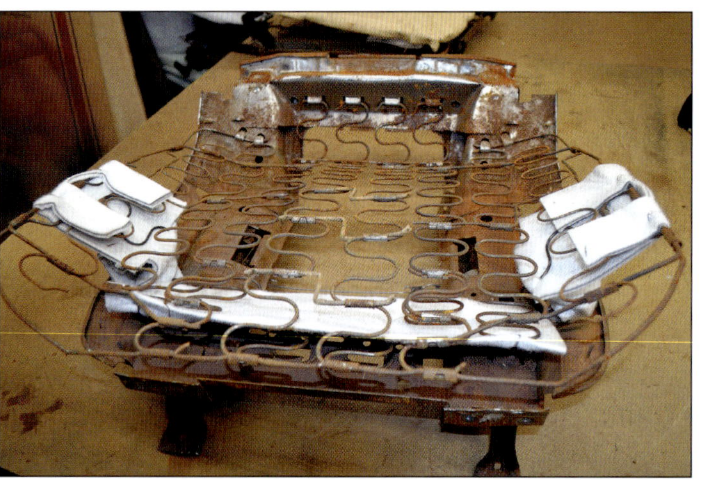

All of the spring silencers have been installed on this lower spring unit, and it is ready to have new burlap installed to tension the springs. The seat will be much more enjoyable to sit on now that it will not creak and squeak.

unit and provide firm support to the passenger. Without the burlap, the springs work individually, making the seat uncomfortable, and they can saw the foam into pieces. Originally, the factory used burlap with wires in it to tension the springs. This flexolator material is not produced any more and can be omitted if you cover the springs from edge to edge. Burlap alone will do the job if it is secured in all directions. The original flexolator only covered the center portion of springs, and they were not secured because of the tempered wires running through the burlap. The factory used this method because it was fast

to install. It was not looking into the future to make the seat last for more than a few years.

Start by cutting a piece of burlap that is 2 inches wider than the spring area in all directions. Begin hog ringing the burlap to the edge wire by folding the excess material back on itself to create a 1-inch border around the edge wire.

The folded material creates an edge roll that will hold a hog ring without tearing. Secure one side and then the opposite side, front and then rear to keep the burlap evenly tensioned over the springs. Finish the corner by pulling forward on the

side and wrapping the front over and around the corner to lock the burlap in place. Add a hog ring a 1/2 inch from each corner to complete the wrap. Continue this process of tensioning the springs with burlap on all of the seat spring units.

When the springs are properly tensioned, there should not be any wrinkles in the surface of the burlap. When the burlap is tight, it will make the springs work in unison and give the proper support needed when they are sat upon. Proper tensioning also helps the springs from over flexing by working together to share the load, which prevents broken springs.

Securing Burlap to the Springs

1 *New burlap is rolled over the seat springs and trimmed 2 inches larger than the outer edge wire. The extra material will be used to create an edge roll around the edge wire. When the burlap is doubled up, it will provide a better foundation for the hog rings and soften the perimeter.*

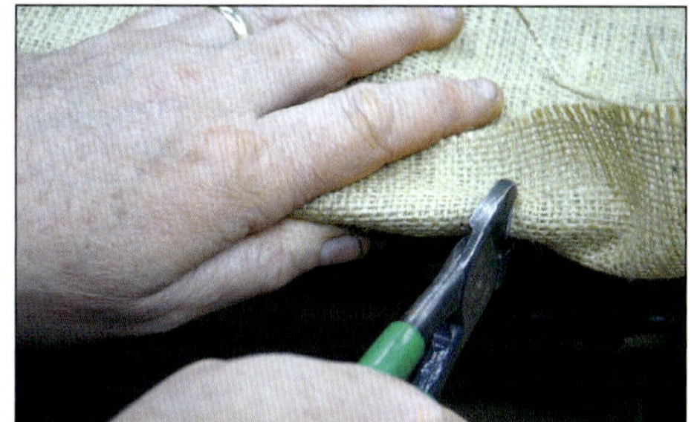

2 *Here the burlap is folded back upon itself to create an edge roll on the edge wire of the seat springs. A hog ring is cinched over the burlap to secure it to the edge wire. Hog rings are placed every 1½ inches to properly tension the burlap across the surface of the springs.*

3 *Creating a neat corner helps eliminate the material from becoming too bulky, which will cause the seat to be lumpy. When the burlap is folded crisply and secured with hog rings from one direction and then crossed over from the other, it will lay flat and form a sharp corner.*

4 *This lower spring unit is now properly tensioned with burlap and is ready for the other support materials to be added before the new upholstery can be applied. Having a solid foundation to build on makes all the difference in the longevity of the seat cover.*

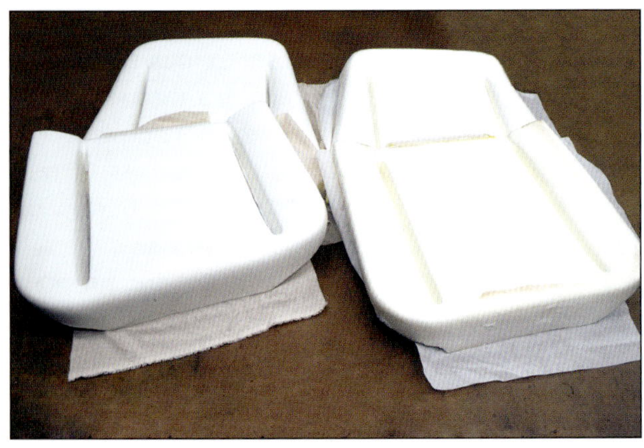

These two sets of seat foam are made by different manufacturers and yet they are designed to fit the same 1969 Impala seat cover. Each has attachment listing materials, and they are almost the same shape. The real difference is in the density of the foam.

A side-by-side compression comparison of the different foam shows that one of the cushions is firmer than the other. This is a matter of personal choice. Softer foam does not have the same support as firm foam and is a little easier to work with. The firm foam will give better support and perform better over time.

Foam

Adding new foam cushions to the seat will not only provide comfort to the passenger but will also fill out the new seat cover and prevent the baggy and wrinkled look caused by worn-out foam. Choosing the type of foam for your project is up to your individual taste. The density of the foam does make a difference in the overall longevity of the seat. Soft foam is cushy and easy to work with. It compresses with less effort and makes a nice seat. Firm foam is dense and is a little more difficult to work with, but it provides a stiffer cushion and tends to last longer.

Fitting the Foam

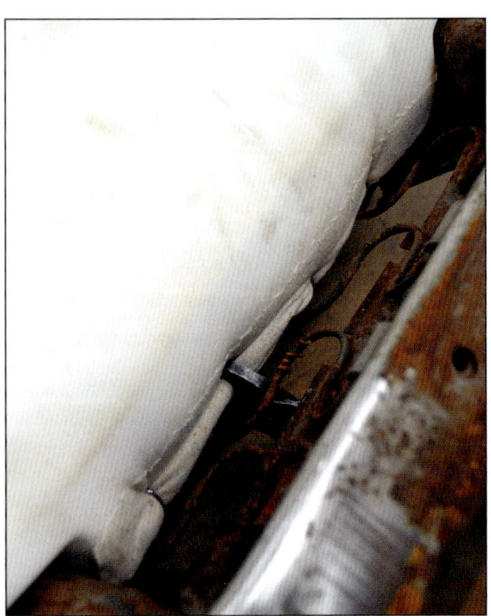

1 *Hog rings are used to secure the rear edge of the foam cushion to the support springs of the bottom seat frame. To prevent the hog rings from tearing through the foam when cinched, a piece of muslin has been added to the edge of the foam to reinforce the soft, spongy material.*

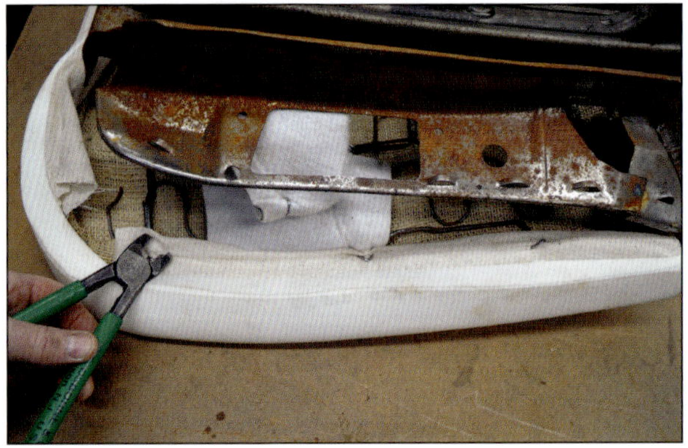

2 *To keep the foam secure, the muslin stretcher is doubled up to create a better surface for the hog rings to bite into without tearing out. Anchoring the foam cushion only takes a few hog rings along the underside of the seat springs to prevent the pad from shifting.*

3 *A Sharpie pen is used to mark the location of the headrest guide posts on the backside of the new foam cushion. Removing this small amount of foam will permit the guide posts to pass through the foam and allow the new seat cover to fit properly.*

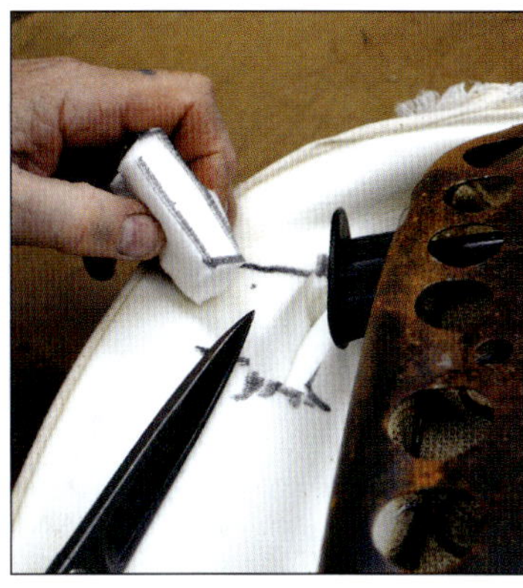

4 A pair of scissors is used to remove the unwanted piece of foam from the top of the cushion. Taking the time to make an accurate cut in the foam will yield a better fit for the seat cover, giving you the desired result of an easier installation and a nice-looking bucket seat.

5 This is what the top of the foam should look like when the headrest guide post has been properly set in the foam. Making the effort to prep the foam ahead of time will allow your new seat cover to look and fit better.

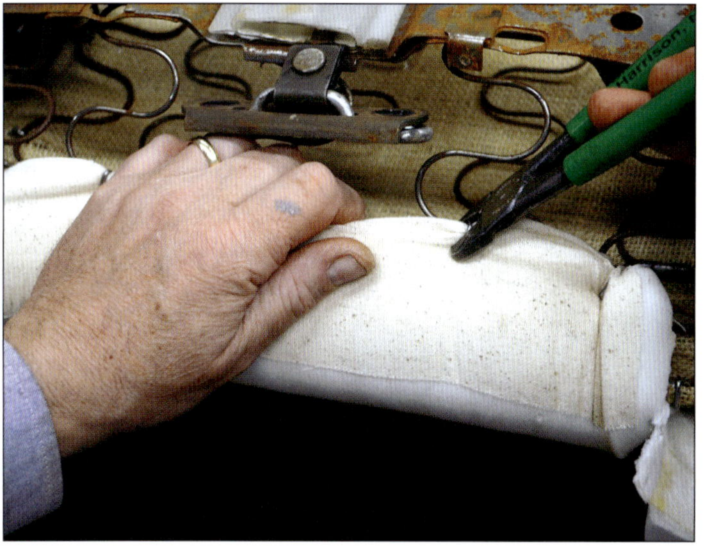

6 Hog rings are added to the fabric-covered bottom edge of the backrest foam to prevent it from moving. The foam must be pulled and adjusted to remove any slack from top to bottom as it is secured to the seat springs.

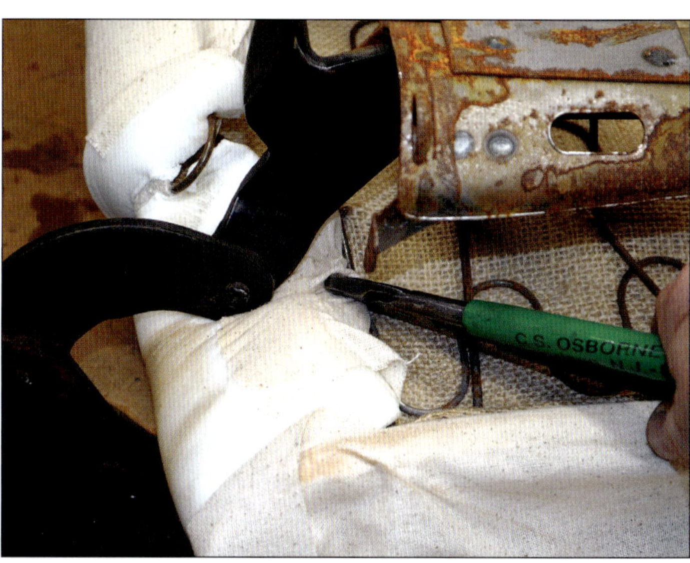

7 Additional hog rings are used to secure the lower section of the side bolster to the seat frame. The foam is neatly tucked into place under the mounting bracket to give the foam the proper shape to fill the lower portion of the seat cover.

Apply a thin layer of cotton over the burlap to level the bottom seat springs. The cotton allows the foam to lay flatter on the springs, which will make the seat more comfortable to sit on. The new foam cushion, or bun, is placed over the cotton and burlap on the seat frame and squared up by aligning the listing channels with the listing anchor wire. There should be a strip of cloth glued to the edge of the foam. This gives support to the foam, preventing the hog rings from tearing through the foam when the hog rings are used to secure the foam cushion to the seat frame. If the foam does not have this strip of fabric, use a 2-inch piece of muslin fabric and glue it to the lower edge of the foam.

Begin by attaching the rear edge of the foam to the seat springs or attachment loops on the inside of the lower seat frame. Flip the seat frame over and look at the underside of the foam. The foam should extend past the edge wire on the front and sides. You may need to pull on the foam to allow the edge wire to be on the inside of the skirt of the foam.

Secure the Foam

Fold the fabric in half to make it thicker and then fasten the fabric to the underside of the springs with a couple of hog rings to keep the foam in place. Secure one side and then the other before anchoring the front. This keeps the foam from bunching up.

The backrest foam is applied a little differently than the bottom on the Strato bucket. Some of the seat models will have headrest guides on the top of the frame. These guide posts must go through the foam and finish flush on the surface of the foam. To make this happen, place the foam bun face down on the workbench and set the backrest on the foam, centering the springs in the foam. At the top of the foam you will have a gap where the headrest guides extend from the metal back. Use a Sharpie pen to mark the location of the shaft onto the foam. Do not mark the flange on top of the guide; just mark the shaft.

This small piece of foam will need to be removed to allow the guides to pass through the foam. You can use a pair of scissors or knife to carefully cut a hole in the foam. Work the guide through the hole until the top of the guide rests on top of the foam. The gap that was at the top of the foam should now be gone and the springs should sit correctly inside of the foam.

With the backrest face down on the workbench, gently pull the foam toward the bottom and wrap the lower part of the cushion around the bottom of the springs and hog ring the edge of the center section of the foam to the seat springs. Make sure you do not pull on the foam enough to distort the upper portion with the guide posts.

Next, secure the bottoms of the bolster section of the foam to the seat springs. It is easier to lift the attachment brackets and then wrap the foam around the springs and tuck the foam under the brackets before securing it with hog rings.

After the bottom is secured, move on to the sides of the foam and hog ring the edges to the inside of the backrest. The fabric along the top section of foam can be either glued in place or the fabric can be attached to the small metal attachment loops in the seat back with hog rings.

Inspect the Seat Cover

Premade seat covers are a quick way to get your worn and damaged seats back to original condition. When your package arrives, inspect the enclosed materials to verify that they are the correct pattern and color for your project. Check the embossed pattern and seams for any flaws that may have gotten past the manufacturer. If you find an issue with the seat cover that cannot be easily corrected, contact the seller immediately to get instructions on how to get a replacement. If you install or alter a part, it may not be returnable.

To get a good fit and finish, you may need to trim the ends of the seams that have a welt cord extending past the seam allowance. This prevents a lump from forming when the cover is fit. Also check the ends of the listings. It is not uncommon that they may have been sewn over during the assembly process. This is not something to be alarmed about. To correct this condition, use a pair of scissors to cut the listing material as close to the seam stitching without

The ends of welt cords may not be trimmed as neatly as they could have been during the manufacturing process. Removing excess material takes nothing more than a snip with a pair of scissors, and the seat cover will be ready to install.

cutting into the thread. When done properly, the listing should move freely. The seat cover can be installed after it has been inspected.

When some seat covers are sewn together, listings and other components can often be over sewn into another seam. Fixing this condition can be as simple as trimming along the stitching to allow the listing to be attached to the anchor listing.

Some listings have a cord sewn into them, and others need to have a wire inserted through a channel. The listing wire or cord provides a substantial anchor to prevent the hog ring from tearing through the listing material when anchored to the seat.

Lower Cushion

Prepare the bottom foam by cutting out the thin layer of material from the listing channel. This material makes securing a hog ring

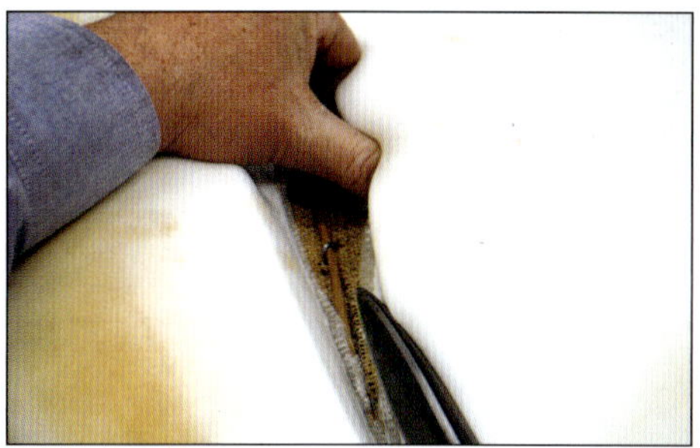

It is much easier to secure the bolster listings to the listing anchor when the membrane in the listing channel of the foam is removed. A pair of scissors is used to cut through the material in the bolster channel of the foam cushion to expose the listing anchor.

through the bolster listing to the anchor listing very difficult. If you secure the bolster listing directly to the underlying anchor, the hog rings will hold the listing better, and it will pull the seat cover into the correct position for the seat foam to fill the cover.

Begin the installation by laying the seat cover on top of the foam and square it up with the foam before you begin to attach it. Insert a listing wire into the rear listing before hog ringing it to the exposed seat springs at the back edge of the foam cushion. With the rear listing of the seat cover anchored to the frame, the bolster listings can then be anchored.

Some bolster listings already have a cord sewn into them to help hold the cover secure. Other listings

may require a listing wire to be slid into the sleeve before it is hog ringed in place. Select a side and begin hog ringing from the rear and work your way forward. Pull forward on the listing and place a hog ring about every 2 inches, joining the listing to the anchor listing wire below the burlap. This will keep tension on the listing and prevent the seat cover from developing a scalloping effect. Repeat on the other bolster listing.

Lift the seat cover and add a layer of cotton to the top of the bolster foam. Tuck the cotton into the listing channel to fill it up and tear the cotton off even with the outer edge of the foam. The cotton will help soften the feel of the seat cover and prevent the foam from chafing and prematurely wearing out.

The new seat cover's alignment to the seat frame is essential to getting a good fit. The edges of the cover need to meet the shape of the foam. Lift the cover to verify that the bolster listings line up with the channels in the foam cushion.

It takes a little finesse to get the rear listing deep into the rear section of the seat. The rear cap panel must be lifted as the listing is pushed down between the seat track channels. The listing wire must be close to the springs so that it can be anchored properly.

The seat cover is first anchored to the seat frame by the rear listing. Slide a piece of wire stake into the rear listing sleeve before it is attached to the rear springs with hog rings. This allows the cover to be pulled forward without losing the alignment.

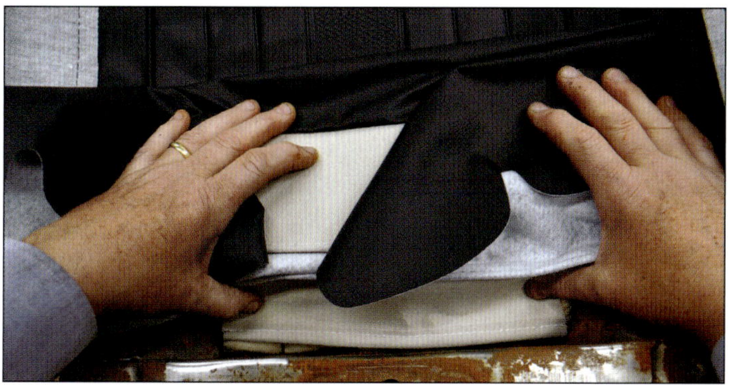

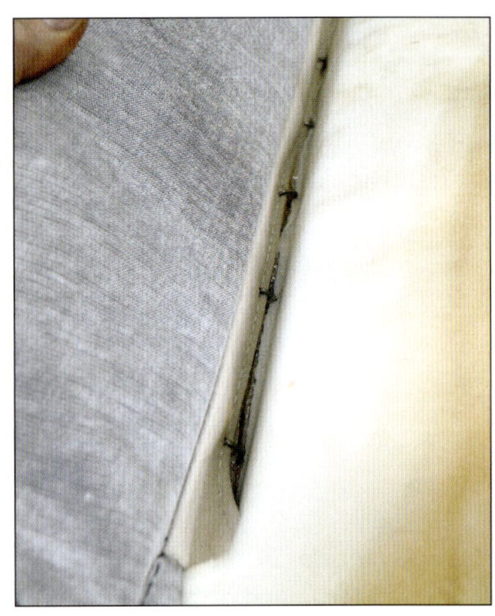

The rear listing of the seat cover is anchored to the seat springs along the rear of the seat frame with several hog rings. This listing keeps the cover from shifting when more hog rings are added to the rest of the seat cover.

To help shape the seat cover, a layer of cotton is applied to the top of the foam cushion and bolster listing channel. The cotton also helps prevent the seat cover from rubbing directly on the foam as it fills out the seat's bolster area.

Deep inside the channel of the seat foam, hog rings are used to secure the bolster listing to the anchor wire underneath the burlap. To keep an even tension on the bolster listing, the hog rings are spaced evenly along the length of the listing.

Fitting the Cover

Pulling the seat cover over the foam can be a bit of a struggle. You can easily tear the material if you yank on it wrong, and it will never fit correctly if you just pull it down on the foam. The seat cover has to be worked into position, and the seam allowance must lie smoothly along the edge of the foam. To make this happen, the seat cover should be inside out with the edge of the seam running along the edge of the foam. Now, inch the seat cover material down over the foam. It will help if you push in and compress the foam to allow the seat cover to come down without tearing. Continue to ease the cover over the foam and then straighten out the boxing by gently pulling down on the bottom listing.

Before the bottom of the seat cover can be secured to the seat frame, a listing wire needs to be

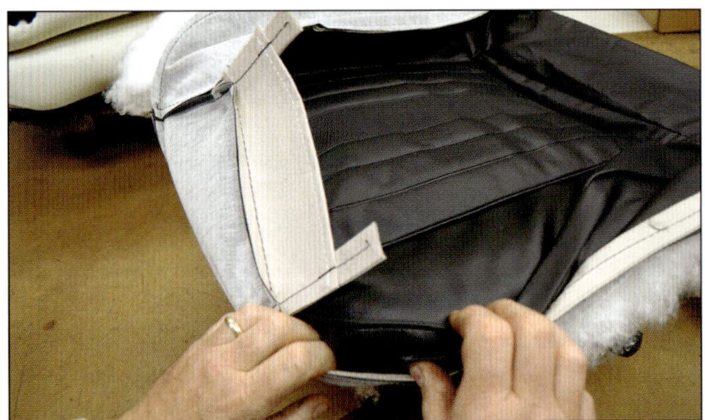

Pulling on the seat cover like this will end in disaster. The resistance on the cover material as it is being pulled will cause the cover to tear. This will result in wrinkles in the cover that can be very difficult to work out.

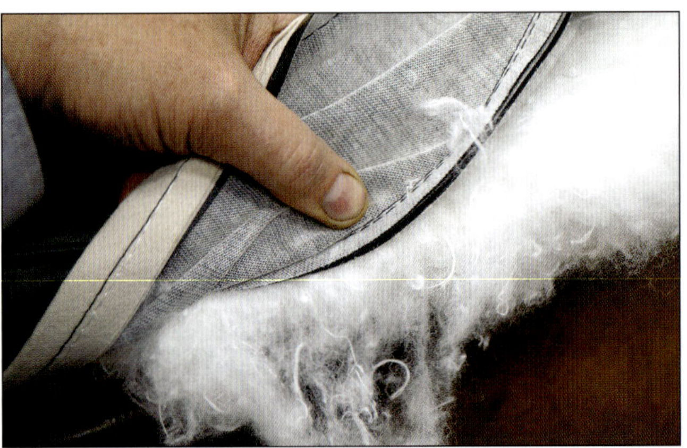

To prevent wrinkles from forming along the welting of the seat cover, the seam allowance is placed at the outer edge of the foam so that the seat cover can flow over the band of material. When properly aligned, the cover material will pull over nicely.

Wire stake is fed through the pocket on the bottom listing of the seat cover. The 16-gauge wire is covered with craft paper that follows the shape of the seat frame and makes an excellent anchor for the hog rings.

Hog rings are added to the front stretcher listing to hold it in place. A listing wire was inserted into the pocket along the leading edge of the stretcher before the cover material is pulled into position and secured.

installed in the perimeter listing. I like to use wire stake for the listing wire because it is strong but flexible enough to conform to the curve around the bottom of the seat cover. Turn the seat face down on the workbench, insert the listing wire into the listing, and trim it to length with a diagonal cutter.

Secure the Bottom

Lift the listing over the edge of the seat frame with the seam allowance flat against the metal frame. Hog ring the listing to the seat frame by cinching it through the raised loop in the frame. Secure the cover with a couple of hog rings and then jump over to the other side and repeat the process.

Move on to the front of the seat cover and insert a listing wire into the stretcher listing. Pull the stretcher until the wrinkles in the front of the seat cover come out. Hog ring the stretcher to the seat springs to hold the tension on the cover.

Continue to add hog rings around the front of the seat cover until the listing is secured and the wrinkles are gone. Finish securing the cover along the sides until all the hog ring loops are used. Turn the seat upright and check the fit of the seat cover. There should not be any wrinkles in the seat cover at this point. If there are any fitment issues, now is the time to address them. You can always cut away some of the hog rings and shift the cover so that it will fit better. You may also need to grab the welt and roll the seam allowance outward to help the seam lay smooth. When you

Working from side to side, the lower edge of the seat cover has been pulled over the bottom of the seat frame and a hog-ring pliers is used to set a hog ring that will pre-position the bottom listing of the cover to the frame.

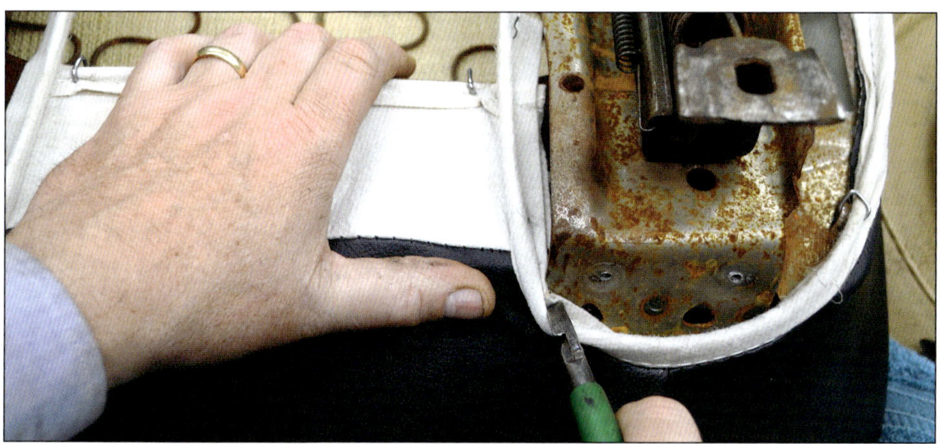

After the seat cover has been set in position, additional hog rings are added to the lower listing to keep the cover from wrinkling. The fasteners are added around the front of the seat frame and extend toward the rear of the seat.

are satisfied with the appearance of the seat cover, the rear cap can be secured.

Rear Cap

With the bottom cushion upright on the workbench, lift the rear cap forward to expose the rear bolster listings. These small listings help keep the proper tension on top of the seat cover. Secure them to the back of the seat frame with hog rings. To get a hog ring in place, use the palm of your hand on the top of the bolster and slide it to the rear. This action will help bring the listing closer to the anchor loops, allowing a hog ring to be easily cinched in place.

Before the rear cap material is pulled over the back of the seat bottom, check the alignment of the seam with the edge of the metal riser. To get the material to lay smoother, the seam allowance should be on the outer edge of the riser. Work the cap material over the back of the seat frame and then turn the unit face down on the workbench.

To protect the seat cover from being damaged, insert the spring liner over the lower back of the seat so that it covers the springs and ridge on the back of the metal seat base.

Pull the rear cap over the spring liner and secure it by hog ringing the stretcher to the seat springs. Pull the cap material to the side so that it wraps around the outside of the track channel. When the material is folded and tensioned correctly, most of the wrinkles will come out. When you are satisfied with the look, hog ring the material to the seat frame. Now, fasten the inside flap in the same way. Secure the center tab by tucking the tab under the seat track and then tighten the track bolt to capture the material.

The outer ends of the seat cover are not attached at this point of assembly. They will be secured after the backrest is attached to the seat bottom.

Seat Bumper

The rubber seat bumpers attach to the top of the bottom riser with small panhead sheet-metal screws. With the seat upright on the bench, use a regulator to pierce the cover material and locate the underlying anchor hole. Insert the anchor screw in the bumper and secure the bumper by tightening the screw.

Seats that have a metal catch for the backrest are also mounted to the rear riser on the bottom seat frame. Locate the mounting holes with a regulator and cut a small circle of material to clear the threaded anchor point. Align the catch to the riser and insert the anchor bolts. Start the bolts by hand tightening them to avoid accidental cross-threading, and then finish tightening the bolts with the appropriate-sized socket wrench.

Additional tension is applied to the seat cover by anchoring the rear inner seat cover listings to the inside of the seat frame. When the seat is used, the small listings prevent the seat cover from sagging and developing wrinkles over time.

Just before the rear seat cap is pulled over the back of the seat riser, the seam allowance is positioned along the outer edge of the metal riser. This prevents the corners of the rear cap from accumulating too much bulk and reduces wrinkles.

Beneath the rear cap is a piece of chip board that is used as a barrier between the seat springs and seat material. Without the spring liner, the seat cover will sustain damage by the flexing of the seat springs and the sharp ends of the hog rings.

When pulled into position, the cap holds the spring liner in place. A listing wire has been inserted into the sleeve on the outer edge of the stretcher and then the trailing edge of the rear cap is fastened to the seat springs with hog rings.

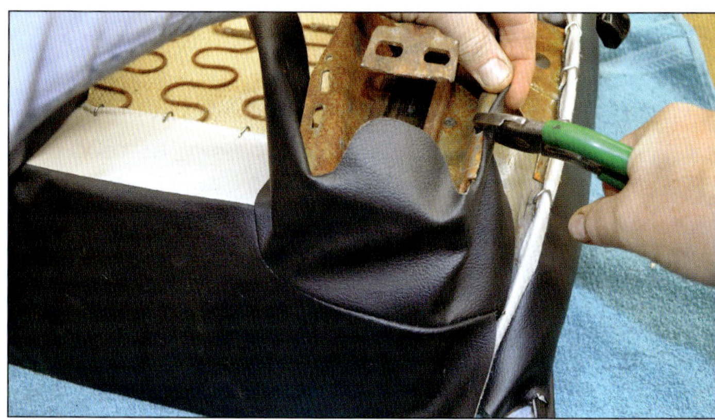

Some extra material has been sewn into the rear cap to cover the rear of the track channels. The wrinkles are removed by folding the top edge of the cover material to the inside, and then the flap is secured to the seat base with hog rings.

Reproduction rubber seat bumpers are available to replace the hard, cracked, and broken bumpers. The new bumpers look the same as the originals but are much softer and provide a better fit and feel to the seat backrest.

This Camaro seat bottom uses a separate metal catch to lock the upper backrest into position and keep it from flopping forward while driving. Before the attachment bolts can be added, the anchor points must be located and opened up.

A small 1/4-inch-drive ratchet wrench is used to tighten the anchor bolts for the final time. The bolts need to be tight, but do not overtighten them, which can cause them to break or strip the threads of the anchor hole.

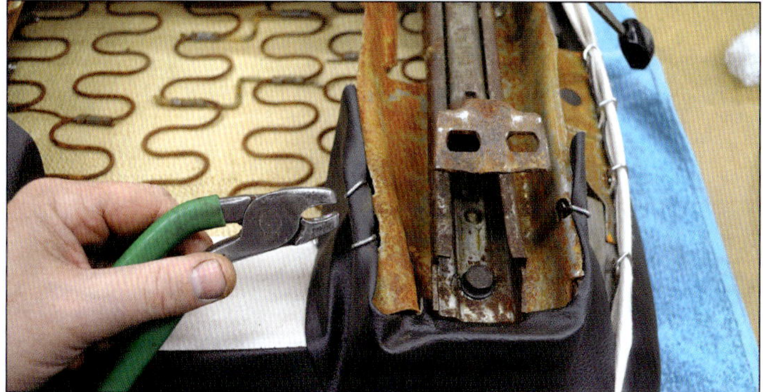

There is no real function to the rear channel cover material other than it dresses up the gaps in the metal seat frame. Additional hog rings are added to hold the inside channel cover material to the set frame. The center tab is held securely by the seat track.

Attachment Variation

The Camaro seat cushion does not use hog rings to secure the cover to the frame. There is a band of nylon sewn into the bottom edge of the seat cover that is inserted behind a metal retainer band inside of the seat frame.

The trick here is to compress the foam, which will lower the seat cover enough to slide the nylon band

Not all seat covers are attached to the seat frame with hog rings. Special fasteners are used on many models. Early Camaros used a strip of nylon tucked under the rim of the frame to hold the seat cover in place.

Some trimming may be necessary to allow the retainer to fit into the retainer slot without binding. When the retainer is inserted correctly, the bottom edge of the seat cover will wrap smoothly around the inside of the seat frame.

behind the retainer in the seat base. The corners are the toughest part to secure, so begin there and work your way around the base. It may be necessary to flare out the retainer prior to installation to make the insertion of the nylon easier.

Backrest Cover

Attaching the backrest cover has some similarities to the lower cushion. The cover is aligned to the foam and the bolster listings are anchored to the frame. The big differences are in the backrest release levers and headrest mounting hardware.

Emblems

After the seat cover is inspected and prepped, the seat emblems need to be installed. Take the recorded dimensions from the teardown and

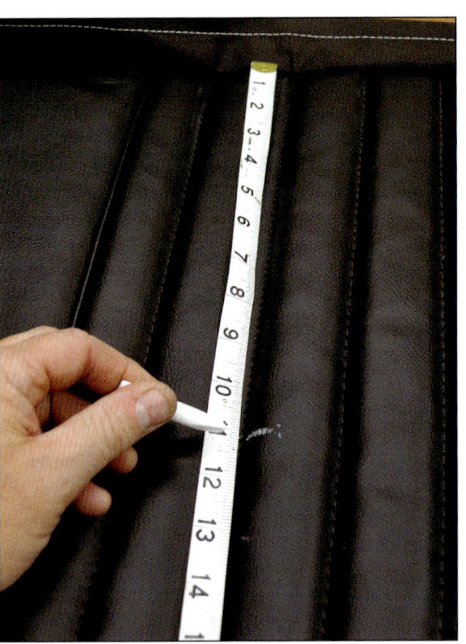

Adding seat emblems to the new cover is rather fun. Careful measuring is required to get the emblem in the correct position, but what a difference it makes to a plain seat cover. Always measure twice before making a hole in your seat cover.

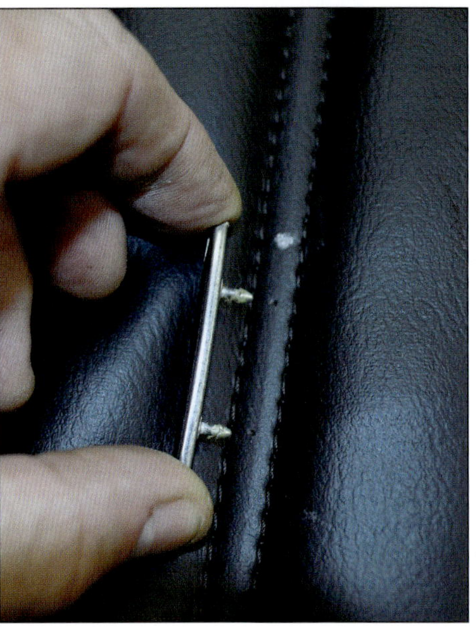

After the location of the seat emblem has been determined, use the actual emblem to make reference marks on the seat cover to minimize any installation error. Mounting holes can now be accurately made in the seat cover.

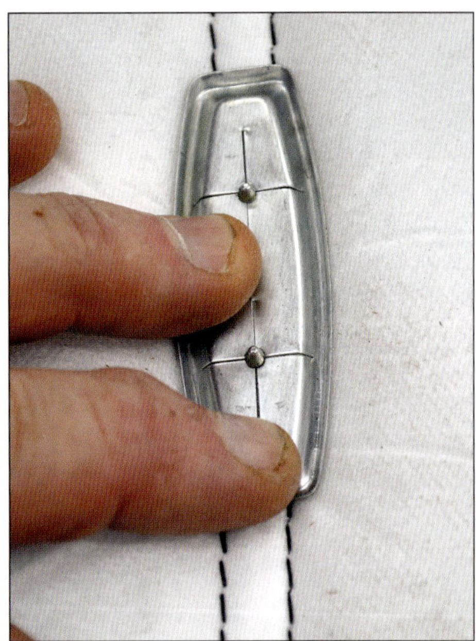

Securing the seat emblem in place is done by a retainer plate on the backside of the seat cover. When the small studs on the emblem extend through the cover material, they are captured in the openings of the recessed backer plate.

transfer them to the face of the insert. You can put masking tape on the cover to write on or just use chalk. Line up the top edge of the emblem with the mark you made and push down on the surface of the seat cover to make a small indent in the material. These marks indicate where the through holes will need to be created.

Use a regulator to pierce the seat cover material. The hole must go through all the layers of material so that the studs will reach the backside of the cover. Insert the emblem into the holes and turn the seat cover face down on the workbench. Make sure that the studs are extended all the way though the material and then position the backer over the studs. Press down hard on the backer plate until the tips of the studs pop through to lock the emblem in place. In the case that your emblem has tabs, they must go through the openings in the backer and then they are carefully bent over to secure the emblem.

Anchoring the Cover

Open the channels in the foam to reveal the anchor listings and then prep the seat cover by trimming the extended welt ends. Secure the bolster listings to the anchor listing with hog rings, starting from the bottom and working upward.

A layer of cotton is then added to the top of the foam bolster to help fill out the seat cover and prevent the material from rubbing on the foam. The cotton should be tucked deep into the bolster channel to fill the gap between the listing and the foam.

When fitting the cover on the front seats, always work the top corners over the foam first. If you fit the bottom before the top, the cover will not be able to stretch over the foam. The seam allowance should lay in the direction you want the cover material to go. Line up the seam with the edge of the foam and inch the cover over the corner.

If the upper corners of the cover look soft or baggy, add some extra cotton in the corners. Use a regulator to work the cotton into the void, taking care to avoid puncturing the seat cover with the tool. Do not secure the cover to the seat frame at this stage.

Securing the seat cover begins with the bolsters. Each bolster listing of the upper seat cover is attached to the anchor listing that is concealed deep within the foam cushion with hog rings. Keep an even tension on the listing as it is fastened.

Depending on the seat design, a little modification to the inner listing is necessary. To prevent an unsightly bulge in the backrest, the bolster listing may need to be trimmed to remove the bulk from the channel in the foam.

It is not recommended to install new upholstery directly over the foam. To enhance comfort and the fit of the seat cover, new cotton is applied over the foam cushion. The extra padding will fill the void in the bolster channel.

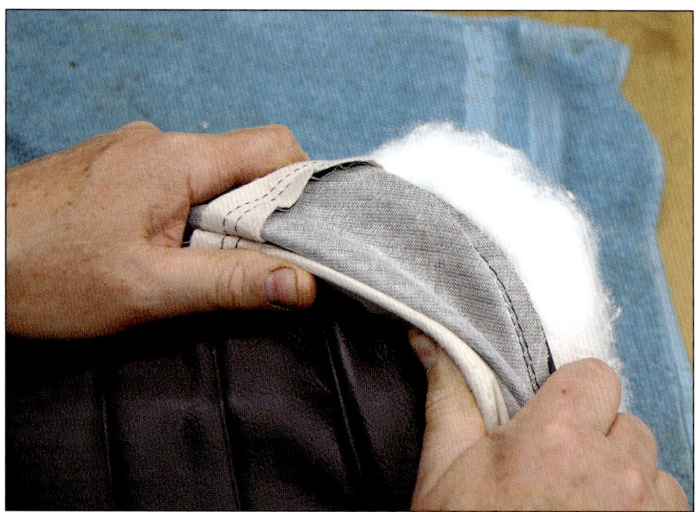

Tugging and pulling on a seat cover during installation can cause the material to tear from all of the friction and stress put on it. Carefully inching the cover over a corner from the top down will prevent damage to the upholstery.

The bottom corner seams of the seat cover are lined up with the edges of the foam before it is wrapped over the seat frame. This will look nicer and prevent the welt from becoming twisted underneath the cover.

After the upper corners are fit, move to the bottom corners and repeat the process. When the cover is worked over the lower corners, the bottom of the seat cover can be secured to the frame. This will tension the seat cover and help pull the wrinkles from the bolsters. Start by securing the inner bottom stretcher to the seat springs with hog rings.

Lower Listings

Before the bottom of the backrest cover is attached to the seat frame, it will help to reposition the back-panel tab. Not all seat frames have this tab, but if you bend it up and out of the way, you will be able to fasten the lower edge of the seat cover to the seat frame with less interference.

The first hog ring will be a tough stretch to get fastened. It helps if you lean on the seat frame to help compress the springs and foam, which will allow you to pull the rear listing into position. Begin the attachment by cinching a hog ring in the center of the panel. Continue working outward on each side by adding more hog rings until the listing is secured. Go back and re-crimp the first hog ring to

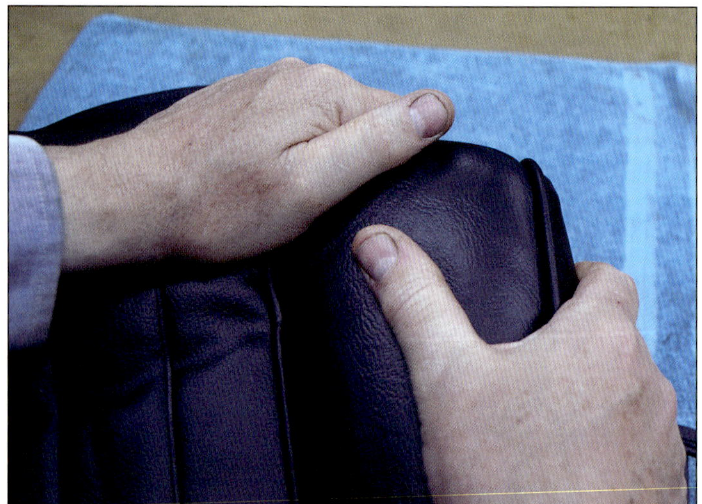

During the fitting of the seat cover, some wrinkles may appear in the bolster of the seat cover. Massage the seat cover with your thumb to help relieve any small wrinkles in the lower portion of the bolster after it has been fitted.

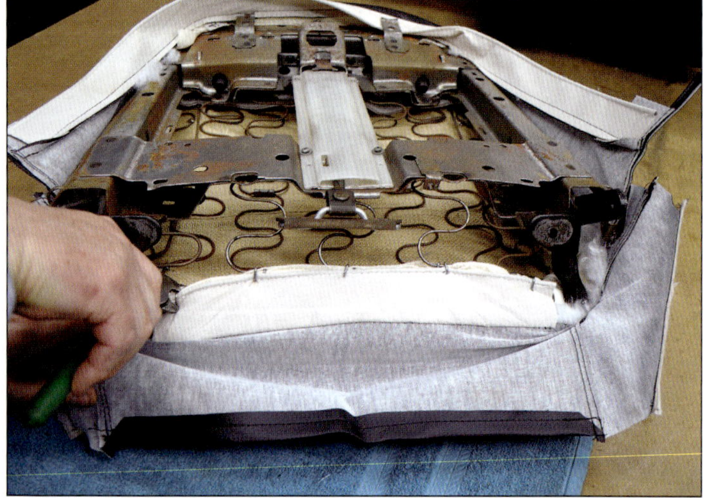

Keep a constant tension on the seat cover to prevent wrinkles from forming and prolong the life of the seat cover. Hog rings are used to anchor the inner stretcher along the backside of the lower springs.

Sometimes it helps to remove or alter some hardware on the seat frame to make the installation of the new seat cover easier. This little tab is in the way and needs to be moved to allow better access to the rear anchor points.

A listing wire has been inserted into the sleeve of the rear panel prior to it being tucked under the seat back tab on the seat frame. The edge of the seat cover is held in place along the rear seat frame with several hog rings.

Tension on the backrest bolsters is established by anchoring the bottom tabs of seat cover. These flaps are worked in behind the seat hinges and attached by hog ringing the sewn-in listing to the exposed springs in the seat frame.

ensure that it is tight. When the listing is attached, the small tab can be tapped back into its original position.

Perimeter Listings

The bottom inside corner of the seat cover has a short listing sewn onto it and it needs to be tucked up behind the seat back hinges. Lift up on the hinge to make room for the flap to lay smoothly. To keep the flap in place, pull upward on the flap, and then hog ring the listing to the backrest springs. When both sides are secured, move to the top of the seat.

Working with the backrest face down, pull on the top listing and work it under the upper back cover anchor tabs. The listing should be pulled until it reaches the anchor loops on the seat frame. Secure the listing to the loop with a hog ring.

Pull on the seat cover material from the top downward along the backside of the backrest to create tension. Hog rings are used to secure the upper perimeter listing to the seat frame anchor points on the upper frame rail.

A good stretch is given to the lower section of the seat cover to remove the wrinkles in the material as it is held in position on the seat frame. Hog rings are used along the bottom edge welt of the seat cover to keep it in place.

Securing the outer cover to the inner frame rail is done by hog ringing the listing to the anchor points along the frame. After the seat cover is completely attached to the seat frame, the hog rings will be hidden by the solid trim cover.

For a better fit along the back inside corner of the seat cover, a fold is made in the corner of the seat cover to allow the material to lay flat against the frame. A hog ring is placed in the corner to prevent the listing from separating.

Now, move to the lower section of the cover and pull the material inward and even with the bottom edge of the backrest frame. Hog ring the welt of the cover to the loop in the frame and add another along the lower inside center frame. Working your way up from the bottom, add more hog rings to the listing along the stretcher to secure them to the inner frame.

When you reach the upper corner, the side should tuck under the top to form a nice sharp fold. Cinch a hog ring at the intersection of the listing to keep the seat cover smooth and tight. Turn the backrest over and check for any wrinkles that may be present. To relax the wrinkles, apply some steam or heat to the seat cover. Stubborn wrinkles can be removed by clipping some hog rings and adjusting the cover to help relieve the material before the hog rings are replaced.

Seat Back Variation

Prior to 1969, the seat backrest had different latching mechanisms with upper trim panel anchor tabs that screwed into the rear top rail of the seat frame. The latch release buttons were located on the outer side of the backrest closest to the door. A base plate for the release button was screwed to the side of the seat frame on top of the cover material. After the trim cover is fitted, the release button and retainer trim plate would be installed with trim screws.

Seat backs that have a lower release lever mechanism have specific driver/passenger-side backrest seat covers that are made with a lever opening designed into the cover. Be aware of this difference prior to fitting the seat cover because the backrest covers are not interchangeable.

When this style of cover is installed, the foam and cotton padding must be carefully positioned to prevent the padding from getting into and jamming the release mechanism. When the cover material is pulled to the inside to be fastened, the opening for the release lever must clear the lever. Secure the cover material to the seat frame with hog rings to prevent it from shifting

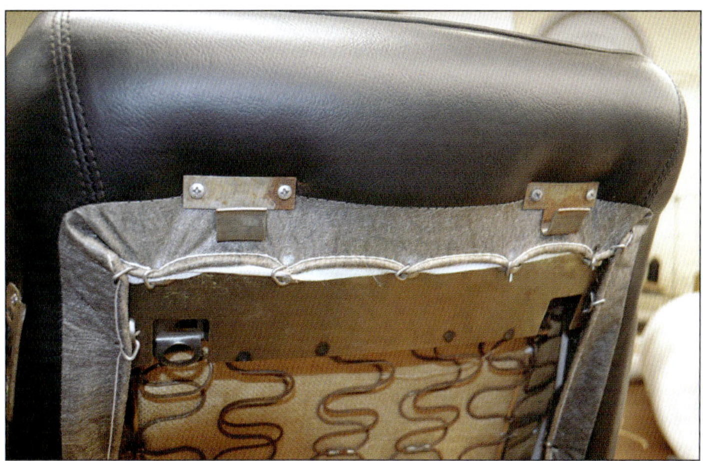

This early Strato bucket seat uses back trim panel mounting hardware that is attached after the seat cover is installed. These variations were common in yearly production and later revised as manufacturing methods improved.

On this side-release button model, a metal base plate is used to secure the seat cover to the frame. Before the retainer is concealed by the trim panel, the cover material inside the retainer is cut away to allow the actuator button access to the mechanism.

Having the latch work properly is a key safety issue. Prior to securing the seat cover to the frame, special attention is taken to prevent the underlying seat cover padding from interfering with the operation of the seat back release mechanism.

This seat cover has been created with an opening to allow the seat back release lever to operate without being obstructed. The cover material has been installed over the lever and is secured with a hog ring.

To allow the latching mechanism of this Camaro seat to work properly, a large opening has been built into the bottom panel of the seat cover. The seat foam and cover have been carefully secured to prevent any movement of the materials.

A thin layer of the original protective jute padding is still attached to the backside of this seat frame. Before the new seat cover is installed, the old pad will be detached with a scraper and then discarded. A modern felt pad will replace the old padding.

This cover is designed with side listings to make the seat cover easier to install. Hog rings are used to cinch the side listings of the seat cover closed. Stainless trim moldings will later be applied to hide the listings.

This style of seat cover uses decorative stainless-steel trim moldings that are applied to the sides of the backrest to conceal the listings and fasteners. A screwdriver is used to carefully tighten the trim screws that hold the moldings in place.

position. Check the operation of the lever to be sure that it works properly before proceeding with the seat cover installation.

Full-Coverage Design

Some seat covers do not have a separate hard cover panel for the back. The upholstery is designed to fit all around the seat back. There are a few things you need to know to get a good fit.

The seat frame is metal, and you will need to replace the worn or damaged jute padding that was once attached to the frame. This padding is not for comfort, but rather to protect the seat cover material from wearing against the sharp metal frame. To get started, remove the old padding by scraping it off and replacing it with new underliner felt. The padding should be glued to the seat frame to cover the metal. Make sure that the padding is applied smoothly over the frame without any overlap along the edges.

The foam cushion and seat cover are fitted the same as most covers. The bolster listings are attached first, and then the cover is pulled over the top of the frame. After the seat cover has been squared up and the cotton padding adjusted, the sides of the cover are joined together with hog rings. The listings and hog rings will eventually be concealed by decorative trim moldings after the seat back is fitted to the bottom cushion.

Backrest Stops

One of the most overlooked items on a car seat is the backrest stop. This is the solid metal item that mates with the rubber bumper that is mounted on the riser of the lower seat cushion. A backrest stop may be adjustable, or it can be as simple as a flat-washer type.

The backrest stop is typically located on the bottom rail of the backrest. Locate the anchor point with a regulator and then cut away a small circle of cover material to expose the threaded anchor point. Insert the stud of the stop and tighten the anchor screw to secure the stop.

Limiting the amount that a backrest can recline is a matter of safety and comfort. Many seats rely on support from a very small device to prevent you from ending up in the back seat while driving. A screwdriver is used to secure this stop to the bottom of the backrest.

Attaching the Backrest Hardware

1 *A special bracket is attached, along with the hinge of the backrest, to the lower seat frame. The bracket not only works as a retainer for the attachment bolts but also provides a place to attach the ends of the lower seat cover and supports the lower trim panel.*

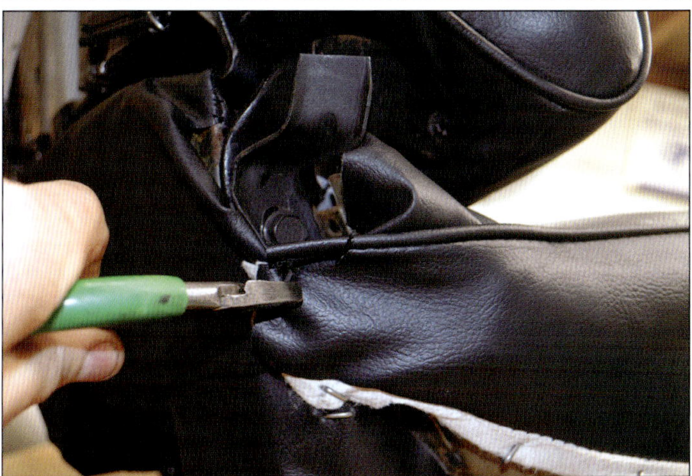

2 *Hog rings are used to secure the loose ends of the bottom seat cover onto the backside of the flanged edge of the retainer bracket. The tab at the top of the bracket supports the trim panel that covers the bracket and raw edges of the seat cover.*

3 *During the installation of the bottom seat cover on a pivot post–style seat frame, the post is intentionally covered. The overall goal is to have the seat cover correctly fit and secured to the seat frame. Gaining access to the pivot is done when fitting the backrest.*

4 *A perfect access hole is created by scoring the cover material around the end of the pivot post with a hammer. This technique allows the material of the seat cover to fall into place without cutting an oversized hole.*

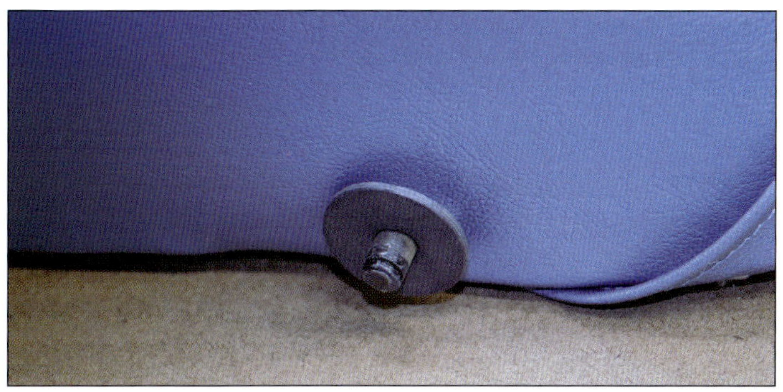

5 *You want the seat cover to last a long time, so pay attention to the little details. This fiber washer acts as a protective barrier between the pivot arm of the backrest and the lower seat cover. Without the washer, the pivot arm will wear through the cover material.*

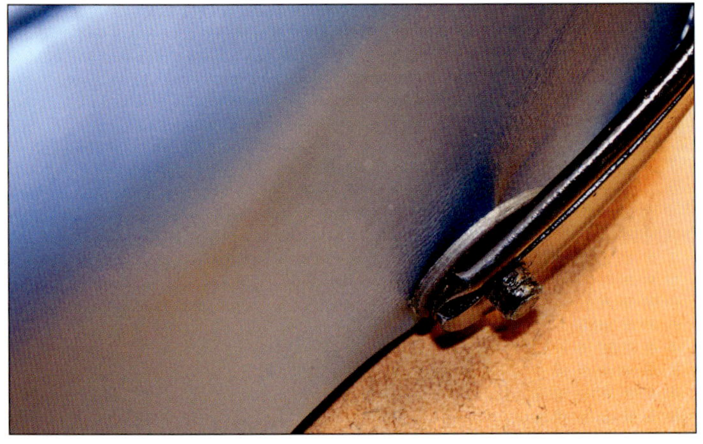

6 *When the pivot arm of the backrest is correctly installed, the large fiber washer will provide a durable barrier between the pivot arm and the lower seat cover. Tilt the backrest forward to verify that the pivot arm will not contact the lower seat cover material.*

7 *A new retainer washer is used to prevent the pivot arm of the backrest from coming off the pivot post during use. These washers are tempered spring steel and may not hold well if they are reused. New retainers can be obtained from many box houses.*

8 *A clean installation of the retainer washer is accomplished by tapping the fastener onto the pivot post with a hammer and a deep socket. The socket should be large enough to straddle the post and yet cover the base of the washer to prevent it from bending.*

9 *The trim panel hides the attaching hardware along the side of the backrest. To hold the stainless-steel trim to the backrest, oval-head trim screws are installed with a screwdriver. Care is taken to prevent damage from overtightening the screws.*

10 *To prepare the trim cap for installation, the retaining tabs inside the cap are altered to a forward position so that they hold the cover securely in place. When the cap is installed, the tabs will bend inward and grip the post.*

11 *A decorative cover is fitted to the end of the pivot post with a deep-well socket. The socket pushes evenly on the rim of the trim pad without damaging the domed surface. It only takes a few taps with a mallet to set the cap in place to cover the end of the post.*

12 *A small, decorative plastic trim cover fit to the pivot arm on this backrest conceals the pivot post and retainer fastener. The barbs on the ends of the split-metal fastener bite into the receptacle in the trim cover to hold the trim onto the pivot arm.*

A folding seat back either has hinges or pivot points, while the front seat of a 4-door car bolts solidly to the bottom seat frame. Most modern cars are equipped with bucket seats that have bolt-on side hinges.

The backrest of the Strato bucket has hinges that are guided onto the open area on the sides of the riser section of the bottom seat frame. To secure the backrest, two bolts are used to attach each hinge of the backrest to the lower seat frame. The bolts go through a metal retainer and into the bottom frame. There is a tab on the upper part of the retainer that is used to support the lower trim panel and a flange on the back edge with oval holes in it that the lower seat cover ends are fastened too.

Pass the two bolts through the retainer tab and then the bottom section of the hinge. Carefully thread and hand-tighten the bolts into the seat frame before using a socket wrench to finish tightening the bolts. After the backrest has been secured, the loose ends of the seat cover can be attached to the flange on the retainer.

Attach the loose edges of the rear cap to the retainer flange with hog rings. Next, pull on the welt of the seat cover and anchor it to the top hole in the retainer flange. Do the same with the lower edge of the seat boxing.

Pivot-style hinges require a little more effort to assemble. The first step is to expose the pivot post on the side of the lower seat frame. Your instinct may be to cut a hole in the cover material with a pair of scissors, but this will create a hole that is larger than necessary. The simple way to expose the post is to tap around the edges on the end of the post with a hammer. This will cut an exactly positioned hole in the cover material.

Before the backrest is slid onto the post, install the large fiber washer to protect the seat cover. The washer will prevent the pivot arm of the backrest from scratching and cutting into the cover material. Fit the backrest to the lower frame by sliding the pivot post into the hole located on the end of the pivot arm. Work on one side at a time and be careful to avoid gouging the cover material with the pivot arms. It helps if you tilt the backrest forward when trying to get the post into the pivot hole.

To secure the pivot arm to the bottom frame, a new retaining washer or E-clip will need to be installed on the pivot post. Use a deep-well socket and a hammer to drive the spring retainer onto the post. If you have an E-clip retainer, align the fastener with the ring groove on the post and then push the clip onto the post until it is fully seated.

A sharp pair of scissors is used to cut holes in the cover material on the seat riser to reveal the threaded anchors for the lock assembly. This step makes the mounting process of the lock base to the seat frame much easier.

The base of the lock assembly has been properly positioned, and the anchor bolts are started by hand to prevent them from becoming cross-threaded into the seat frame. A socket wrench is used to tighten the bolts and secure the base plate to the riser.

Post Covers

To cover the post and fastener, there are different trim options that were used. Some seats had a decorative stainless or chrome molding that covered the post fastener and side of the backrest. These moldings were secured with oval-head trim screws along the side of the backrest. A small acorn-style trim cap was used to cover the end of the pivot post.

The trim caps available today are a push-on type. They need to be modified a little before you install them. Inside of the trim cap are either several small teeth or four larger tabs. These retainer tabs need to be bent outward just enough to get the cap started on the post before it is set in place. If you do not flare out the tabs, they will fold inward and the cap will fall off of the post. After the modification is made, the trim cap can be tapped onto the post. To prevent the cap from becoming dented during the installation, use a deep socket that is larger than the cap but still can fit on the rim. Use a rubber mallet to tap on the socket to set the cap in place.

Some seats have a smaller pivot cover that is screwed onto the pivot arm or held in place by a retainer clip from the backside. The retainer clip is inserted through the pivot arm with the prong end extending to the outside. The cover is then slid over the end of the arm to capture the tip of the arm, and then the upper end of the cap is tucked under the seat cover. When properly positioned, the retainer clip is pushed into the small anchor post inside of the cover to keep it from falling off the pivot arm.

Support Hardware

Attachment of the backrest lock assembly mechanism is next. This device is attached to the riser with two bolts. Use a regulator to locate the threaded anchor points in the top of the riser and cut away a small circle of material to allow the attaching bolts to pass through. Insert the bolts through the base plate of the lock assembly and tighten the bolts with a socket wrench.

Installing the Seat Trim

1 *Damaged or broken trim panels will spoil the look of your new seat cover installation. You can obtain a new set completely assembled at most box houses. Reproduction cover panels are a very good replacement for the factory originals.*

2 Large molded trim panels are needed to cover the seat cover fasteners and mechanical elements of the car seat. Several small screw fasteners are used to hold the large covers tight to the seat frame, preventing them from coming loose.

3 Decorative-head sheet-metal trim screws are used when the trim cover fasteners are exposed and visible after installation. A Phillips-head screwdriver is used to carefully tighten the trim fasteners without distorting or cracking the molded plastic cover panel.

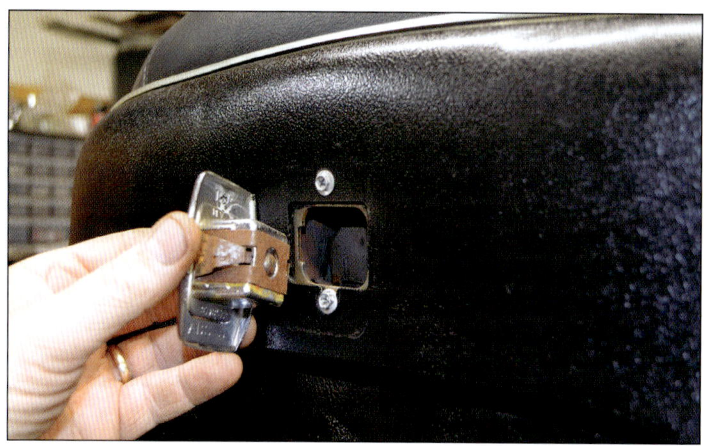

4 The backrest release button is installed by pushing it into the opening in the upper back of the seat. A retainer spring clip holds the button firmly in place, and the casing of the release button is designed to follow the contour of the trim panel.

5 Use a regulator to position the lower skirt and locate the anchor points for the trim screws that are used to keep the trim panel from moving. Carefully tighten the trim screws with a Phillips screwdriver without distorting the panel.

6 A soft plastic mallet is used to secure a new chrome-plated knob to the seat track adjustment lever. A metal hammer will cause damage to the finish on the plastic. It only takes a good blow with the mallet to jam the knob on the lever.

7 *With the help of a regulator, the base plate for the headrest lock is located to the top of the backrest. After the mounting holes are located, secure them in place with long screws. This will provide a strong foundation for the other components.*

8 *The section of the seat cover material that covers the inside of the lock base is cut away with a small knife to allow for the passage of the headrest post. The base plate prevents the seat cover from shifting position and this makes trimming an accurate opening possible.*

9 *This seat is ready for a final inspection, and then it can be installed in the car. With a little care, the new seat cover will perform for many years of driving fun. The best part of finishing the seat cover installation is that you did it yourself. Congratulations!*

Covering the large open areas of the newly upholstered seat is achieved with decorative trim panels. These panels can be very ornate and vary in design and construction depending on the model and manufacturer. Some panels are constructed from metal and painted or covered with the same materials as the seats, while others are simple panels molded from plastic.

To fit the backrest panel, begin by slightly bending the upper mounting tabs outward. This will make it easier to hang the panel. Start the installation by aligning the rear cover panel just above the upper tabs and slide the panel downward to capture the tabs into the pockets in the backside of the panel.

Use a regulator to locate the anchor points with the openings in the panel and insert the fasteners. Secure the cover to the backrest with the correct screws and hardware. Do not overtighten the hardware as this can cause damage to the trim panel.

After all the attaching hardware has been tightened, the release latch button can be installed. Look on the backside of the button bezel for the word TOP. This will help you with the correct orientation of the button. A spring clip is attached to the button case and is the only fastener that holds the button in place.

Push the release button into the opening of the upper backrest panel until it is fully seated against the trim panel. Check the operation of the release latch to verify that it works properly. Make any necessary adjustments to ensure proper operation.

Seat Skirts

Fitting the lower seat skirts is done much like the seat back cover. Hang the upper rear of the skirt on the retainer tab and work the cover around the front of the lower seat frame. Align the panel to the frame and insert and tighten the correct hardware.

Now is a good time to install the seat adjustment knob. Place the knob on the seat track adjuster lever and tap on the knob with a plastic mallet to lock it onto the lever. Release and adjuster knobs designed with a set screw are slid onto the lever shaft, and the set screw is then tightened with the appropriate tool.

Headrest Trim

Headrests can have one or two posts, and some have none at all because they are built into the seat. Some have locking mechanisms that allow them to be raised or lowered by pushing a button located on the trim cover, or they can be adjusted by directly pulling them up or pushing them down.

Locating the post holes is done by feeling through the seat cover. After you have identified the features of the underlying guide post, place the base plate on top of the guide post and use a regulator to line up the anchor screw holes. Insert the long flathead screws into the guide post and secure the anchor plate to the top of the backrest.

Use a hobby knife to remove the small piece of cover material from the center of the base plate. Without clearing the opening, the headrest post cannot be inserted into the guide post. Fit the locking cover piece on top of the base plate and secure it in place with two oval-head trim screws. The plastic cover can easily become distorted by overtightening the trim screws. Check the spring-loaded locking button to ensure that it works properly.

Insert the posts of the headrest into the backrest and verify the function of the locks and headrest. Go back and inspect the overall appearance of the seat. Use a steamer or heat gun to help relax any small wrinkles that might be visible.

Skirts and Backs

The outer trim panels on a Strato bucket can be reused if the plastic is still sound. Often the surface of the

Reconditioning Skirts and Backs

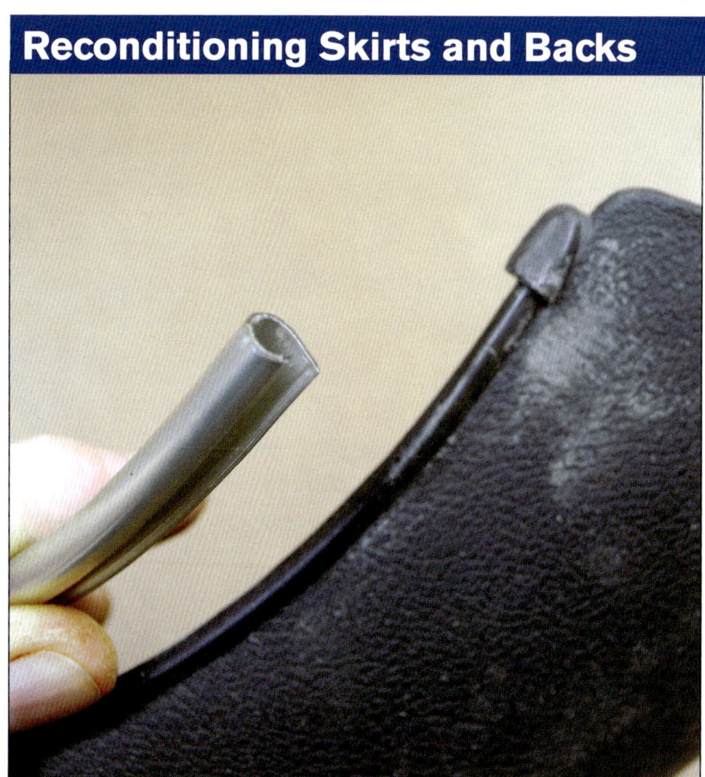

1 The original extruded plastic molding used mylar film to achieve its chrome appearance. This molding often shrunk and turned yellow as it aged. After the molding is unclipped, the trim panel can be cleaned in preparation for restoration.

2 The bullet end is left in place as a disc grinder is used to flatten the retaining bead that held the original extruded chrome molding to the trim panel. Extreme caution is needed to prevent nicking the textured surface of the trim panel.

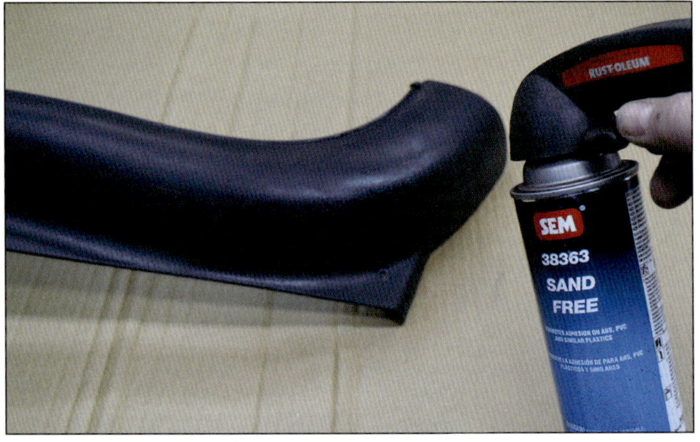

3 Getting the new color coat to stick to the plastic trim panel takes a good cleaning and an adhesion promoter. SEM makes an excellent product called Sand Free to draw the new color coat onto the surface of the plastic.

4 A light dusting coat of color is applied to the plastic trim panel and allowed to flash to provide a strong base for additional light coats. A SEM satin color coat is the perfect choice to blend with the sheen of the vinyl seat cover.

5 A package of standard door edge guard is all that is needed to replace the damaged or faded chrome trim on the seat back or skirt of a Strato bucket seat. One package of trim contains enough material to restore the trim panels of two bucket seats.

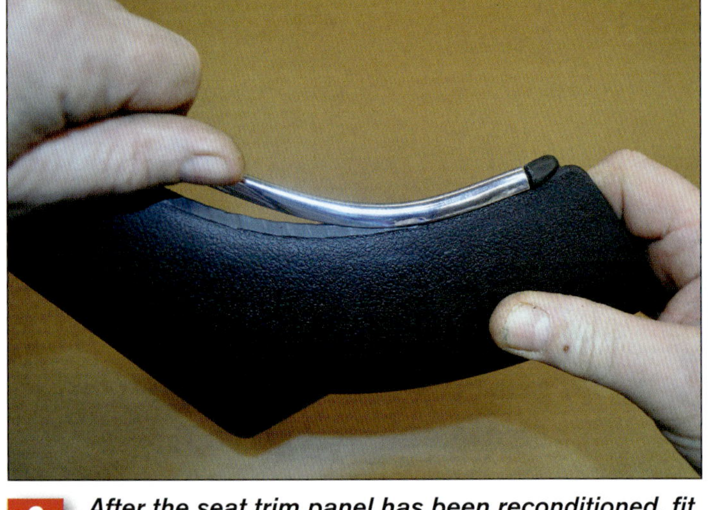

6 After the seat trim panel has been reconditioned, fit a new piece of chrome trim molding onto the edge of the panel. There are no special tools needed to install the molding. It is pressed into place with your fingers and cut to length with a wire cutter.

7 The finishing touch to the trim is done by adding a bullet cap to the cut end of the molding. Apply masking tape to the pliers to prevent harming the stainless steel as is used to secure the tip onto the panel.

plastic has dry rot from overexposure from the sun or it has become gouged and worn beyond an acceptable appearance.

Making the old panels look new is something that can save you money if you are willing to put in the effort. If the plastic is solid and in good condition, it can be prepared for a new color coat after a thorough cleaning to bring it back to life. Adding new chrome garnish molding to outer edges will give the panels that factory look.

Begin by inspecting the overall condition of the piece. Use your fingernail to do a scratch test on the surface of the plastic. If the plastic has not become chalky and shows no sign of scratches, the plastic can be made to look like new again.

Panel Preparation

Begin by removing the chrome trim molding from the edge of the trim panel. The molding may be brittle and crack as it is removed, but new molding will be reinstalled after the panel has been restored. The old molding can be removed with a twisting and pulling motion and then discarded.

The surface of the plastic must be clean in order for the color coat to adhere properly. Wash the panels with soap and water and then dry them completely. The original chrome edging trim fit over a raised bead on the outer edge of the panel. This style of molding is costly and hard to find. Replacement molding will not fit well on the panel unless it is modified.

To make the installation of the new chrome trim easier, the raised bead will need to be flattened. A right-angle grinder fitted with an 80-grit disc is the fastest way to knock down the bead. This can be a messy procedure and can cause damage to the plastic if you are not careful. Work slowly and try to keep from melting the plastic as you are grinding. When you have the edge flat and smooth, the panel is ready for a final cleaning.

Wipe down the outer surface of the panel with lacquer thinner to remove any fingerprints and other contaminants that may be on the surface. Place the clean panel on a piece of cardboard to prevent overspray from getting all over the shop.

Restoring the Color

To bring the panel back to life, spray a new coat of color onto the plastic. There are many types of coatings you can use, but for the best results I recommend SEM products. The SEM Color Coat products are formulated to have enough elasticity to withstand any flexing of the plastic. When used correctly, the results will last and give your panels a new appearance for a long time.

Before you begin spraying, wear protective eyewear and a respirator. Begin by following the manufacturer's application directions. Spray a wet coat of SEM Sand Free onto the surface of the panel. While the Sand Free is still wet, apply a dusting coat of the color and allow it to dry before adding any more color. Apply several color coats to the panel until the surface is evenly covered. After the color coat has dried, the chrome trim can be added.

If you plan to change the color of the trim panel, it may take several extra light coats to hide the old color. New plastic panels and pieces are usually black, and they will need to be sprayed to match the seat cover. To achieve the best results, always use light coats. They tend to dry faster and cover better. The thin coat is also less likely to crack or peel.

Adding the Trim

If you buy your chrome trim from a box house, follow the product's installation directions that are on the product. Most aftermarket suppliers use the same extruded door edge guard for the seat trim panels made by Cowles Products and others. This product can be purchased from most auto parts stores in a package that contains 18 feet of chrome molding.

The trim is installed by pressing the molding onto the edge of the panel and trimmed to fit with a pair of diagonal cutters. The molding should fit snug to the molded bullet end in the trim panel. Trim panels used prior to 1969 had stainless-steel bullet caps to finish off the ends of the chrome trim. These little trinkets often fell off and were difficult to mount securely to the trim.

Installation of the chrome tips is straightforward. Slide one over the end of the trim molding and use a curved jaw pliers to crimp it onto the molding to conceal the cut end. Because the tip is made of metal, it is difficult to get it to stay in place without denting the part. It helps if you put a few wraps of masking tape on the jaws of the pliers to help protect the tip from accidental damage. It may also be necessary to add a little contact cement to the underside of the tip to help it stay in place.

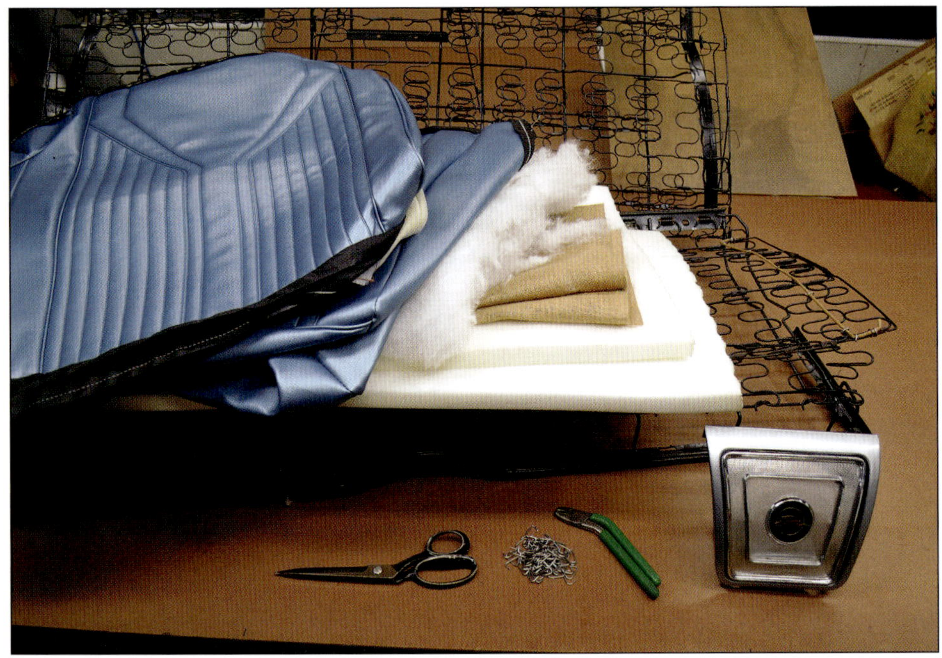

With the rear seat frame cleaned, repaired, and painted, all new materials will be used to restore the seat back to its original condition. The supplies and simple tools needed to install the rear seat cover are available from local and online suppliers.

To make the attachment of the bolster listings easier, use a pair of scissors to cut open the cotton padding covering the anchor listing. Care must be taken to avoid cutting into the burlap as this will compromise the function of the burlap and comfort of the seat cushion.

Rear Seat

Attaching the rear seat cover is a much simpler task than the bucket seat. The most obvious difference is that it is a wide bench-style cushion that may have bolster listings but most likely will be a simple pullover cover that attaches to the perimeter of the seat frame. Other variations that may be part of the rear seat backrest include a fold-down armrest and/or a center-mounted speaker grille.

Teardown is the same as with any other seat. Remove the hog rings that secure the cover and discard the old foam, cotton, flexolator, and burlap. The frame and springs need to be inspected for broken and damaged components. Clean and repair any compromised components before painting the springs.

Replace the listing anchors with new wire-stake before the new burlap is applied to the surface of the springs.

The burlap will give the springs the proper tension and a solid base for the new cotton and foam rubber cushion materials. To make the new seat cover installation easier, use a marker to highlight the location of the underlying listing anchors.

Add a base layer of cotton over the burlap to level the springs before the poly foam cushion is applied. The cotton should be cut or torn to reveal the anchor listing below. When the poly foam is positioned and secured, cut access slits in the foam to allow the seat cover listings to pass through.

Bottom Seat Cover

Use the same technique as with the bucket seat to attach the new

Old, tired listing wire can break or bend and cause a loose seat cover condition. To prevent the new seat cover from bagging, replace compromised listing wires with new solid 16-gauge wire. The listing wires are cut to size from craft paper–wound wire-stake.

You will eliminate the gaunt look at the bolster welt by adding cotton into the bolster channel before the seat cover is pulled over the outer edge of the seat. Make sure the cotton lays smoothly over the foam before the seat cover is pulled over.

Adding a loop end to the perimeter listings is not necessary because it only creates extra bulk in the listing. Before the wire stake is inserted into the listing pocket, apply a piece of masking tape to help it slide without snagging or tearing through the listing material.

seat cover. The listing wires should be solid and rust-free, so you may need to make new listings to secure the seat cover to the frame.

Place a layer of cotton over the top of the foam to help fill out the seat cover. Work from the center of the seat cover outward, securing the inner listings first. Tuck the edge of the cotton into the listing channel to fill the gap in the foam, and then roll the cover over the top of the cotton. Secure the outer listing and add more cotton to the outer bolster, and then work the seat cover over the edge of the seat frame. Make sure that the welt seam lays smoothly along the seat frame before adding hog rings to the perimeter listing.

Securing the Seat Cover

The rear edge of the seat cover should be secured first. A new length of wire-stake needs to be inserted into the listing sleeves before it can be hog ringed into place. It helps to apply masking tape over the end of the listing wire to help it pass

Hog rings hold the rear listing of the bottom rear seat cover to the seat frame. The method of working from the center point outward will keep the seat cover from migrating too far to one side. This helps the embossed pattern of the seat line up properly.

through the listing sleeve without snagging and hanging up inside of the listing.

The listing wire can be inserted into the listing sleeve and gradually advanced until the end appears at the other end, and then it can be cut to size. Start at the center and work outward by hog ringing the rear listing to the seat springs to keep the seat cover in place.

Work the seat cover over the front and sides of the seat frame and then turn the seat face down on the workbench to gain better access to the perimeter listing. A new listing wire needs to be threaded through the perimeter listing so that the cover can be anchored to the seat frame. Pull the bottom edge of the seat cover over the edge of the seat frame and check that the corners line up correctly. Start hog ringing in the center and proceed outward to the corners.

When you get to the corner, use the hog-ring pliers to bend the listing

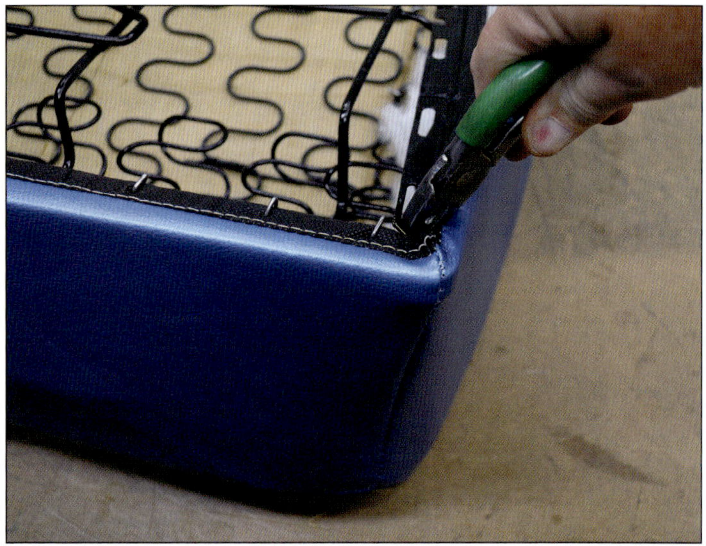

The rear bottom seat cover is worked over the padding, and the lower edge of the boxing is wrapped under the seat frame. Hog rings are used to attach the perimeter listing to the openings in the frame's inner rail.

The underside of the seat cover should look as nice as the rest of the seat. Getting the seat cover to conform to the frame is as simple as making a sharp bend in the listing wire to shape it to match the angle of the seat frame.

To avoid winkles along the bottom edge of the seat, the seam allowance from the perimeter listing should lay flat against the bottom of the seat frame. Hog rings are used to cinch the listing to the oval openings along the inner rail of the seat frame.

wire 90 degrees and continue fastening the cover until you get to the end. Secure the tail of the listing wire before it is trimmed to fit.

Back Cushion

Wrestling the rear seat backrest cover into place is usually awkward to fit because it is so large. Just when you get one corner to fit, it will pop off when working on another. This process should help alleviate the stress of installing the new upholstery.

Spring Tensioners

For the seat cover to fit properly, the top of the rear backrest springs must be tensioned so that they are within a finger's thickness of the speaker housing. To get the correct measurement for the spring

Upper spring position on the rear backrest is determined by visually mocking up the final height needed to make the seat cover look and fit properly. Once the height is determined, accurate measurements can be taken to create the new spring tensioner.

A measuring tape is used to get an accurate measurement for the correct positioning of the backrest's upper spring height. If the springs are not tensioned properly, you will have trouble getting the seat cover to fit properly.

Many measurements need to be taken to ensure that the spring tensioner will be made correctly. Although the tensioner is a simple device, it is a foundational piece that is integral to the structure of the seat.

tensioner, fit the speaker housing into place on the seat frame and measure from the edge wire down to the surface of the inner seat frame. Next, measure an inch past the corner to the edge of the speaker grille housing. These measurements can be transferred to a new piece of burlap. Add an additional inch of material to the top and bottom of the tensioner to allow for a listing cord.

Roll out some burlap on the workbench and use a ruler and Sharpie pen to mark the dimensions of the tensioner. Double check that you have measured and marked correctly before cutting the material, and don't forget to make two tensioners.

Now, it is time to sew. (If you do not sew, do not panic. Contact a local upholstery shop to make the tensioner.) Take the cut pieces to the sewing machine and sew in a jute cord to act as the listing wire. Fold the edge inward 1 inch to capture the cord. The cord is then sewn in just like a welt cord. Repeat this step for the other side of the tensioner. Measure the tensioner again to confirm that it is the correct size you need, and then make a second tensioner for the other side of the seat frame.

Position the new tensioner along the top of the seat frame and begin attaching the lower edge to the frame with hog rings. There is no strain on the tensioner at this stage, and it makes cinching the lower hog rings easier. Next, pull up on the tensioner and hog ring the tensioner to the top edge wire of the springs, placing them opposite of the lower fasteners.

A new set of spring tensioners are drawn out on a fresh piece of burlap with the measurements taken from the backrest. The markings help during the sewing process and will not be seen after the new seat cover has been installed.

The burlap is folded over a strong fiber cord and then sewn directly into the stretcher. The cord will become the listing used to anchor the tensioner to the seat frame and springs. Without the cord, the burlap would not be strong enough to keep the springs in place.

An inspection is made of the tensioner to ensure that it has the correct dimensions and that the anchor cord has been securely sewn into place. The process of making new tensioners is not difficult but necessary to complete the project.

Hog rings are used to attach the bottom of the tensioner to the small loops in the seat frame. Adding a little side tension to the stretcher will help keep it from becoming loose as more pressure is put on it by the springs.

Pushing down on the springs will make it a lot easier to align the edge wire with the upper edge of the tensioner. The tensioner is then secured in place by hog rings. You should notice a big difference in the firmness of the backrest.

Burlap has been fastened to the frame to create tension in the backrest springs. This makes a solid foundation for the padding material. Diagonal cuts are carefully made in the burlap to create an opening for the fitment of the speaker housing.

The edges of the speaker housing opening have been rolled and then secured with hog rings. This step will help preserve the tensioning of the backrest springs. If the burlap is loose, the springs will not be able to support and provide comfort.

Cotton is used as padding on this backrest. It takes at least three layers of the synthetic cotton to reach the proper depth to fill out the seat cover. Listing channels have been created in the cotton to allow for the attachment of the seat cover.

Cover the springs with a piece of burlap that extends 1½ inches past the spring edge wire. To get a smooth and tight surface, fold back the edge of the burlap upon itself and fasten it to the edge wire with a hog ring to anchor it at the center point of one end. Now, move to the opposite end, put a little tension on the burlap, and anchor the burlap to the edge wire. Add a hog ring about every 3 inches as you work your way out from the center anchor point. Secure the bottom edge of the burlap, and then the top edge.

To secure the burlap around the speaker opening, make a diagonal cut into the corner of the opening, but stop cutting about a 1/2 inch from the inner corner. Fold the material back upon itself and secure it to the perimeter of the opening with hog rings.

Cotton Padding

The backrest on most rear seats typically use several layers of cotton padding to support the seat cover instead of foam rubber. The cotton is laid out on top of the burlap and sometimes covered with cheesecloth to keep the cotton from bunching up when the seat cover is installed.

After the cotton has been built up to the desired thickness, the anchor listings can be located and the cotton torn away to allow the seat cover listing to reach the anchor.

Installing the Cover

1 *Always attach the bottom of the backrest cover to the seat frame first. Use hog rings to anchor the seat cover in place, creating a foundation to work against. Now, the seat cover can be stretched over the top of the frame without it coming loose.*

2 *The top of the seat cover has been fit over the seat frame, the seam is lined up with the corner, and a couple of hog rings are used to help hold the cover in the correct position while the rest of the cover is fit in place.*

3 *More hog rings are added along the top listing of the seat cover. During the process, pressure was put on the cover material to minimize wrinkles and the underlying cotton padding was stuffed back into place to maintain the shape and fullness of the backrest.*

4 *A few small wrinkles have formed in the cover material during the attachment of the side boxing. This is caused by a lack of support behind the cover material, and it is nothing to be worried about. Once the seat is installed in the car, this area will not be seen.*

If your seat cover has bolster listings, they need to be attached to the anchor listings before the cover can be pulled over the frame. Simple wrap-over covers can be fit to the frame and anchored along the bottom to give the cover stability before the top is pulled over the top.

Attach the bottom listing or stretcher to the bottom edge of the seat frame. Work from the center point outward to avoid the seat cover shifting too far to one side. After the bottom of the seat cover has been secured, turn the seat face up on the workbench and work the top corners of the seat cover over the springs and top of the frame. Adjust the cover so that the end seam is lined up with the corner before you secure the listing to the underside of the seat frame. Continue to hog ring the top seat cover listing to the backside of the seat frame.

Attach the sides of the seat cover to the frame in the same manner as the top and bottom. Some wrinkles in the outer ends will be inevitable, but they can be worked out with a little heat.

Rear Speaker

The rear speaker in the seat is one variation that was a popular option for cars of the 1950s and 1960s. An opening in the rear seat frame allowed a space for a stamped-metal frame that held a speaker for the radio and was most likely adorned with an ornate logo for the make and model of the car.

A listing has been sewn onto the inside perimeter of the speaker pocket and hog rings are used to attach the listing to the seat frame. The newly created opening will now allow room for the placement of the metal housing.

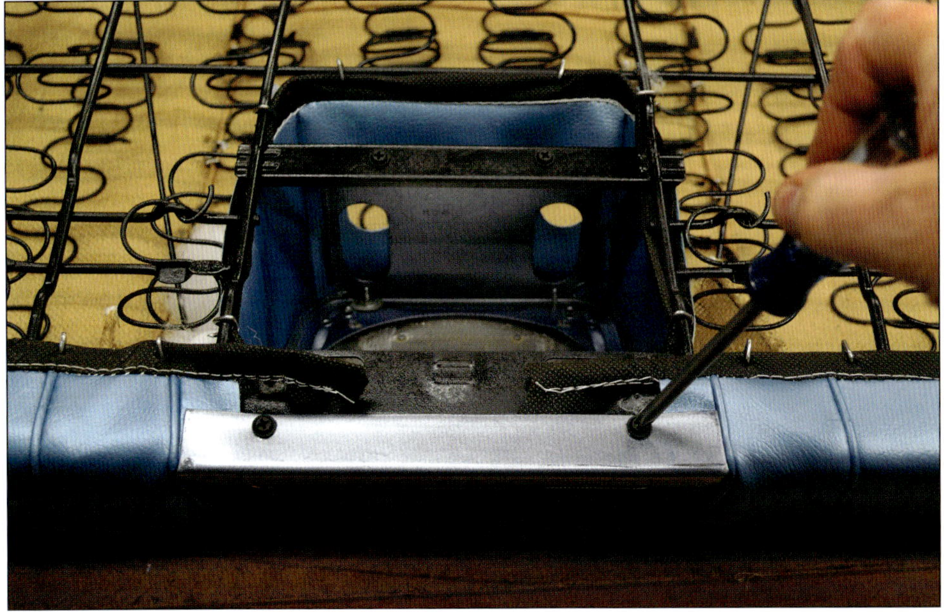

A lip on the speaker housing slides over the top of the seat frame and conceals the raw ends of the seat cover. After the housing is seated in the pocket, small sheet-metal screws are used to secure the metal housing into the opening.

Overall, the fit of the speaker housing looks good on the initial inspection. The housing sits nice and tight across the top of the seat, and there is just a small gap that can use a little more padding along the bottom.

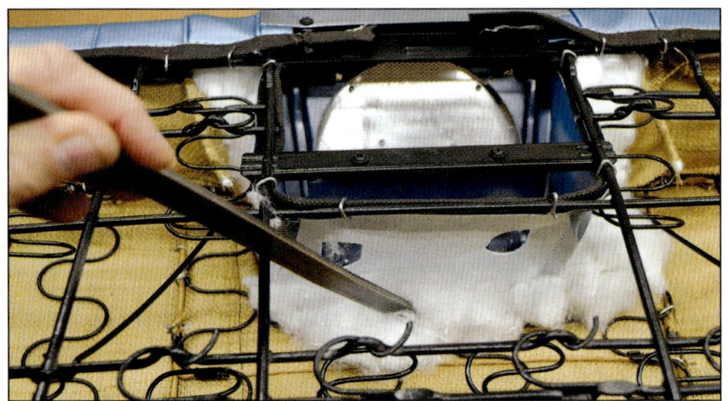

Working from the backside of the seat, add a small amount of cotton padding along the bottom of the speaker housing. A blunt-end piece of bar stock is used as a stuffing tool to push the cotton in and around the opening in the burlap.

When using the center point on the frame as a key reference point to work from, the embossed pattern lines up as it should. After a quick wipe down to remove fingerprints and a little heat to soften a small wrinkle, this rear seat is ready to be installed.

Rear Seat Installation

1 *Before the seat is installed, a new trunk divider panel has been fit into the rear of the car. This panel will separate the trunk area from the cab and protect the open back of the rear seat from objects that could poke through the seat cover.*

2 At the bottom of the inner wheel tub is a small tab that threads through a loop on the lower corner of the backrest frame. When the tab is bent over, it locks the corner of the seat firmly in place to prevent the seat from coming loose.

3 The main attachment devices of the rear backrest are a pair of loop retainers that can be adjusted to fit the anchor point on the floor of the car. A combination sheet-metal bolt and washer is then used to secure the seat in place.

4 A pair of retainers are welded to the floor of the car and designed to catch a loop in the frame of the lower rear seat cushion and keep it from sliding out of place. The seat is captured by pushing the seat frame backward and down.

5 After all that hard work, all that is left is to give the seat a quick clean and vacuum the carpet. Now that the backseat area of the car is complete, it is time for some fun. Just imagine loading up the kids and taking them for ice cream.

The seat cover also has a special pocket sewn into the center panel of the cover. This pocket provides a place for the speaker housing to be installed. Hog rings are used at the outer corners of the pocket to help shape the opening. Install the speaker housing at this point. There should be four small sheet-metal screws that hold the housing to the frame.

Turn the seat cover face up to check the fit of the speaker housing. The cover should fit snugly around the casing. If you see gaps around the perimeter of the housing, add some additional cotton by tucking it in and around the pocket.

Check the overall fit of the seat cover. Make any alterations that are necessary, and if you need to remove any small wrinkles that still may be present, you can use a heat gun to help relax them away.

Installation of a rear seat is simple, but there are some things that must be observed prior to fitting the seat. If your car is in need of a new package tray, now is the time to install one. The front edge of the package tray is glued to the seat riser.

Without the backrest in place, the task of fastening the retainer strip is much easier. Rear-deck speakers can also be added or upgraded since the rear seat is out of the car.

Many cars have an open framework that does not isolate the cab from the trunk area. This open partition requires a larger piece of panel board that separates the two areas. The rear seat trunk divider panel hangs on small tabs welded to the cross-braces or off the backrest hangers. The panel provides a physical barrier between the two spaces.

Backrest Installation

If your car has rear armrests, they may need to be removed so that the backrest can be set in place. To set the backrest, press the frame against the seat riser and lower it onto the hook-shaped fasteners that are attached to the riser. Press down on the top of the backrest to settle the frame onto the fasteners.

To prevent the backrest from coming loose, it is fastened to the floor. There may be metal tabs at the lower corners and on the floor that pass though loops or slots in the backrest frame. The metal tabs are then bent over to lock the frame in place.

Loop retainers may also be used to secure the backrest to the floor with a washer and sheet-metal bolt. Whatever type or combination of fasteners your car uses, be sure to secure the backrest before installing the lower seat cushion.

Bottom Cushion Installation

The rear lower seat cushion is held in place by friction or a loop catch that is welded to the floor. To set the seat, tilt the frame by lifting the front edge of the seat and slide the back edge of the frame under the bottom of the backrest.

To prevent the cushion from coming loose, a loop in the frame slides into a pocket on the floor or is hooked by a bracket on the bottom of the floor. When the cushion is pushed backward, the loop will fall into the retainer and be held in place by the forward pressure on the seat frame. After the seat has been fit, the inner rear armrests can be remounted to complete the installation.

DOOR PANELS

A door panel typically refers to the decorative upholstery that is attached to the inside of the door and serves to conceal the inner workings. The door panel also provides a buffer from outside noise to help keep the cab quieter. Construction of the door panel varies by manufacturer, but most are traditionally made from a heavy paper or Masonite base material. Modern panels are also being built on an ABS plastic base using vacuum-forming equipment.

Every era of automobile used different methods to secure the door panel to the inside of the car. Panels can be attached to the door with nails, spring clips, and screws. Other applied elements, such as armrests and window cranks, also keep the door panel in place.

Why Replace a Panel?

Reproduction door panels are a simple solution to replace original worn or damaged panels. A combination of age, weather, and abuse factor in the deterioration of the original panel, which will lead to its replacement with a reproduction panel. When rain enters through the glass opening, water can get on the backside of the panel, which causes the base material to warp. Ultraviolet rays from the sun can also lead to the discoloration and deterioration of the outer panel materials. This happens when body oil from your skin

This reproduction 1969 Impala door panel looks and fits just like the original factory-installed upholstery. Most of the work was done by the manufacturer, but the final assembly details and installation are left to you.

Warpage is a tell-tale sign that water has caused this panel to fail. As a result, the metal trim on the panel lifted from the surface, was caught on a pant leg, and sustained significant damage. The addition of electrical tape to repair the damage was not much help.

A Word of Caution

There are many precut openings on the backside of an aftermarket door panel. Do not remove all of the knockouts. Some of the through holes are for features your car may not have and are not needed on your application. Always compare the original door panel with the replacement panel to verify what is necessary. Use caution when removing the knockout so the cover material is not disturbed. The cover material should not be cut until the trim pieces are dry fit for location. This will prevent any oversized holes in the door panel that will not be covered when the panel is installed. ■

Nothing fits better than original parts. This 1964 Impala door panel was created with the reconditioned cap panels from the old door panels. All that is left is to install the door panels onto the car.

is left on the panel covering. After many years of service, the panels show signs of wear from normal use, and sometimes they are cut up to accommodate an added speaker for an upgraded audio system.

When you shop for new door panels, you may encounter two versions. One is a fully assembled panel that is ready to install, and the other is a standard version that needs to be put together with some of the original components of the old door panel.

Preassembled

The best choice for the DIYer is the preassembled door panel. This version is complete and ready to install right out of the box. The premium panels come with all the stainless trim moldings attached, along with the lock knob ferrules and inner window sweep. All of this comes at a higher cost compared to the standard replacement door panels. So, if you are not handy, this option may be best for you.

Depending on the model of your car, some manufacturers may not have patterns or enough demand to recreate the metal caps to make a complete ready-to-install door panel. To make your new door panels, the manufacturer may require you to send the original metal caps from the old panels for them to install onto the new panel board.

Removing the old cap is pretty straightforward. Begin by removing the window sweep and lock ferrule; then, peel back the old cover material. The metal cap can then be separated from the panel board and cleaned up before sending it off to be

added to the new door panel. If the supplier has to prep the old metal to be usable on your new panels, you might be charged an additional fee for reconditioning.

Many panels are made with new metal or plastic caps. These are not always desirable due to the fit and quality of the reproduction. The metal is often thinner and can easily be bent or dented, causing them to fit poorly and look damaged once installed. The plastic caps tend to

The final touches needed to complete the assembly of this door panel are door lock ferrules, window sweeps, and panel fasteners. To prevent assembly delays, these items should be ordered at the same time as the door panel set.

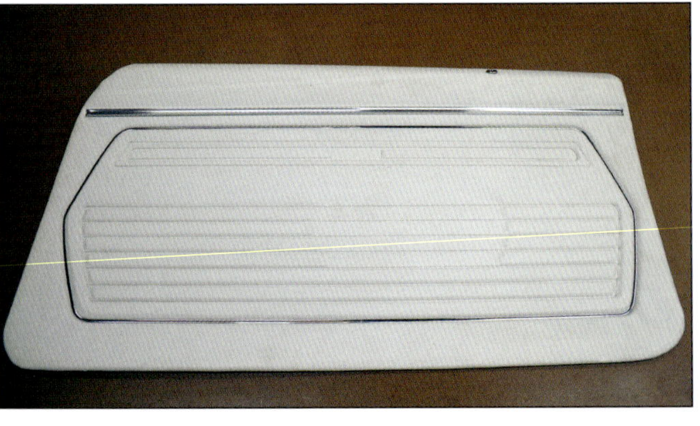

Replacing a worn or damaged door panel doesn't get any easier than pulling a new, exact reproduction from a box. The only thing that you will need to do before installing this in your car is to put the panel clips on the back.

be thicker than the original metal. This added thickness can make the glass more difficult to raise and lower because the window sweep fills up more of the glass opening. Do not stress over these issues. The door panels will fit with a little finesse.

Standard Door Panel

For those who have a desire to be more hands-on and save some money, you may choose the standard door panel option. These require the restorer to install the original metal caps onto the new panel board and finish covering the upper portion of the panel with the allotted material included with the panel.

The restorer must also acquire the additional hardware (at an additional cost) along with the tools and supplies needed to finish the panel before it can be installed in the car. As stated earlier, this second option can save you some money, but it will require a good amount of time and some skill to complete the panel so that it will look like it was factory built.

Hardware

Removal of a door panel varies by make and model. There are several items that need to be taken off of the door panel before it can be lifted from the car. Most cars have an upper panel cap that holds the panel along the top of the door. This cap is either a separate painted piece or it can be integral to the panel. The cap usually has an inner window sweep that is attached horizontally along the window side of the panel, as well as a door lock button ferrule that prevents wear to the door panel when the lock button is depressed or pulled up.

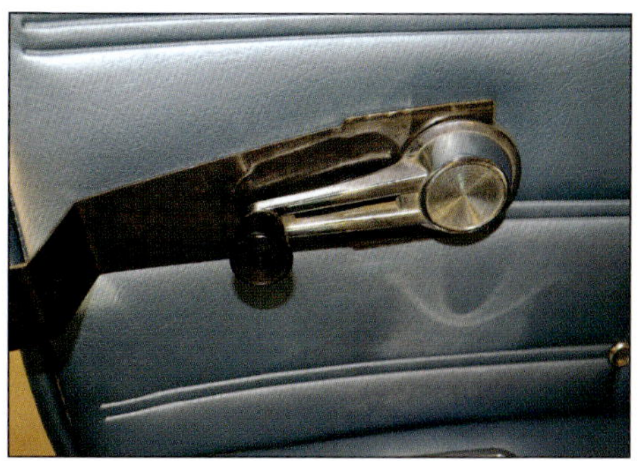

This simple tool is designed to make the removal of the window crank almost effortless. The crank will come off the splined regulator post when the small retainer spring clip is pushed out of place from the backside of the crank.

Lock Knob and Cranks

The lock knob must be unscrewed and removed to allow the panel to be lifted from the door. Window cranks must also be removed from the face of the door panel. These can be held in place with small screws, pins, or clips. Retaining screw removal is a straightforward operation performed with an appropriate screwdriver or Allen or hex wrench. The removal of a pin or clip requires a specialized tool designed to push the retaining device from the shaft of the handle.

To use the window crank clip removal tool, insert the device between the base of the window crank and the protective escutcheon. Align the tool from the same direction as the crank knob and

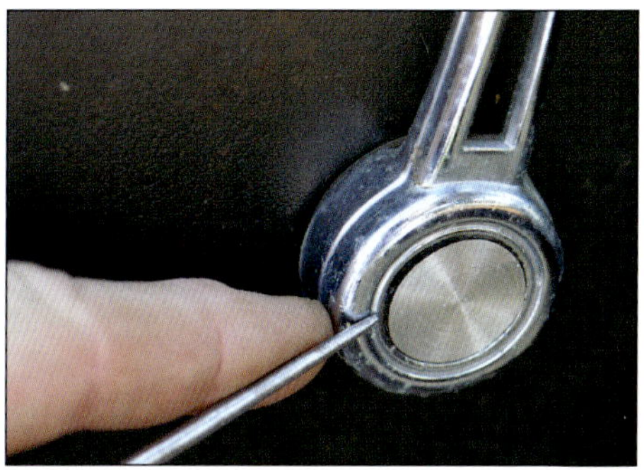

A razor blade or upholsterer's regulator can be used to lift off the self-adhesive disc that will allow access to the retainer screw underneath. Damage can occur during removal of the disc, but new replacements are readily available.

push it inward until it makes contact with the post on the underside of the window crank. Use a slight back and forth motion on the tool until it locates the retainer clip slot in the post of the crank. The tool will advance slightly to dislodge the clip and free the crank from the regulator shaft. The crank can then be removed along with the escutcheon.

Some Ford models have a foil disc that covers the retainer screw. This decorative disc must be peeled back to access the retainer screw underneath. Once the screw is exposed, it can be removed from the regulator shaft.

Armrests

Another item that may be applied to the surface of the panel is some

Two or three large sheet-metal screws are used to anchor the armrest base to the door. A #3 Phillips screwdriver is needed to remove the screws, allowing the armrest to be removed from the surface of the door panel.

Before the inner door release handle can be removed, a socket and ratchet are used on the small machine screw so that it can be removed. After the retaining fastener is removed, the handle can be pulled from the door.

sort of door pull. This can be a strap or an armrest. These are held in place by heavy screws that anchor the center of the panel. Use a #3 Phillips screwdriver to loosen the screws that hold the armrest base to the door.

Behind the armrest base is the inner door release handle. These handles are removed the same as the window cranks. After the retainer screw or clip is removed, the handle can be slid off the door latch actuator shaft.

Door Panels

The bottom of the panel is typically fastened to the door with screws. Usually there are four or five oval-head screws along the bottom of a panel. Screws are used in this location instead of clips because they can hold the panel securely and withstand the abuse of being kicked by the passenger as they exit the vehicle. Remove the screws with a #2 Phillips screwdriver.

Separating the door panel from the inside of the door requires the use of a panel-lifting tool to get behind the concealed fasteners. Without the proper pry tool, you will most likely cause damage to the door panel if you pull it off of the door.

Starting from the bottom outer edge of the door panel, insert a panel-lifting tool between the door panel and interior surface of the door. Carefully slide the tool upward until you locate a panel fastener. Pull back on the tool until the fastener clears the retaining socket in the door. Continue upward until all the fasteners have been released, and then do the same with the inside edge of the panel to free it from the door.

Grab the door panel and pull it away from the bottom as you lift it upward and away from the door to remove the wrap-over cap from the top of the door. Panels that tuck under a trim piece are pulled downward to release them from the door.

Under the Door Panel

A waterproof membrane called a water shield is located directly under the door panel. This barrier is needed to prevent moisture from causing damage to the door panel. Without the barrier, water can enter through the glass opening, which can get onto the backside of the door panel and cause damage from warping and mold.

Check the condition of the door panel clip anchors located along the front and rear edges of the door. If these small plastic clip cups are found to be cracked or missing, add them to your list of items to order. The clip anchor is needed to hold the door panel securely to the door.

Other items you may find are window crank handle springs. These helical devices apply a small amount of pressure to the backside of the door panel to prevent a gap between the door panel and the base of the window crank.

When it comes time to service the inner workings of the door, the door panel will need to be safely removed. A special removal tool is used to lift the door panel from the surface of the inner door without causing any damage to the panel or car.

Care is needed when removing the door panel from the car to prevent the panel fasteners from scratching the painted surface of the car. Watch your fingers and arms because the fasteners are sharp and can harm your skin and clothing.

A piece of plastic sheeting has been used to replace the original water shield on this door. Duct tape and asphalt caulking have been used to fasten the water shield to the inside of the door. This will be removed, cleaned, and replaced with the correct materials.

After a close inspection, the door panel clip anchors are in usable condition. Someone has painted over them, which does not alter their effectiveness. It just shows that these plastic fasteners have been installed in the door for a long time.

These small, cone-shaped springs prevent gaps from occurring between the base of the window crank and surface of the door panel. When fitted around the regulator post, the spring creates just enough tension against the backside of the door panel.

Disassembling the Panel

1 *From the underside of the door cap, a small screwdriver is used to lift the fastening tabs on the door lock ferrule. If the lock bezel is in good condition, it can be reused on the new door panel. Damaged pieces can be replaced with new reproduction parts.*

2 *A slight twisting action is needed to free the retainer clip from the armrest backer. The spring clip is designed to grip the through tab when it is pushed on. When the tension on the small inner teeth of the clip is reduced, the clip will be able to be removed.*

3 *Preserving the retainer spring clips is a must on these door panels because new clips are not readily available. It only takes a few seconds to reshape the clip to restore it to a useful condition. Once restored, it is easily reinstalled on the new panel.*

4 *A little upward pressure is placed on the decorative trim molding as it is cut away from the old door panel. A fresh knife blade and a lot of care is needed to prevent damage to yourself and the molding. With a little cleanup, the molding can be reused.*

5 *Door panel moldings have relied on these prongs to hold the decorative trim to the face of the panel for many generations. When fitted through the panel, the tabs are bent over to secure the molding. Age, corrosion, and previous removals can cause the tabs to become brittle and break.*

6 *This medallion is in good condition and will be reused on the new door panel. There aren't any visible mechanical fasteners to remove, so a stiff-blade putty knife is used to lift the emblem from the old panel. It can be prepped for reattachment after it's removed.*

Many of the original components of the old door panel will need to be removed. Some of these pieces can be reconditioned and reused in the assembly of the new reproduction door panel. Pieces that are not viable for reconditioning will be replaced with new parts that can be obtained from a box house to complete the restoration.

With the door panel removed from the car and placed on the workbench, begin disassembly by removing the applied elements. The first component to be removed is the door lock bezel. The bezel is either pressed in and can be pried off, or it is secured in place with small tabs from the backside of the door panel cap. From the underside of the door cap, pry the tabs up to release the bezel.

Door panels adorned with armrest base plates have to be removed. These chrome-plated plastic items are usually worn and cracked from years of service. They are held to the door panel with small retainer clips on the backside of the panel. It can be difficult to remove the clip without breaking off the through tab or clip, but if the backing plate is in poor condition and needs replacement, it is best to break the through tab to save the clip. If you use needle-nose pliers and give the fastener a slight bend, it will come off easier.

After the clip has been removed, reshape the clip to its original condition so that it can be reused. These clips are not always available, and care must be taken when removing them.

Stainless Moldings and Emblems

Special trim moldings are applied to the surface of the door panel to divide and conceal the edges of dissimilar materials. Older car models used stainless-steel and chrome-plated castings for the trim moldings. Later models used applied moldings that were either extruded rubber covered with a mylar film or directly embossed onto the surface of the door panel.

Attachment of these moldings to the door panel changed as manufacturing techniques improved. Most of the metal moldings relied on sharp metal tabs to hold the trim in place. These tabs often broke off when removed or rusted away to leave the trim unusable.

The modern trim does not have any physical fasteners because it is attached by embossing it directly to the surface of the door. Removing this type of molding requires cutting it off of the door. Stainless-steel moldings can be reattached with special mounting tape, but extruded moldings tend to develop wrinkles in the mylar coating when it is flexed, so it is best to replace these with new self-adhesive moldings.

Special decorative emblems may need to be carefully removed and reused because they may not be available as a reproduction item. The emblems may have posts on their backside. Threaded nuts, push-on speed nuts, and adhesives are common locking devices used to secure the emblem to the door.

Window Sweeps

Window sweeps run horizontally across the upper inner edge of the door panel or door cap window molding. They are called by many different names: door felts, fuzzies, cat whiskers, and those door window things.

Whatever you decide to call them, they serve a very useful function. Window sweeps are designed to prevent damage to the glass as it is raised or lowered. Some sweeps are made of felt, rubber, cloth, or a combination of the aforementioned materials.

Industrial staples are the most common type of fastener used to attach the window sweep to the door panel. Small screws are also used to hold the sweep in place. A small screwdriver, die grinder, or diagonal cutter can be used to detach the fastener and free the old sweep from the panel. New sweep sets are available for most cars along with bulk lengths of sweep material for models that are not available as a prefabbed kit.

Door Cap

After all of the applied elements have been removed from the door panel, the cap is next to be removed. To ensure the proper fitment of the door cap on the new panel, an alignment line will need to be scribed onto the metal cap. This will give you a reference point for the new panel placement.

Use a regulator to scratch a line on the metal cap by following along the edge of the old panel board. It

Be Careful with Emblems

Always check to see how the emblem is attached before you try to remove it. If the casting or plastic becomes damaged during removal, it may be difficult to find a suitable replacement. ■

may be helpful to take a picture of the ends of the panel and refer to it when fitting the cap to the new panelboard. Peel back the cover material from the door cap. There will be some padding material under the cover that will need to be removed. Use a stiff-blade putty knife to loosen the padding from the surface of the cap.

Removing and Repairing the Door Cap

1 *Before the door cap is removed, a reference line should be scribed onto the inner surface of the cap to help with the correct alignment and placement on the new panelboard. Photos can also help refresh your memory when it is time to reattach the door cap.*

2 *A spun Dacron padding that is bonded to the metal door panel cap was exposed when the cover material was peeled back. To remove the padding, use a stiff-blade putty knife to scrape the material from the surface of the metal.*

3 *Separate the metal cap from the old panel board with a little twisting and pulling action. This will dislodge the small star-like crimps underneath the lower edge of the metal that are embedded into the panelboard.*

4 *A lot of scraping and cleaning is needed to prepare the metal door cap so that it can be reused on the new door panel. Just a few strokes from a wire brush will remove the old glue residue and leave the surface of the metal bright and shiny.*

5 *Quick work is made by refurbishing the flared-out crimp fasteners by synching the points together with a pair of diagonal cutters. This action will make flattening the metal much easier without causing the metal to distort and warp when hammered flat.*

6 *A machinist hammer is used to flatten the crimp fastener points on the metal cap panel. The flat surface of an anvil makes an exceptional surface to hammer against and prevents the thin metal from distortion and becoming unusable.*

7 *A 1/8-inch die is fitted into a Whitney punch, and holes for pop rivets are created every 5 inches in the edge of the metal door cap. The punch tool is easy to use and makes precise holes faster and cleaner than a drill bit.*

Preparing the Cap

There are many small crimped fasteners along the bottom edge of the door cap. Separating the cap takes a little effort by rocking the metal cap back and forth to loosen it from the cardboard panel. Be careful when working the cap loose because the metal edges may be sharp.

The surface of the cap needs to be cleaned and prepped before it can be installed onto the new door panel. Scraping the old padding and glue off the metal will remove the large pieces of material. A wire brush makes quick work of getting the surface clean.

After the metal is cleaned up, the crimp fasteners need to be flattened. Hammering the points flat or grinding them off may seem like a good option, but it is best to preserve as much metal as possible without warping the part. Begin by raising the flared-out metal with a pair of diagonal cutters. Squeeze the tabs opposite of each other together to make them stand up. This may be a tedious task, but it goes pretty fast.

Next, place the edge of the metal cap on an anvil and hammer the raised points flat. Try not to distort the metal when hammering. The object here is to get the edge of the cap as flat as possible without ruining the metal cap.

Use rivets to attach the cap panel to the new panel board. To prep the cap panel for the rivets, 1/8-inch holes need to be made in the metal to allow the rivets to secure the cap. You can use a drill bit to make the holes, but I prefer to use a Whitney punch. The punch makes a perfect hole in the metal without any distortion and is safer to use. A drill bit can grab and spin the metal out of your hand if it is not clamped securely. The rivet holes should be located about 5 inches apart. Holes are then made halfway between the scribed line and bottom edge of the cap while being centered between the flattened points.

Panel Assembly

Cover the surface of your workbench with a soft protective towel and take the new door panels out of the box and place them on the workbench. Compare the details of the old door panel with the new to make sure they are a match. If you encounter an issue with the new panels, contact the manufacturer before you begin to glue or cut into the material.

Turn the new panel face down on the workbench and line up the scribe line on the metal cap to the panel board. Temporarily clamp the front and rear of the pieces with a small vise-grip pliers to prevent it from shifting position. Turn the panel face up and mark the location of the rivet holes onto the panel board with a Sharpie pen. When you are satisfied with the fit and location of the cap panel, remove it so that through holes can be made in the panel board.

Use a 1/8-inch hole punch to make a through hole in the panel board. As an alternative method, a rotary punch will work much easier. Place a suitable backer under the panel board and line up the punch over the mark you made on the panel board. Strike the punch to make a clean and crisp hole in the panel board. Do not accidentally punch through the cover material, as this will spoil the door panel.

Attaching the Cap

After the holes have been made in the panel board, place the cap under the panel board and check the alignment of the rivet holes. Make any adjustments necessary to the holes before any rivets are set.

I prefer using 1/8-inch aluminum rivets with 1/4-inch grip range to fasten the pieces together. The rivet is inserted through the panel board and then into the metal cap. The rivet is intentionally installed this way to eliminate any extra bulk from backer washers. Use a pop-rivet tool to set the rivet.

After the cap has been secured to the panel board, address the bulk left over by the pop rivet. The rivet needs to be flattened in order for the cover material of the door panel to lay properly. To flatten the rivet, place an anvil under the head of the rivet and tap the protruding side of the rivet down with a machinist (ball-peen) hammer. Do not smash the rivet into the metal, but make it as flat as possible. The padding material of the door panel will hide the slight imperfection and become invisible when the panel is finished.

Reinstalling the Door Cap

1 A lot of care is taken to prefit the metal door cap onto the new door panel. After the alignment of the panel is set, clamps are placed at the ends of the metal door cap to hold it in position on the panel board so that the rivet locations can be marked.

2 Take the time to accurately identify the rivet hole positions to make reassembly much easier. Use a marker to indicate the hole positions on the panel board by filling in the punched holes in the metal door cap.

3 *The door panel cover material has been safely repositioned to prevent accidental damage when through holes for rivet fasteners are cut into the panel board with a rotary punch tool. Each 1/8-inch hole is carefully made to ensure they align with those in the metal door cap.*

4 *Aluminum pop rivets are inserted through the panel board and into the metal cap panel that has been positioned underneath. The head of the rivet holds the panelboard to the cap, and the flared end is secured by the metal panel after being set by a rivet tool.*

5 *Further flattening of the rivet ends is required to prevent unwanted bumps from appearing in the finished door panel. With an anvil positioned under the rivet head, the end of the soft aluminum rivet can be hammered down to level it against the metal cap.*

Edge Banding

General Motors built many of its door panels with a metal edge that served a few purposes. The first was to anchor the door covering material to the panel. Small prongs pierced the material and were folded back to lock the door skin in place. The edge band added stiffness and some protection to the panel board.

A secondary feature was the panel fasteners spot welded to it. These were small ring-shank nails that, when inserted into the retainers in the door, held the panel securely to the surface of the door. Due to the frail nature of the fastener design, the nails often broke off and caused the door panel to become loose and result in damage to the panel.

Reproduction panels do not always use this method to secure the panel or skin. Many panels have slots cut into the panel board to accommodate a nail fastener, and the cover material is glued to the backside of the panel.

New edge banding is available through some manufacturers, but it is not a common reproduction item. If you can get new banding for your project, I would recommend it, but you can finish the door panel without this metal edging.

Reconditioning the Band

Removing the old panel covering from the edge banding involves lifting the edge of the cover material straight up to free it from the sharp fastener points that run along the length of the band. The exposed metal band can be pried off of the panel board with a broad knife or flat-blade screwdriver. Care should be used during removal so that the metal is not damaged.

After removing the metal band, it needs to be cleaned and straightened so that it can be reused on the new panel. A thin, flat-nosed pliers is best suited for reshaping the metal. An upholsterer's regulator can be helpful to help raise the small tabs for straightening. Be aware while handling the banding that you can cut or poke yourself on the sharp edges of the metal.

Installation of the Banding

Now is the time to check the size and edge profile of the new door panel. This is done by placing the old door panel on top of the new. Look for differences in the width and height of the panel board. Use a pencil to mark any variations in the profile so the new panel can be altered for an exact fit. Be careful when trimming the panel board to avoid accidental damage to the cover material.

When you are satisfied with the edge profile, the banding can then be slid onto the new panel board and lightly tapped into position with a small hammer. Once the banding is in position, use a flat-nosed pliers to crimp the metal onto the outer edge of the panel board.

Reinstalling the Edge Banding

1 *From the backside of the door panel, the cover material is lifted up from the retainer points and away from the edge, exposing the metal banding that runs along the outer edge of the panel board. Remove and recondition the edge band for use on the new panel.*

2 *A screwdriver is used to carefully lift the metal edge band from the old door panel so that it can be reconditioned. The metal is fragile enough, and it will need to be cleaned and straightened before it is reinstalled onto the new door panel.*

3 *A wire brush works well to clean the metal banding before it is straightened for reuse. Working with a pair of pliers, the many small sharp points along the band can be raised and flattened with very little effort. All this prep work will make installation a breeze.*

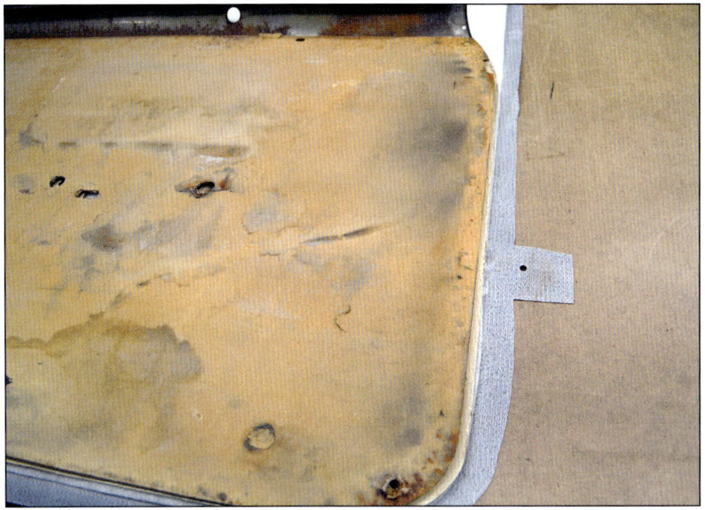

4 To prevent any fitment issues, the profile of the door panel should be compared to the original panel board. Check the overall size and contour of the new panel and make any necessary adjustments to the panel board to ensure an exact fit of the banding.

5 Adding a little contact cement to the edge of the panel board before the edge banding is applied will help keep it from shifting position. After a few taps with a hammer, the banding can be cinched to the edge of the panel board with a pliers.

No Edge Banding

Many reproduction panels do not have edge banding, or when the original is not reusable, the manufacturer will provide a slot in the panel board for the nail fastener. These slots are not always in the correct position and you may need to make an adjustment to get the panel to fit your car. Always measure for the best fit and placement of the fastener.

Panel Nail Repair

During the installation of the banding, you may encounter missing or damaged nail fasteners. These need to be replaced before the cover material is secured to the panel. Replacement panel nails made by Au-ve-co Products can be obtained from your auto trim supplier.

To determine the position of a missing nail fastener, look for the telltale sign of a spot weld or missing piece of metal. Another way to locate a fastener position is by transferring the measurements from the retainer locations on the inner door. This method is most useful if the metal banding is not used.

Setting the Fastener

Before a new fastener is inserted into the panel board, an accurate measurement of the nail position is needed. This position is determined by measuring from the inside edge of the nail retainer base to the center of the nail shaft, which is about 3/16 inch. This distance will guide you to where a slot in the panel board needs to be cut.

Next, determine the center point of the original fastener and mark the offset onto the panel board. If you do not know the original position of the fastener, the location can be obtained by measuring the center point of the retainer from the edge of the inner door. These measurements will give you a better fit when installing the prefabricated door panel.

Fastener placement on many of the prefabricated door panels is close but not always spot on. This can lead to the misfitting of the panel when it is installed to the door. The slots are cut long to allow for adjusting the fastener, but there is not an adjustment for the in-and-out positioning.

To correct the placement of the fastener, cut a new slot in the panel board. Be careful when making this modification because it is easy to cut through the surface material and ruin the door panel. Begin by sliding a 3- or 4-inch metal broad knife under the panel board. This will create a solid barrier between the panel board and the surface material and padding when you cut through the panel board.

Use a fresh blade in your utility knife when making this cut. The new blade will give you a cleaner cut without tearing the material, and it will easily glide through the panel board. Use a straightedge ruler as a blade guide when making the cut. Center the cut on the fastener position and make the slot about 1½ inches long. This will allow for some adjustment of the fastener in the opening.

Insert the new fastener into the slot on the panel board and recheck the measurement to verify that it is correct. Tap down the edges of the metal base with a small tack hammer to lock the fastener in place, and then remove the broad knife from under the panel board. Turn the panel face up on the workbench and be careful of the nail fasteners.

Nail Repair and Fastener Placement

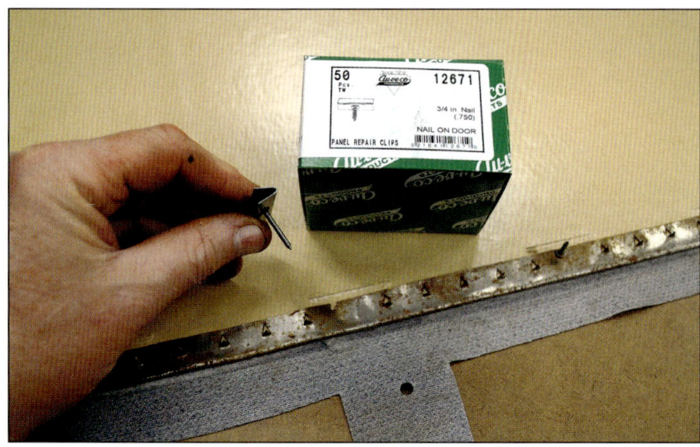

1 *New panel nails are available to replace the missing and damaged fasteners. These components are necessary to secure the new door panel to the door and should not be overlooked. It will only take a few minutes to install a new fastener.*

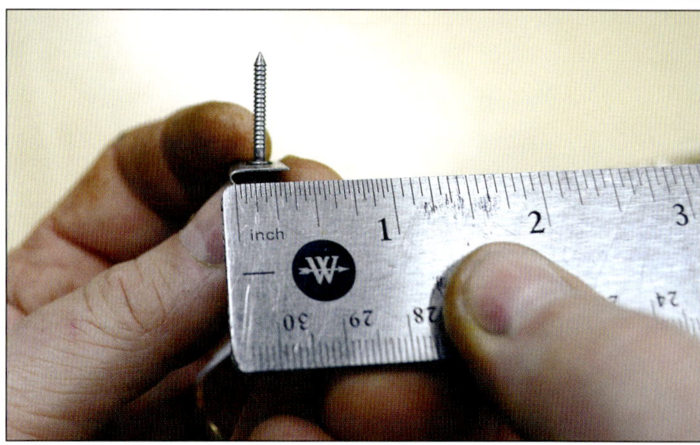

2 *There is not much margin for error when fitting the nail fasteners on the door panel. Take careful measurements of the fastener offset to help you get the placement right. This is essential to make the door panel fit correctly on the car.*

3 *Transferring the fastener offset measurements to the door panel will allow you to make the correct placement of the new fastener. You can see the how far off the fastener mounting slot is on the prefabricated panel.*

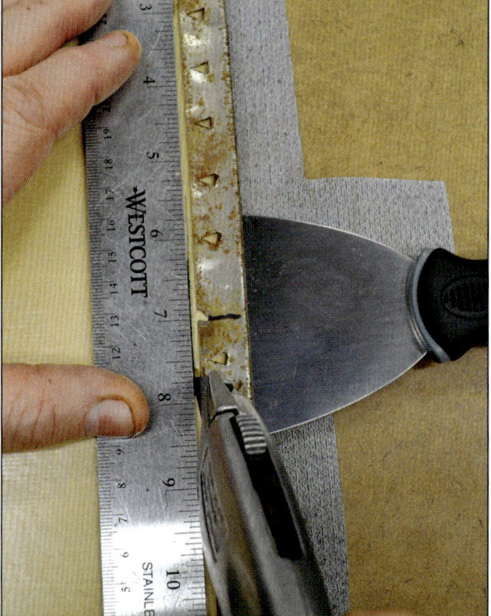

4 *A broad knife is inserted between the cover material and panel board to prevent accidentally cutting into the surface of the door panel. A metal ruler is placed parallel to the edge of the panel to help keep the new slot perfectly straight.*

5 *After the new nail fastener is fitted into the newly cut slot on the panel board, it is secured in place by flattening the edges of the base. The fasteners can still be adjusted from side to side if needed to make it align with the retainer/receiver in the door.*

Wrapping the Panel

1 Attaching the cover material to the panel board requires the use of a quality contact cement that can be sprayed as well as applied by brush. Most aerosol spray adhesives are not well suited for this application as they tend to let go after a short period of time.

2 Cardboard is used as a glue shield to prevent accidental overspray of glue onto the surface of the door panel and work surface. Taking this precaution will save you a lot of time from cleaning glue off of the cover material.

3 To prevent wrinkles from forming, an even amount of tension is put on the cover material as it is pulled over the door cap. Over stretching can leave puckers in the cover material along with dimple marks from excessive glue application.

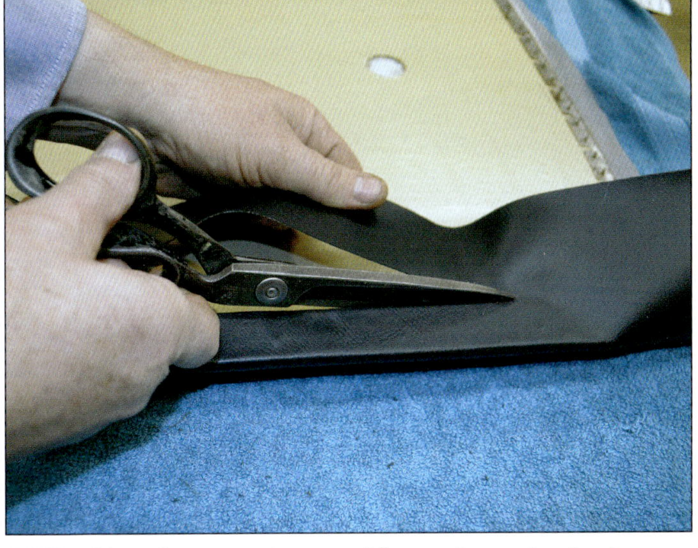

4 After the contact cement has set, a pair of scissors can be used to trim the excess cover material flush to the edge of the door cap flange. Proper trimming will help the panel fit better when it is installed on the door.

5 A cardboard glue shield is used when adhesive is sprayed onto the backside of the door panel and outer edges of the cover material. Coating both surfaces evenly with glue will allow the materials to achieve a better bond when pressed together.

6 *It is very important that you prevent any bulk from forming along the backside of the door panel. Making a relief cut in the cover material will help it form around curves and fasteners without any bunching or wrinkling.*

7 *The small, sharp gripper points on the metal edge banding easily pierces the cover material as it is pulled over the edge of the panel. After the material has been positioned over the metal points, they are bent over to secure the cover material to the panel.*

8 *A little extra contact cement is brushed onto the surface of the panel to help secure the corner flap of the cover material. The trick here is to let the glue dry to the touch before you stick the material down. If the glue is not dry enough, the material will let go.*

Panel Wrapping

The first section of the door panel to be wrapped is the cap. Begin by placing a cardboard shield under the door panel to prevent any overspray of glue from getting onto the workbench. Spray a light, even coat of contact cement onto the surface of the metal cap and backside of the pad material. Allow the glue to tack.

When the contact cement is just dry to the touch, turn the panel over and pull the padding material over the top of the cap and smooth it onto the cap. You do not want any wrinkles in the padding as they will show through when the cover material is applied. After the glue for the padding has set, trim the excess padding close to the edge of the metal cap and leave about 1/16 inch to cover the edge.

Repeat this process with the cap material. It is a good idea to place another piece of carboard behind the cover material when spraying to prevent glue from getting onto the surface of the door panel. When the glue is ready, wrap the cover material onto the cap. Again, avoid getting wrinkles in the cover material.

Turn the panel face down and apply an additional light coat of glue to the back flange on the metal cap and cover material. Allow the adhesive to tack. Flip the panel over and pull the cover material taut as you work the material onto the flange of the cap. When the glue has set, the excess material can be trimmed flush against the bottom edge of the flange.

Wrapping the Edge

Finishing the edges of the door panel consists of trimming the pad to the correct reveal and then pulling the cover material over and fastening it to the backside of the panel. There are some variations on finishing the edges of door panels that are composed of multiple layers and different materials. These panels require some additional details to make them look right.

Simple Cover

A basic panel has a one-piece cover material design that extends all the way around the door panel. Attaching the material along the edges is very basic. The key to get the panel to look right is to have a tight and sharp edge without any wrinkles or bulk.

Begin by trimming the pad material to 1/16 inch from the edge of the panel board. The small amount of extra material will give a soft appearance to the edge without carrying onto the backside of the panel. Excess padding on the underside will make the installed panel sit high on the surface of the door. This will interfere with how the door closes, resulting in pinching of the panel materials and eventually developing holes in the surface material of the door panel.

Contact cement works the best at securing the cover material to the backside of the door panel. A light coat of adhesive can be sprayed or brushed onto the backside of the panel board and cover material. When the glue is dry to the touch, pull on the cover material just enough to give it that snug appearance on the surface of the panel as it is wrapped around the edge, and then the glued surfaces get pressed together.

Do not pull too much on the material because that can cause a condition known as scalloping. Scalloping is a wavy appearance in the cover material. You want the material to be tight and smooth.

Mechanical fasteners are also great at keeping the material in place. To set the cover material, it should be pressed onto the triangular spike, piercing it and then bending the spike back to hold the material securely on the panel. When you encounter metal banding fastener nails, a small relief cut needs to be made in the cover material so that it will lay around the nail fasteners without any bulk.

Multilayer Panels

Deluxe door panels are comprised of different types of materials that include carpet, fabric, and vinyl along with stainless-steel trim moldings, cast emblems, and embossed trimmings. These ornate panels tend to have a lot of bulk at the intersection of the dissimilar materials. The layers add thickness to the surface of the panel that can interfere with how the door closes by binding and rubbing on the door jamb.

Thinning the layers of materials at these junctions will not only reduce the risk of damage to the

Production techniques have left too much material that will end up in the seams of this 1965 Impala panel. With a little careful trimming and gluing, we can make the cover material on this door panel look and fit a whole lot better.

surface of the panel but will also look better. When assembling the panel, it only takes a few minutes to make minor adjustments that will improve the overall fit of the door panel.

Relief Cuts

Trimming away some of the seam allowance will help minimize the bulk. It is very important to take your time when cutting the excess material from the seam. You do not want to cut into the thread. If this happens, the panel pieces will open up and it will be harder to make a proper repair.

Angular cuts work well to prevent materials from doubling up when they are folded back on themselves. This method works great when you have a metal edge band along the edge of the panel. Door panels that do not have a metal edge band are easier to work with. You can make a V-notch into the edge of the panel board to allow the extra material to fall into. This will also give you a level and uniform appearance on the door panel. Glue is brushed onto the backside of the material and is neatly folded and pressed into place.

Take care that the stitches are not snipped while small relief cuts are made in the seam allowance on the lower corners of the carpet binding. This helps the material lay down smoothly without bunching up under the turned binding.

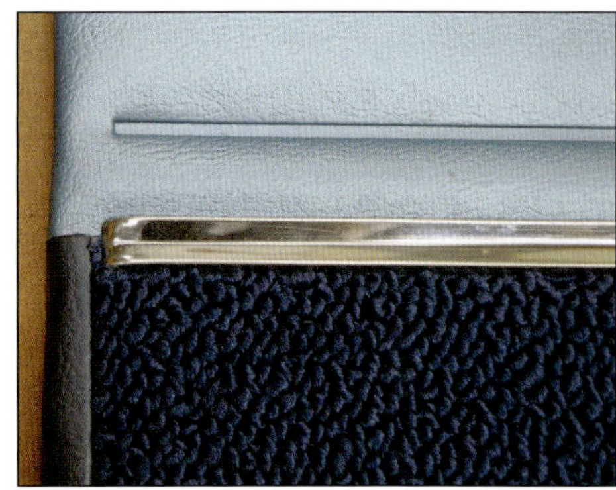

This is the result of making an effort to reduce the bulk in the layers of door panel materials. The appearance of the door panel is greatly improved, and the transitional joint disappears from view when the stainless trim molding is applied.

Wrap the Edge

After all the bulk has been removed from the seam allowance, contact cement can be brushed onto the backside of the panel board and binding. When the glue is dry to the touch, pull gently on the cover materials and wrap them around the outer edge of the door panel to secure them. Pay attention to the joint between the carpet binding and main cover material. You want the material to lay as flush as possible with the edge and appear flat and smooth along the surface of the panel.

Adding the Sweeps

Keeping weather from entering the car requires special seals. The window seals are attached to the top inner flange and the outer window sill. Outer window sweeps are attached to the door with special clips and/or small sheet-metal screws. Factory attachment of the inner sweep onto the door panel was done with heavy industrial staples. Pop rivets and small screws are often used to secure the replacement aftermarket seals.

You can obtain premade reproduction window sweeps for many

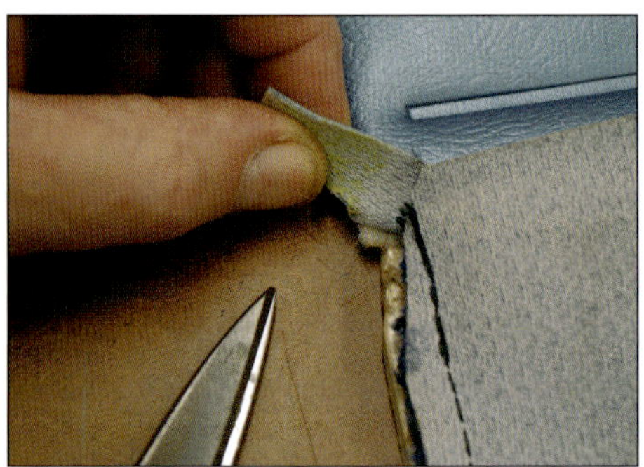

Excess material is cut away from the seam allowance to reduce bulk. A small notch is cut into the panel board to make room for the trimmed lower layer to disappear into. Glue will be applied to the material to secure it to the backside of the panel board.

Most window sweeps are ready to install straight out of the box, and the bur left over from manufacturing can be removed from the ends of the sweep with a few strokes from a fine file to make it look and perform better.

It is difficult to fasten window sweeps with industrial staples because it's hard to get them crimped tightly enough. When the sweep is aligned and in the correct position, drill a series of holes through the sweep and base material to accept rivets.

cars from a lot of suppliers. These sets are available in several configurations. Most sets contain eight pieces: four outer and four inner seals. Kits are also available as just inner or outer sets.

The quality of the window sweeps varies on which manufacturer makes them. Some sets are labeled as "original" and others as "replacement." The original sets are manufactured to be as authentic in detail as possible to what came with the car from the factory, while the replacement seals are generic in fit and finish. What you need to ask when ordering the seals is, "Are these returnable if they are not the correct fit for my car?" Whichever set you order, it will most likely need to be dry fit and refined before it is installed on the car.

I have always taken the time to soften the outer ends of the stainless trim bead with a fine file to remove the sharp edge left by the manufacturer. This small detail of rounding the ends will prevent any accidental snagged clothing or scratched skin when you brush up against the win-

dow sweep. This modification will also make the part look nice after it is installed on the car.

Securing the Sweep

There are many methods to attach the window sweep to the door panel, and it is up to you to decide what works well for you. The simplest way to secure the sweep to the flange of the door panel is to use pop rivets. Aluminum pop rivets are easy to use and hold the sweep without fail.

I prefer to use 1/8-inch aluminum rivets with a 1/8-inch grip range. This is the shortest pop rivet available that will not protrude into the glass or hang up on the upper edge of the door opening.

Pop rivets require a hole to be drilled through the materials you wish to join. After positioning and clamping the sweep on the cap flange, use a 1/8-inch drill bit to make a hole in the sweep and flange. Insert a rivet into the through hole and secure it with the proper setting tool. Continue to drill and set rivets about every 4 inches along the distance of the window sweep.

After the rivets are installed, it may be necessary to go back and flatten the rivet with a flat-jaw vise-grip pliers to minimize the bulk of the rivet on the flange. Taking the time to do this now will help the cap panel

Adding black enamel paint to the heads of the rivets can make them disappear. Use a hobby brush to control the amount of paint applied to the rivet head without getting paint on the surface of the window sweep.

fit better when it is hung on the door.

To reduce the visibility of the aluminum rivet, apply a drop of black paint to the head of the rivet. Take a small scrap of cardboard and spray some black semi-gloss paint onto the cardboard until you have a small puddle of paint. Use a small craft paint brush to apply the paint to the rivet head.

Installing Trim

Many adornments can be added to the door panel that not only make it more attractive but also have a practical purpose. These include door lock ferrules that cover the raw edge of the panel cover material and provide a smooth guide for the door lock knob.

A simple pop-rivet tool is used to secure the window sweep to the door panel. Additional enhancements can be made with a Vise-Grip pliers to flatten the rivet, helping with the fit of the door panel to the top of the car door.

Before the lock ferrule is installed, the mounting hole is opened up by cutting away the cover material that conceals the opening. A small hole like this is best cut with a hobby knife. The smaller blade is easier to control, which helps prevent overcutting.

After the ferrule is positioned, the small tabs protruding on the backside of the door cap can be flattened to hold the ferrule in place. The ferrule should fit snugly in place without any movement. Loose or poor fitting guides can be secured by brushing on a little contact cement.

You can see the effect of what 50 years or service can do to a piece of chromed plastic. Oxidation has taken its toll on the original armrest backing plate. New reproduction plates are available, and they look and fit exactly like the originals.

A small variation in the mounting points can throw off the fitment of the molding and spoil the whole project. Use the old door panel to verify the location of the armrest base and make any corrections necessary to ensure a perfect installation.

The reconditioned spring clip retainers are used to secure the armrest baseplate to the door panel. This is done by pushing the clip onto the mounting stud that protrudes through the backside of the panel. This will hold the trim tight.

The ferrule is inserted into the larger hole of the door cap trim, and it reduces the size of the hole to better fit the door lock knob. If the ferrule opening is not already accessible, it needs to be opened by cutting away the cover material to expose the opening. A small razor or X-Acto knife can be used to carefully cut away the cover material and pad to allow the insertion of the lock ferrule.

Lock ferrules vary in appearance by year and manufacturer. Some are made of plastic, metal, or a combination of both materials. Some ferrules snap into the hole on the door cap, and others are secured by bending back small tabs on the bottom of the ferrule.

Armrest Base

When chrome-plated plastic armrest bases and base plates were introduced, they added a new level of beautification to the interior of the car. The problem with these parts was how they aged, which turned out to be poorly.

Unlike its chrome-plated metal counterparts, the plastic cracked and the chrome wore off or tarnished, leaving the piece in an undesirable state. Many of these pieces are being reproduced and at a higher level of quality than the originals. Although the chrome is still subject to aging, with a little care, these pieces will last for a long time.

To prepare the door panel for installation, check the indexing and mounting holes against the original panel for size and location. If alterations are necessary, carefully make adjustments to the panel board without cutting into the cover material.

To fit the baseplate to the door panel, a sharp hobby or X-Acto knife

will be useful to make the through holes in the cover material. When setting the baseplate, turn the panel over and secure the piece to the panel with the clips that were saved during removal. Carefully align the clip to the mounting stud and press it onto the stud until it settles and holds the panel snugly in place.

Emblems and Moldings

The look of the door panel is enhanced by jewel-like emblems and shiny stainless-steel moldings that are applied to its surface. These fragile pieces take patience and some skill to apply correctly.

Many prefabricated panels already have reference marks on the door panel to help you position the emblems. For panels that do not have these guides, it will take accurate measurements to get the positioning correct. I recommend using ridged rulers when determining the center mark and attachment points of the emblem. Before affixing an emblem to the door panel, apply some painter's tape to the area. The tape will allow you to draw alignment guide lines on the panel without leaving unwanted marks.

Emblem Attachment

New emblems will have retainer tabs or threaded studs on the backside to secure them onto the panel. To affix a new emblem, carefully align the emblem on the door panel and gently press the emblem into the panel to create impressions from the posts. These marks will guide you as to where the mounting holes need to be made.

Create the through holes in the door panel with a small punch or regulator. This will allow the mounting posts to pass through to secure the

emblem. Pierce the door panel and dry fit the emblem to ensure that the holes are large enough to allow the emblem to sit flush on the surface of the panel.

Turn the door panel face down on the workbench and secure the emblem with the proper fastener. Use a small socket to push the spring-type lock washer onto the mounting shafts. Threaded posts use a washer and a locking nut to retain the emblem by carefully tightening the nut against the panel board. If you overtighten the nut, it can break off and you will have to get creative to secure the emblem.

Preparing the Emblem

Reconditioning an old emblem may require some effort to get it to fit the new panel. On the project 1969 Impala, the original door panel emblem is not available, so we will have to alter the old part.

When the emblem was first applied to the original door panel, three mounting studs were peened back to secure the emblem onto the aluminum skin of the door panel. Our new panel is made from vinyl and the emblem will not be able to be attached in the same manner as the factory. A Dremel tool with a cutting bit can be used to remove the flared portion of the mounting stud. It only takes a few passes to remove the unwanted metal, leaving a straight post that will keep the emblem from rotating.

Indexing the emblem on the door panel is done by squaring up the emblem with the guide lines that were made on the painter's tape. When you have the emblem in the correct position, press on the emblem just enough to leave small indentations in the surface of the tape. Use a small hole punch and hammer to

---

pierce the surface of the door panel to allow the emblem to lay flush on the surface.

To affix the emblem to the door panel, apply a high-quality silicone adhesive to the backside of the medallion and set the piece into the panel. Use some masking tape to hold the emblem tight to the surface of the door panel while the silicone adhesive sets. Do not remove the tape until the glue has fully cured. Any excess silicone that oozes out from the edges can be carefully removed when the adhesive has set.

Applying a Door Emblem

1 *Alignment lines are made on the door panel to help determine the precise position of the decorative emblem. Tape is used to create a temporary grid on the door panel. Remove the tape after the layout is determined.*

2 *It only takes a few minutes to accurately position and set the door panel emblem. The anchor posts of this panel emblem are used to make small dents in the surface of the door panel to be used as a guide for making the mounting holes.*

3 *To prevent the mounting posts of the emblem from bending or breaking during installation, a regulator is used to prepunch a hole all the way through the panel board. When the emblem is fit, add retainer clips to hold the emblem securely.*

4 *There are many types of fasteners used to secure an emblem to a door panel. This emblem uses small spring clip retainers to hold it on the door panel. A deep-well socket makes an excellent tool to push the clip in place.*

 INSTALLING AUTOMOTIVE INTERIOR KITS

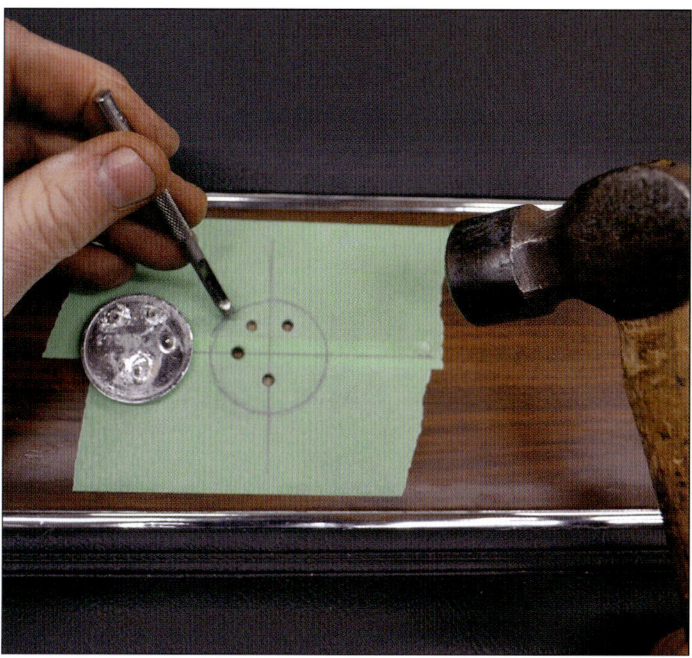

5 *New emblems are not available for all projects, and some reconditioning of the original cast emblem is necessary. By carefully preparing the mounting studs, the old emblem can be reused and mounted on the door to restore its original appearance.*

6 *An impression has been set into the protective tape, making it possible to create new mounting points for the emblem studs. Use a hole punch to make the recessed pockets in the door panel for the indexing studs to set into.*

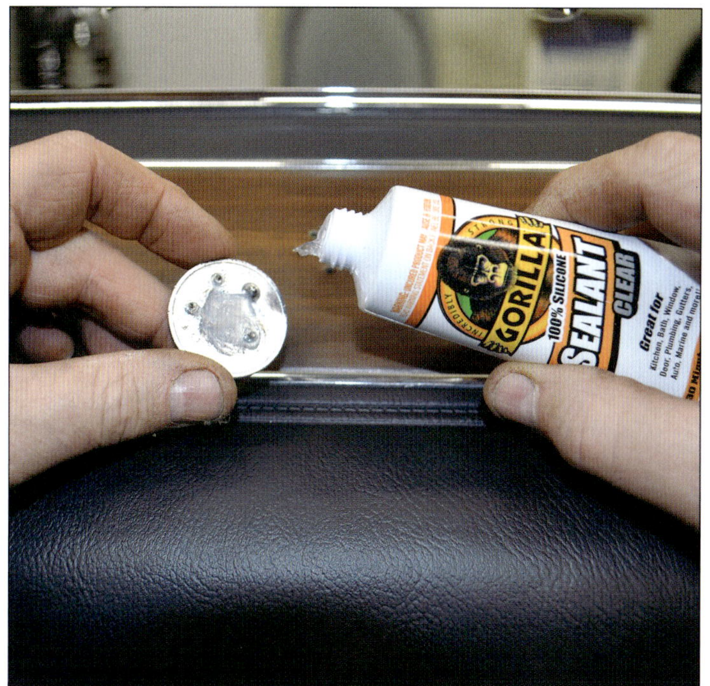

7 *After removing the protective masking tape from the door panel, secure the emblem to the surface of the panel with a strong silicone adhesive. When the adhesive is set, the emblem will be permanently bonded to the door panel.*

8 *To prevent the emblem from lifting or shifting position, use masking tape to keep the trim piece in place while the adhesive cures. Follow the adhesive manufacturer's guide for drying time before removing the masking tape.*

Molding Options

Transitional moldings are not only decorative, they also conceal the joint between the dissimilar materials often used when the door panel is created. Older stainless-steel moldings used small tabs or pins to secure the molding onto the door panel. The tabs were stamped from a strip of steel, and then the strip was embedded into the backside of the molding. Pins, or trim nails, are spot welded to the molding. These fasteners often break off or rust away over time, leaving the molding unusable.

Installing the Trim

Stainless can be repaired and polished to look new. After it is reconditioned, the moldings can be fit to the door panel. Rest the tabs of the stainless molding on the center line of the transitional area. Press the tabs into the cover material just enough to make a reference impression. Remove the molding and make a hole through the door panel to allow the tabs to pass through.

Reset the molding by placing the tabs into the through holes and press the molding flat to the surface of the panel. Turn the panel face down on the workbench and secure the molding by bending the tabs over. The tabs are delicate, and it only takes a

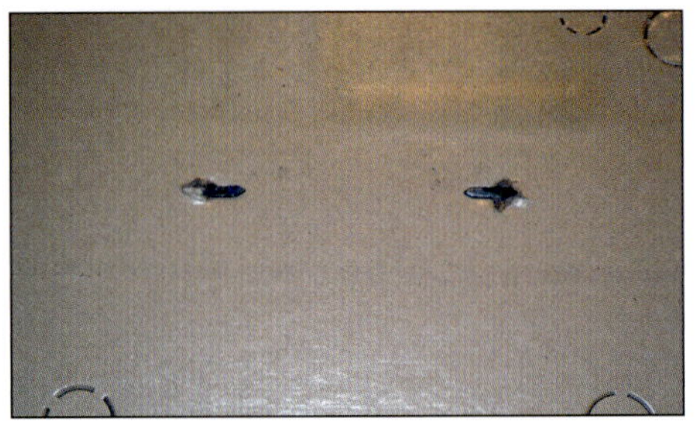

Retainer tabs from the stainless molding have been flattened against the backside of the panel board to hold the molding in place. When the tabs are bent over, I like to alternate their direction to ensure that the molding doesn't shift.

few light taps with a tack hammer to lock the molding in place.

Repairing the Molding

Repairing the molding can be accomplished with many processes or methods. Most often, a hole was drilled through the molding and a screw is used to reattach it. Not only does this choice of installation result in an ugly fix but it also adds further damage to the molding.

One method of replacing broken tabs is to cut a new metal tab from sheet metal and use epoxy glue to hold it to the back of the molding. This process only works if the surfaces of the materials are thoroughly cleaned and the glue bonds to the metal.

Welding a new tab to the molding is the best solution, but it can discolor and damage the stainless. An alternative to welding is soldering the tab in place. SolderWeld makes an excellent product that works well and will not harm the molding.

The low melting point of the special solder combined with its Hot Block heat shielding material allows you to make a strong repair without causing more damage to the trim. The solder can also fill previously made holes in the molding, which makes an acceptable repair until a better replacement molding can be found.

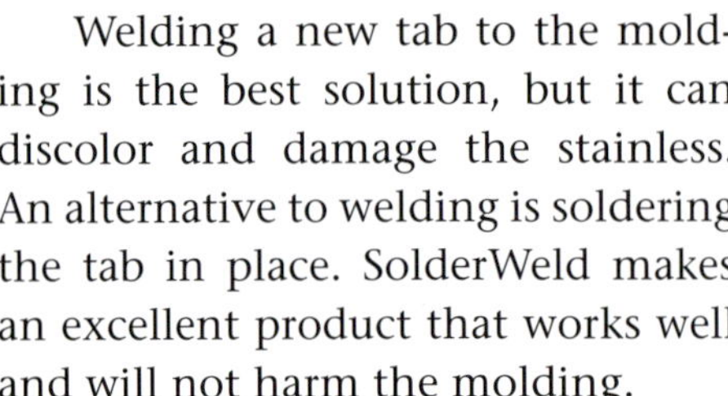

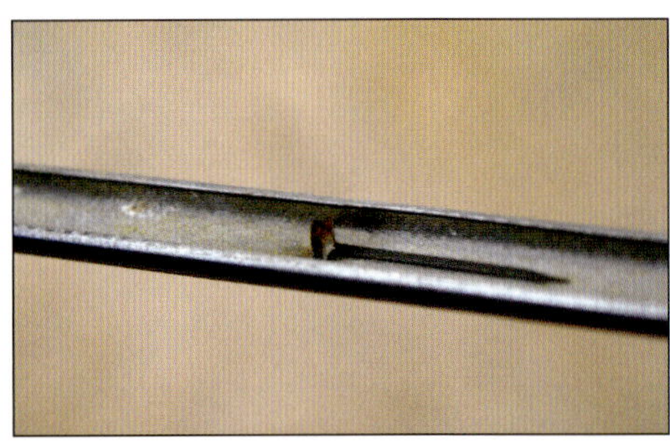

This broken fastening tab is a common problem with traditional trim moldings. Too often a tab is missing or breaks off when it is removed from the old door panel. Many upholsterers find this an impossible situation to deal with.

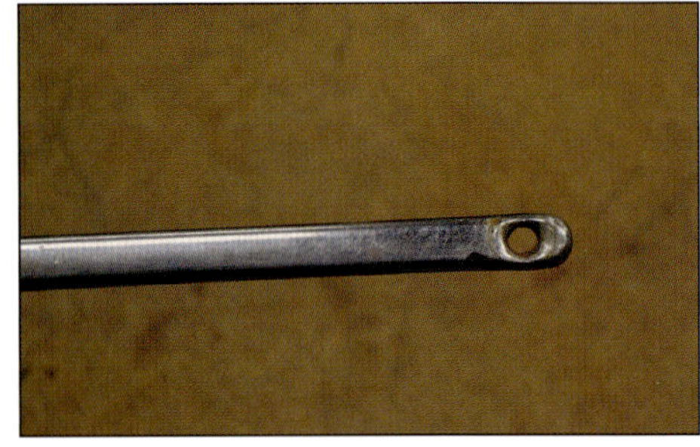

This molding will cover the line between the edge of the carpet and upper door panel. It is being used to mark the position for the fastener tabs that will hold the molding in place. Holes will be prepunched in the panel to prevent the molding tabs from breaking.

All too often, I find a molding that has been attached to the door panel with a screw. Someone has drilled a hole in the end of this molding, and it is destined for the scrap pile. With a little effort, this molding can be repaired and put back into service.

Fixing a Piece of Molding

1 *A new metal retainer tab has been cut and formed from a piece of 22-gauge sheet metal. The metal is not only strong enough to hold the decorative molding to the door panel but also soft enough to be worked without any special tools.*

2 *Making a permanent repair to damaged molding can be accomplished with some basic tools. Special solder and flux products made by Solder-Weld can make the task of attaching new fastening tabs to a molding almost effortless.*

3 *After the surface of the molding has been properly prepared, a new metal tab can be secured to the backside of the molding with a little heat. With the use of special solder products, moldings can be repaired without further damage.*

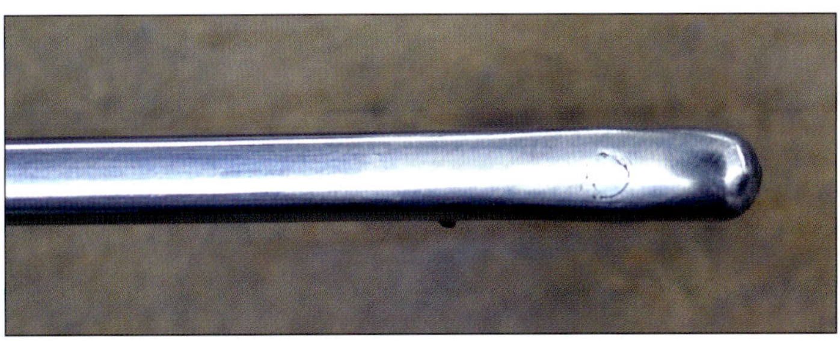

4 *After this hole was filled with the SolderWeld Multi Sol product, it was filed smooth and sanded before it was buffed to a shine. This repair took only minutes and cost less than a dollar in materials. At a glance, the repair is almost unnoticeable.*

Modern Moldings

Not all moldings are made of stainless steel. When a modern door panel is created via a dielectric process of stamping a pattern or pleats, chrome accents can be added to the surface of the door panel. These accents are most likely made of a rubber or vinyl base with a mylar finish applied, which gives the appearance of a stamped-metal molding.

Other methods of attaching a molding to the door panel is with emblem-mounting tape. This product has a strong adhesive tape on both sides of a closed cell foam rubber base tape. After the tape is applied to the backside of the molding, the trim can be positioned on the door panel as the protective cover film is removed to expose the adhesive on the outer side of the tape and pressed into place. When the surface area for the molding is properly prepared, the resulting adhesion is almost permanent.

Severely damaged metal moldings can be replaced with an extruded self-adhesive molding. Many styles

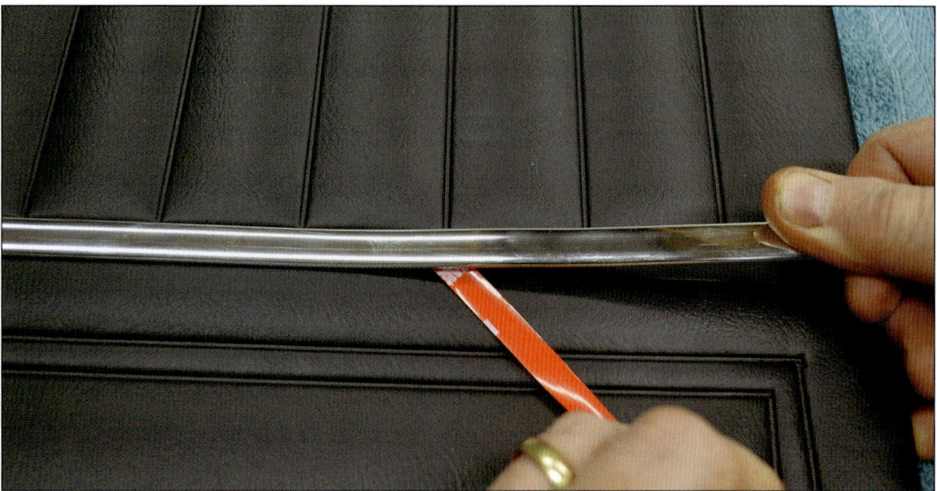

The key to a successful installation of an extruded molding is to first clean the surface of the panel with an alcohol wipe prior to installing. Exposing only a small amount of the adhesive strip at a time will ensure a great bond with the panel.

Emblem-mounting tape works well as an alternative to physical fasteners for holding ridged moldings to the face of a door panel. Be sure to choose a width and thickness of mounting tape that is appropriate for your particular molding.

Prepackaged extruded moldings come in many sizes and profiles. These products can save you a lot of time and money on your project. You can find a variety of these products by searching online or at your favorite auto parts supplier.

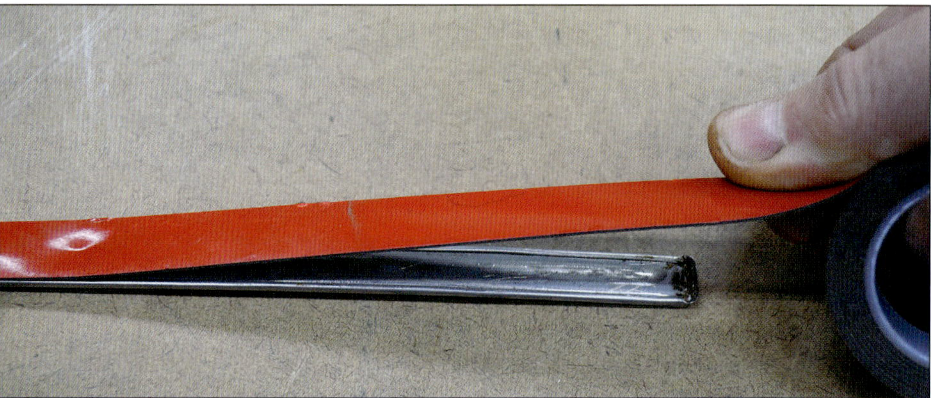

Using the correct size and type of emblem-mounting tape will make a difference on how well the installation will look and perform. The tape should be no wider than the molding it is applied to. This ensures that it will not show.

and sizes are available to make an acceptable repair. If you decide to use one of these products, always follow the manufacturer's installation instructions and surface preparation before installing the product to achieve the best results.

Final Preparation

On the backside of the door panel are many precut knockouts that need to be removed before the door panel is installed on the car. These die-cut shapes allow for an easy pass through of window regulator posts, door latch handles, remote mirror controls, and power window actuators. Not all of the knockouts need to be removed. Only remove the knockouts that are necessary for the installation on your car.

Use a flat-blade screwdriver to get under the knockout and carefully lift it away without damaging the underlying padding and cover material. It is not recommended to precut through the cover material at this time. An exact hole can be made after the door panel is installed.

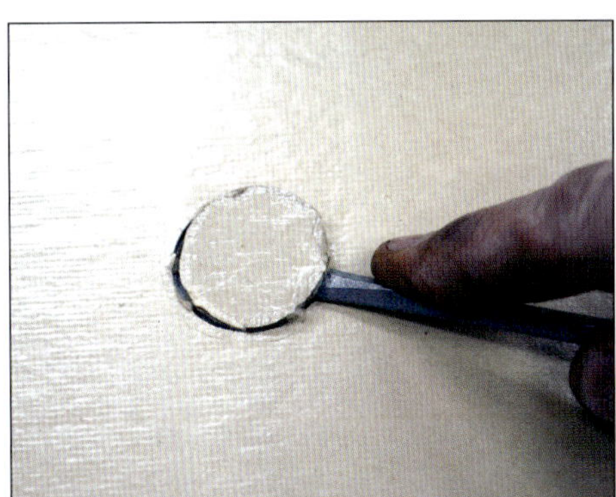

To make the installation of the window cranks and other applied items easier, the appropriate knockouts are removed from the backside of the panel board. Once the door panel is installed, the cover material can then be cut away to allow access for the attachment of the accessories.

After a few hours of work, we have a completely assembled door panel that is ready to be installed in the car. After the new panel is fitted, the remaining hardware and accessories can be attached and enjoyed for years to come.

Some panels may need to have the fastener retainer knockout holes opened. Use the same technique to remove the die-cut material as with the other knockouts. Pay close attention during the removal so that the cover material is not damaged. Install the metal spring clip or plastic Christmas tree fasteners into the door panel.

Water Shields

Now is the time to install the window crank handle springs. Set the spring on the regulator post with the small end of the coil inward toward the door. The larger end will push against the door panel to help support the panel board against the base of the window crank.

Protecting a newly installed door panel from being water damaged is done with a simple barrier. A water shield is made up of a plastic-coated paper that is applied to the inner surface of the door with body putty or tape. The shield limits the amount of rainwater that can get on the backside of the door panel through the stamped access holes in the inner door skin. When properly installed, the shield will keep your new interior looking great for many years to come.

Panel Installation

Fitting the new door panel onto the car takes a little finesse. Dry fitting the panel will prevent unforeseen issues with the alignment of the panel fasteners. If the fasteners do not line up directly with the fastener receptacle, now is the time to re-clock the clip or make an adjustment to the panel board to ensure the fastener will work properly. Centering is also key to preventing damage to the edges of the cover material, so check the end alignment of the panel. If you are happy with the overall fit, the panel can be fastened in place.

It helps the installation process if the door glass is lowered into the door for full-coverage door panels. Door panels with an attached cap fit over

This water shield has been installed on the wrong door. The rubberized coating should face the interior surface of the door. Another installation error to note was duct tape being used to secure the water shield to the door's surface.

the top of the door and are locked in place by retainers mounted to the top of the door. The window sweep should rub lightly onto the inside of the door glass when it is raised or lowered. Remember to insert the door lock rod through the lock ferrule before fully setting the panel onto the door. Door panels that do not have an attached cap panel are slid under the retainer molding on the door.

Panel Fasteners

Early-model wood-frame cars commonly attached a trim panel with small headless nails called brads. The brad pierced the fabric cover of the panel as it was driven through the panelboard and into the hardwood frame of the car. A curved needle was used to lift the cover material over the nailhead to conceal it. To remove the panel from the car, a tack lifter was used to pry the panel off the brad and leave it embedded in the wood. The brad was then removed with a pliers or claw hammer.

Steel-body cars use a variety of fasteners to attach the panels. Some panels use a metal edge band with ribbed nails attached. These nails mate with a nail cup along the outer ends of the inner door. Spring loaded wire clips are another popular fastener used to secure the door panel in place. The fasteners are clipped onto the backside of the panel and inserted into a small hole in the metal surface of the door.

Modern plastic door panels are held in place with Christmas tree fasteners. These are single-use fasteners that push into the metal door and hold the panel securely in place.

Installing Clips

Most door panels have precut openings in the panel board to allow

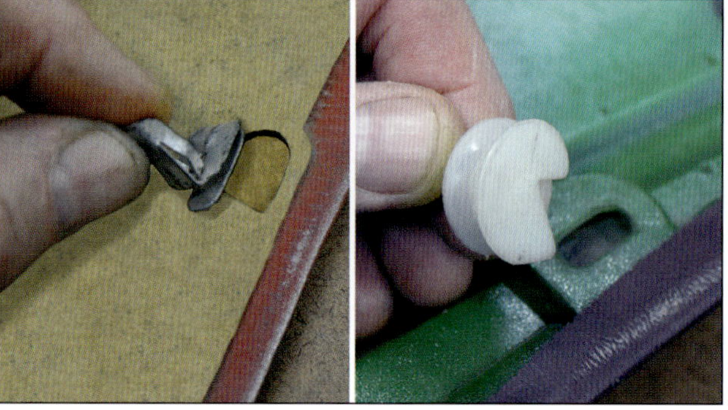

This door panel is keyed with a flat edge on the keeper hole to indicate the proper indexing of the metal door panel fastener. The plastic Christmas tree fastener simply turned into an oval slot on the plastic molded door panel.

the insertion of a panel fastener. The positioning of the clip is usually determined by the direction of the cutout. Panels that have a round opening are a little more difficult to align until they are matched up with the receptacle opening in the door. The clip can easily be re-clocked to mate with the receptacle to allow a precise fit.

It's best to prefit the fasteners in the door panel while it is still on the workbench. Cover the workbench with a towel before placing the door panel face down on the bench. Insert the lower leg of the clip into the fastener hole and advance it until it is fully seated against the edge of the opening. If the panel board is thicker than the gap in the leg of the clip, spread the clip open a little to allow it to slide over the panel board without damaging the panel.

After the clips are installed, the door panel can be fit onto the door. Visually check the alignment of the fastener to the receptacle. If the fastener is in the wrong position, it can be re-clocked to help it mate with the anchor point. In the case that the fastener still does not reach the anchor, you may need to alter the panelboard to allow the fastener to align properly.

Insert the Christmas tree fasteners into the panel by twisting them into the fastener hole. The fastener

holes are usually elongated to allow for some variance in the fastener anchor point. These are usually a one-use fastener, so be careful when anchoring the panel.

Setting the Fastener

Once the door panel is properly aligned, the tips of the fasteners should be set into their respective anchor points to ensure that they will go directly into the door. You do not want to cause any damage to the surface of the door panel, so it is best to use a soft rubber mallet to lightly tap the fasteners to fully seat them. Please take a word of advice from a veteran in this trade: avoid using your fist as a mallet. This will save you from a lot of pain in the years to come.

Anchor Screws

One feature that is very common with many door panels is the use of trim screws to secure the bottom edge of the panel. Due to the use of a foot to help open the door, this rough treatment causes most fastener clips or blind cleats to fail. A stronger method of attachment was needed to keep the panel in place.

Typically, there were four or five trim screws evenly spaced across the bottom of the panel. When you are ready to fasten the bottom of the panel, it may be quicker to measure

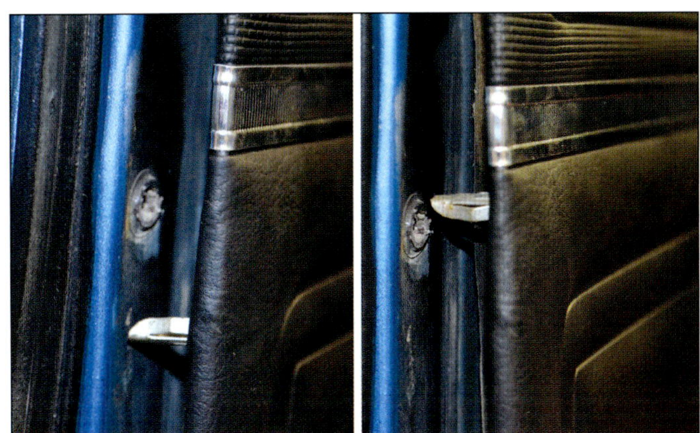

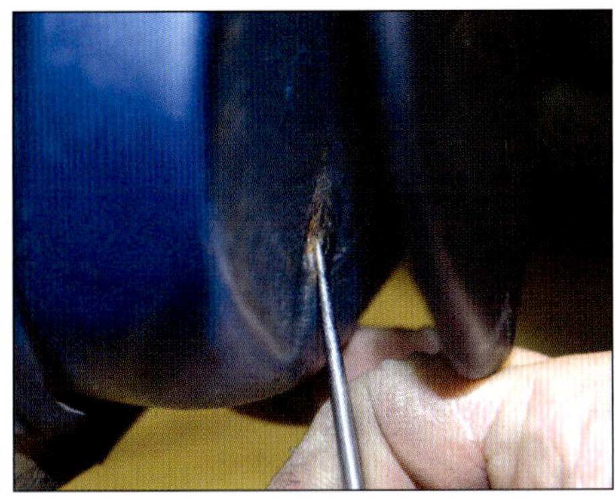

This door panel fastener was inserted in the wrong position to mate with the door anchor when it was installed on the panel. After the panel is removed from the car, the clip can be rotated 180 degrees to correct the problem.

The position of the door panel anchor holes along the bottom of the door are located with the help of a regulator. Indexing the distance from the bottom edge of the door will give you a good idea on where to make the hole in the door panel.

and drill new holes in the door. However, locating and using the original anchor points is not difficult and is more authentic to the installation.

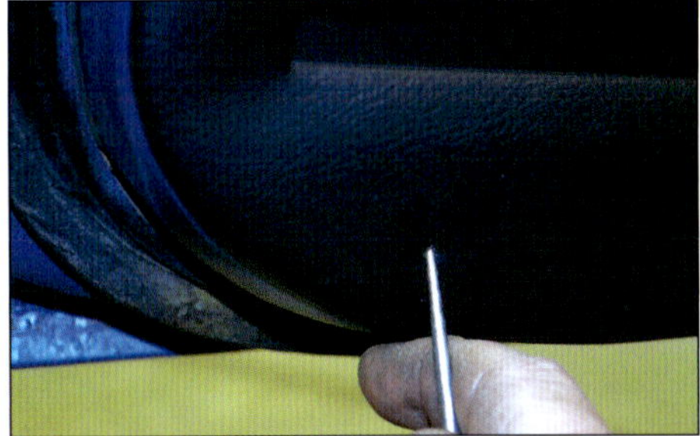

The anchor screw position is located onto the front of the door panel by transferring the recorded position of the anchor hole with the regulator. Keep the measured distance as accurate as possible to prevent error in the screw placement.

The original anchor holes can be located by using a regulator. If you lift the bottom of the panel, the anchor point can be indexed by placing the tip of the regulator in the screw hole and pinching the shaft of the regulator along the bottom of the door.

This measurement can then be transferred to the face of the door panel by realigning the regulator in the same vertical position. At this juncture, push the tip of the regulator into the door panel and pierce the panel board. After the regulator has passed through the panel, the screw hole should be very close to the new hole in the panel. If not, move the tip of the regulator in a small circular motion to locate the screw hole.

A 3/4-inch #8 oval-head trim screw with a flush washer is then inserted into the hole and tightened with a Phillips-head screwdriver. The screw should hold the panel securely to the door without dimpling the cover material.

Fitting Door Hardware

You should be able to see a small lump in the cover material of the door panel to indicate the location of the window regulator post. Use a pair of scissors to cut away a small circle in the cover material to expose the post. The hole should be large enough for the splined shaft to come through and yet small enough to

Using the correct hardware during the installation of the door panel will give your project the authentic appearance that it came with from the factory. Wrinkles should not appear on the surface of the panel if the trim screws are tightened properly.

No detail has been overlooked during the door panel's assembly and installation. A final inspection is necessary to check for proper fit. You don't want any premature damage or wear on the panel from rubbing or misalignment.

cover the opening with the window crank.

A protective escutcheon is placed behind the window crank to protect the door panel cover material from wear when the crank is rotated. This simple nylon disc is often forgotten or ignored when the crank handle is installed. For the small cost of the escutcheon, why wouldn't you want to keep your interior from wearing out before its time?

One thing to keep in mind when the escutcheon is installed is that the cover material of the door panel should be cut away just enough to allow the recess in the escutcheon to rest inside. This will allow the crank to fit properly and turn without any binding.

Prior to the window crank being installed, the window needs to be raised so that the crank can be clocked correctly. Make sure that the retainer clip has been removed and the escutcheon is behind the crank when the window is raised. Install a new retainer clip in the window crank to prepare it for installation. The C-shaped clip is inserted into the small slots in the internal shaft of the crank with the open portion of the clip facing toward the handle or knob end of the device.

Place the escutcheon behind the base of the window crank, index, or "clock," the handle or knob end of the crank at 2 o'clock, and press it onto the splined window regulator shaft. When properly seated, the base of the window crank will rest flush with the surface of the door panel.

Attachment of a window crank with a screw-type fastener is the same as described above with the exception of inserting the screw to secure the crank to the regulator post. Some cranks also require the application of a foil decal disc to cover over the screw fastener. Verify the function of the window by rolling it up and down, and make adjustments if necessary.

Installing the Window Crank

1 After locating the window regulator post, cut a small hole in the door panel to reveal the splined end of the post. The window can now be rolled all the way up to allow the proper position of the window crank.

2 This thin plastic disc is designed to protect the surface of the door panel from abrasion when the window crank is turned. The escutcheon will also help protect the door panel from damage when a window crank removal tool is used.

3 A retainer clip should have some movement when seated in the shaft of the crank to allow the spring action of the clip to operate properly. The open end of the clip should face forward toward the knob end of the window crank.

4 To prevent your knee from hitting the window crank, install it at any comfortable position to give you room to operate the window. For visual uniformity and usability, the window crank on the driver-side door is usually set at the 2 o'clock position.

This lever-style door release handle was pushed onto the exposed actuator shaft. A small spring clip keeps the handle from falling off of the post. An armrest base will be installed over the post to conceal the base of the release handle.

Details, no matter how small, are very important. Worn and shabby pieces will spoil the overall appearance of the door panel. Something as simple as threading a new chrome-plated lock knob onto the lock knob shaft will brighten the interior of the car.

Door Release Handle

Note that some release handles are completely exposed, and others are partially concealed by the armrest base. The fitment of the door release handle is similar to the window crank. First, locate the bump in the door panel and cut a small opening in the cover material to allow the splined shaft of the door opener to come through. Carefully enlarge the hole to be no larger than the shaft of the release handle. The edges of the hole should be trimmed neatly.

Insert a new retainer clip into the slots in the post of the lever and push the release lever onto the shaft. A variation of securing the lever is to use a machine screw to hold the lever onto the post.

Armrest Base

Depending on the type of armrest base your car requires, there may be two or three large sheet-metal or machine screws needed to hold it onto the door. Door panels that do not have precut mounting holes in the cover material for the armrest will need to be cut to allow the locating posts on the base to index with knockouts in the panel.

Begin by feeling for the relief left by the knockout and use a regulator to locate the anchor holes in the underlying door. Cut away the minimum amount of cover material to allow the armrest base to sit flush with the panel. The cutout will allow the mounting screw to reach the inner door without being obstructed. Tighten the screws just enough to hold the armrest firmly to the door without distorting or cracking the plastic.

Final Details

The last item to be installed is the door lock knob. This screws onto

Use large sheet-metal screws to secure the armrest base to the door. A regulator is used to help with the location of anchor holes. After the screws were started, the base was adjusted for fit, and then the screws were tightened.

the lock post. Most of these devices are made of plastic and can crack if tightened too much. It is a matter of judgement on how far down to screw the lock knob. The top of the knob should be within 3/4 inch from the surface of the ferrule and yet easy enough to grab when in the down or locked position. The base of the lock knob should not extend above the ferrule when in the up or unlocked position.

Check the fit of the door panel and wipe off any smudges, grime, and fingerprints that were left behind during the installation. Make sure the door is unlocked and check to see how the door closes. Slowly close the door and watch for any pinching or binding along the edges. Roll the window up and down to ensure that it functions properly. If adjustments need to be made, loosen the panel and shift it to achieve a better fit.

Rear Trim Panels

There are some variations to consider when installing new upholstery to the rear section of the car. Cars with four doors have door panels that are installed just like the two-door models. Installation of rear quarter trim panels differ by bodystyle. Many cars may or may not have an armrest. The armrest can be a bolt-on type or a filler type that extends into the cab of the car.

Removal

Access to the rear trim panel is gained by removing the rear seat from the car. Push in on the lower edge of the bottom cushion to release it from the floor of the car. If your car has applied rear armrests, they will need to be removed to allow for the removal of the backrest. A #3 Phillips screwdriver is needed to remove the anchor screws holding the armrest base to the inner panel of the car.

After the lower cushion and rear armrests have been removed, you will be able to see the attachment hardware that secures the rear seat backrest to the car. Typically, there are two anchors that hold the seat frame to the rear floor. These fasteners are either metal tabs that are bent over a loop in the seat frame or sheet-metal screws with large attached washers

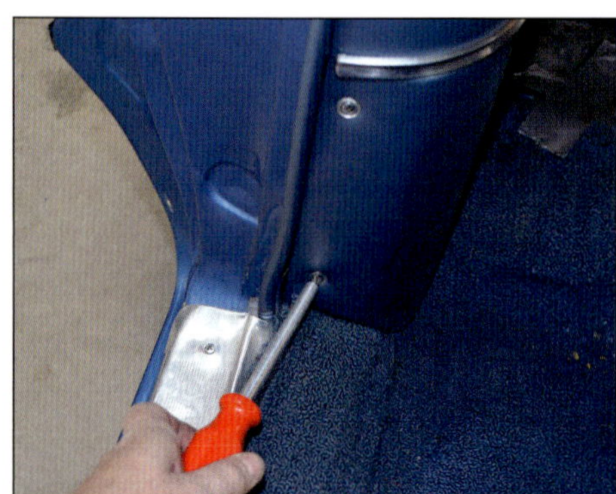

Decorative oval-head washer trim screws hold the armrest in place. These screws anchor into small brackets that protrude into the cab area. An appropriate screwdriver is used to remove the screws in the front of the armrest.

that lock the backrest in place. Larger seats may also have a metal tab that threads through a slot on the lower outer seat frame. This tab can be lifted to allow the seat to be freed from the floor. After the backrest fasteners are lifted, the cushion can be lifted upward and out or the car.

Lower Armrest

Cars, such as convertibles and coupes with a short-width rear seat, most likely have a lower or filler-style rear armrest. The width of this armrest compensates for the inner wheel tub and conceals hydraulic cylinders used for moving the convertible top.

The exposed trim screws in the lower rear armrest have a decorative washer attached to the screw. The washer prevents the head of the screw from digging into the cover material, and it is made in such a way that it cradles the head of the screw, making it appear flush with the surface of the cover. A Phillips-head screwdriver is used to remove the trim screws.

There is another screw located near the rear edge of the panel that will need to be removed. After the retainer screws are removed, the panel can be lifted out of the car.

Upper Rear Panel

An additional filler panel may be secured to the back edge of the trim panel. Remove the fasteners on the inner backside of the trim panel and set the panel aside. Cars that have an upper window trim molding or a B-pillar molding will need to be removed to allow the panel to be lifted from the inner quarter panel. Remove the window crank so that the quarter trim panel can be removed.

The rear panel may have a top cap, or the top edge of the panel may be tucked under a trim molding.

There are many different ways the panel can be attached to the car. One configuration uses panel clips to hold the front edge of the panel in place while the front edge of the panel butts up to the rear wind lace. Use a panel-lifting tool to get under the fasteners to separate the panel from the car. When the panel is removed, you will be able to remove the wind

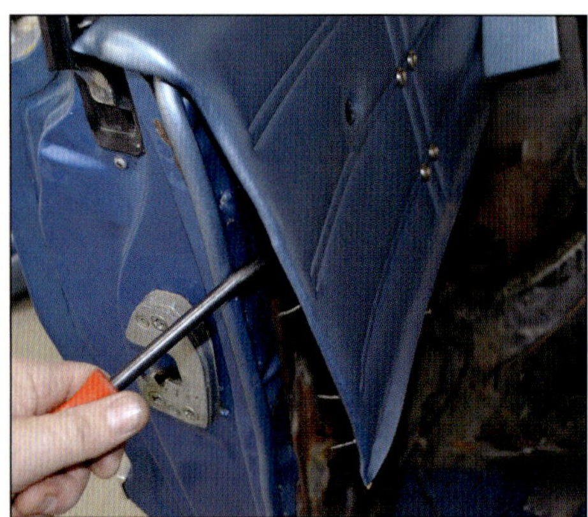

This panel was attached to the car with nail-type fasteners. The ring shank fasteners were imbedded into a tack strip, and a panel-lifting tool is used to pry the panel free. The new trim panel will be installed in the same manner.

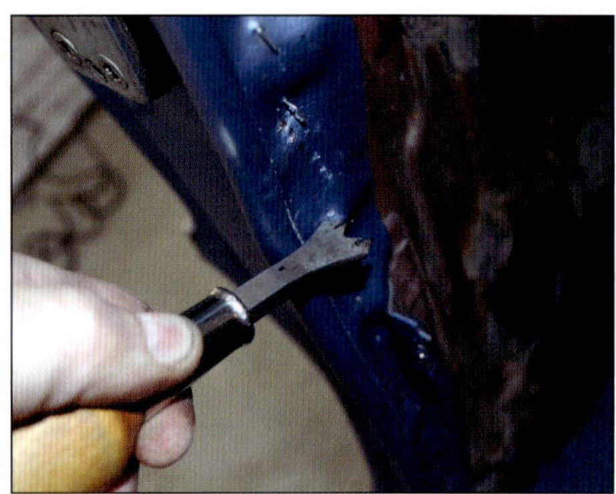

Staples were used when this wind lace trim was installed. When the staples are removed, the wind lace can be removed to allow inspection of the underlying tack strip. New tack strip can be installed, if necessary, to ensure a good bond for the new wind lace and trim panel.

lace from the edge of the door jam and replace it if necessary.

Another option uses the leading edge of the panel cover material wrapped over the pinch weld of the door jam and secured in place with a quick-edge wind lace. First, remove the sill plate to access the bottom of the wind lace. Carefully lift the lower end and pull it forward and off of the pinch weld. The cover material can now be pulled loose from the body of the car and the panel can be removed.

Panel Covers

There is a variation on some cars as to how the rear panel is fastened to the car. Cars with a soft-core wind lace will need to have the underlying tack strip inspected for viability. It must be in great condition so that it can hold a staple or tack. If it is damaged, it must be replaced.

Sewn foam-core wind lace is installed around the door opening before the headliner and door panel are installed. The seam of the wind lace runs along the edge of the pinch weld of the door opening, and the selvedge is attached to the tack strip with tacks or staples.

Installation of the rear trim panels is not very different than the installation of a door panel. The

Because the tail section of this rear panel extends into and overlaps the package tray area, a new package tray was installed before the new rear trim panel was aligned and fit to the inner rear of the car. The new panel fits just like the original.

water shield is installed and then the panel is fit to the inner panel of the car. It helps if the new package tray has already been installed and the rear quarter window is in the lowered position.

Fit the trim panel to the rear quarter and check the alignment of the front edge of the panel board so that it does not extend past the pinch weld of the door jam. When you get the panel positioned correctly, it can be set onto the rear quarter window ledge.

Fastener Variations

Panels with nail fasteners take a little more finesse to attach. The front edge of the panel should butt up to the edge of the foam core and just cover the stitching of the wind lace. Working the panel from the top down, place the nail fasteners on the

tack strip and drive them into the tack strip with a dead-blow hammer. Use gentle taps to prevent the nails from breaking off when setting them into the tack strip.

Spring clip fasteners secure the front of the panel by lining up the tip of the fastener with their respective retainers. When the clip is positioned correctly, a light tap with a soft mallet will set the fastener into the receptacle.

Panels that are held in place by a quick-edge type of wind lace will need to be attached by applying contact cement to the leading edge of the panel material and pinch weld.

This panel is secured in place by wrapping the leading edge of the cover material around the pinch weld of the door jamb. A little glue is brushed onto the mating surfaces to help keep the panel in place until the pinch weld molding can be applied.

Rear trim panels require a water shield to protect the upholstery from damage. New water shields are available from most supply houses and are easy to install. They are worth the few dollars they cost to protect your new interior investment.

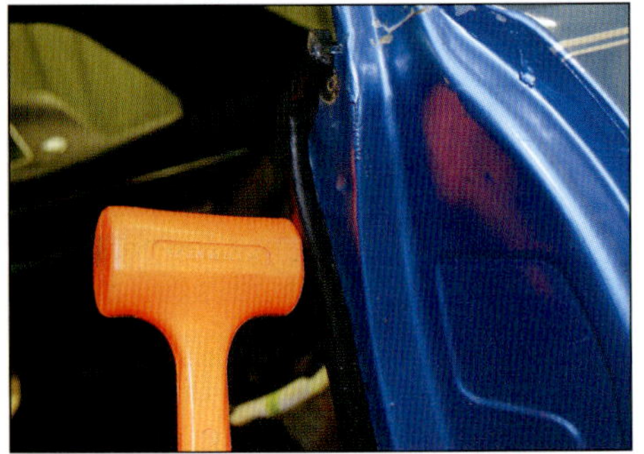

Inside of the quick-edge wind lace is a gripper bead and a metal spring core that helps hold the molding to the pinch weld of the car. A dead-blow hammer is used to help set the wind lace onto the wrapped edge of the pinch weld.

After the glue has reached a dry tack state, the material is wrapped around the pinch weld. The quick-edge wind lace is then applied over the panel material and pinch weld. Start at the top of the pinch weld and place the quick-edge trim over the cover material. Begin to tap the molding onto the pinch weld with a soft mallet to set it into place.

Cars with a post may have a trim panel that covers the metal. Once the quick-edge is secured, install the

A trim panel has been applied to the inside of the B-pillar to cover the rough structural metal on this sedan. A screwdriver is used to tighten the small finish screws that hold the decorative trim in place.

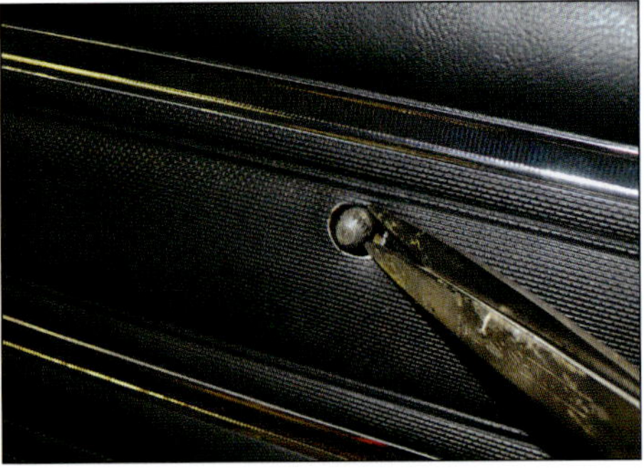

After the rear trim panel has been secured, cut an access hole into the cover material on the panel to reveal the splined window regulator post. A window crank handle will be fit to the post to raise or lower the window.

B-pillar trim panel. Use a regulator to locate the anchor holes and secure the small panel with the correct trim screws.

Appling Hardware

Expose the quarter window regulator post by cutting around the lump in the panel. A sharp pair of scissors or razor blade works well to create the opening. The post hole will be covered by the window crank so do not make the opening larger than the base of the window crank.

Before the window crank is installed, roll the window up to ensure the proper installation position of the crank. Use an escutcheon

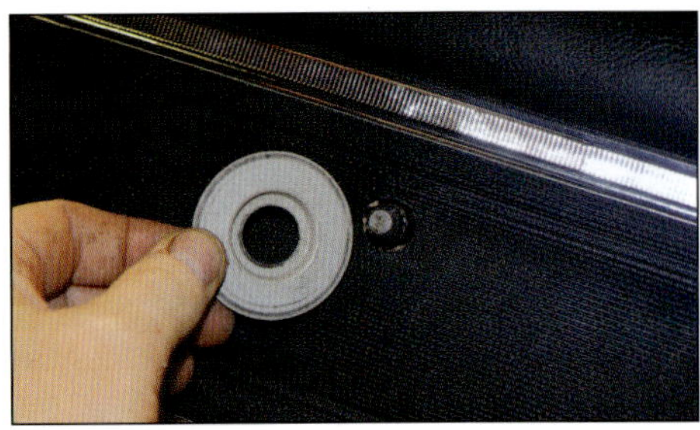

This thin plastic disc is called an escutcheon. It's used to protect the surface of the door panel when the window crank is turned to raise or lower the window. The escutcheon is installed behind the base of the window crank.

to protect the cover material of the door panel from the friction created by turning the window crank. Check to see that the spring clip has been removed from the crank and roll the window up. Remove the crank from the regulator post and reinstall the spring clip in the window crank. With the escutcheon behind the base of the crank, press the base onto the regulator post with the handle at the 2 o'clock position.

Armrests

There are many styles and types of armrests. Some are built into the door panel, and others are applied to the face of the panel. Most likely the

This rear trim panel and all of its components were compiled from new reproduction pieces. By taking the time to make small adjustments and paying attention to the details during the assembly and installation, the installation turned out well.

armrest in your car is an applied type. These are attached to the door with large sheet-metal screws. The screws go through the base of the armrest and anchor into the door.

The style of the armrest will vary from make and model of car. Solid armrests are one-piece units that are molded, and when the pad goes bad, they are difficult to repair and most likely will need to be replaced.

Multi-piece armrests have an upholstered pad that is attached to a molded base. When the pad wears out, it can be repaired with a new foam pad and vinyl, or it can be replaced with a new piece. The base can also become damaged and need to be reconditioned or replaced. Cracked bases are a good candidate for replacement. Chrome-plated or painted bases that have a faded finish can be reconditioned, but it is almost always better to find a suitable after-market part to replace the worn part.

Front Armrest

It is not very difficult to replace the base and pad of the armrest. There are many quality replacements available for the more popular cars, and it only take a few minutes to install the new parts.

To replace a worn pad, turn the base face down on the workbench and remove the retaining screws from the pad. Dry fit the new pad to the base to verify that it is the correct part. There are many side-specific pads and bases, and you can easily

Armrests are a high-impact surface on a car, and they wear out fast. They begin to crack and discolor when body oil gets on the surface of the cover material. Solid molded armrests can easily be replaced with new and two-piece units can be rebuilt.

New door panels were installed to replace the worn and tattered originals on this Camaro. The deluxe interior option has a built-in armrest pad that is not serviceable if it becomes damaged. This style of panel deserves special care to keep it looking nice.

An older armrest can be reconditioned, but it will save you a lot of time and frustration if it can be replaced with a new part. Original-style individual and complete restoration components are readily available from most suppliers.

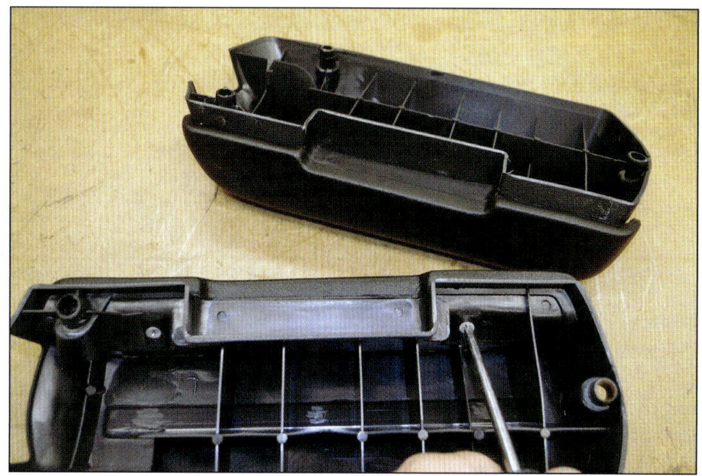

Installation of the replacement pad is the opposite of the removal of the old, worn pad. Use a screwdriver to remove the retaining screws from the backside of the armrest base. Fit the new pad to the base and reinsert the screws.

get them turned around, so always check the fit.

With the new pad in place, reinstall the retaining screws and tighten them to hold the pad securely to the armrest base. Be careful that you do not overtighten the screws. Take the new armrest assembly to the car and install it on the door with the correct mounting screws.

Rear Armrest

A feature that is found on convertibles and coupes are the large lower armrests that fill the space between the end of the rear seat and quarter trim panel. These armrests usually have an ashtray embedded into the top section, and many have a small courtesy light in the lower front.

This trim panel is covered in a matching upholstery and may need to be recovered to bring the entire interior back to that factory-new appearance. Once the panel has been removed from the car, the old cover materials can be stripped off and the base tins can be cleaned and recovered.

Old Materials

Age, weather, and neglect have taken a toll on the interior panels and their components. The old materials will need to be removed so that the underlying base can be reconditioned for use. Disassembly begins with the removal of the upper cylinder panel on convertible models.

To remove the trim pieces, turn the panel face down to get at the fasteners. From the backside of the trim panel, locate the retainers that hold the attached components in place. Lift out the ashtray from the retainer bezel and set it aside. Use a small prying tool to lift the retainer tabs on the ashtray bezel and lift the bezel from the panel.

If your panel has an applied trim molding, carefully lift the tabs and remove the trim. Take care when working on the trim moldings as they are sharp and fragile. The molding will need to be reconditioned before they are reapplied.

Glue was typically used to secure the old cover materials to the metal trim panel. From the backside of the panel, work the edge of the material loose from the edge of the panel and peel it away until the cover material is free from the base metal. Under the cover material will be some dried-out cotton padding that must be scraped off. Wear a dust mask to protect yourself when removing the padding.

The top of the base will have a thicker layer of padding. This may be cotton, jute, or foam. It will all need to be removed and discarded. After the bulk of the padding has been removed, clean the metal with a wire brush to remove any smaller debris and rust scale. Wipe the bare metal down with lacquer thinner to clean off any old oil or glue on the surface of the metal.

If the bottom edge of the panel has been damaged by rust, make repairs to the metal to bring it back to its proper shape. Hammer out any dents and give the panel a coat of paint to prevent any future corrosion.

Removing Old Armrest Material

1 *The old panel hardware is removed by accessing and lifting the fasteners from the backside of the armrest panel to free the part from the panel. A staple puller is used to pry up on the bent-over retainer tabs on the ashtray bezel.*

2 *Decorative stainless-steel moldings were attached with small tabs that went through the panel and were bent over on the backside of the trim panel. The delicate tabs are gently raised with a tack puller to remove the trim molding.*

3 *The original cover material was held in place with contact cement after it was wrapped over the edges of the armrest base. A scraper can be used to get under the old cover to separate it from the inside of the base, and then it can be lifted off.*

4 *To make the rear seat experience a little more comfortable, the factory used multiple layers of cotton to pad the top of the armrest. Over time this material has become compacted and water damaged. Remove the cotton by scraping it off, and throw it away.*

Installing a New Cover

Preparing the metal base starts by making new armrest pads. You can use a variety of materials for this, but I like to use jute carpet pad. The jute pad is soft but will hold up longer than foam or cotton. Roll out the padding on the workbench and lay the top of the base on the jute padding. Use a Sharpie pen to trace the perimeter of the panel. You want the pad to be at least 3/4 inch thick, so cut enough pieces to cover both trim panels.

Cut the padding from the roll and dry fit it to the base. To make the installation of the accessories easier, cut out for the ashtray and power window switch if your car is equipped with these options. After trimming the pad, spray contact cement onto the mating surfaces and align the pad to the base.

Look at the new presewn cover to determine if it has a built-in underliner. If it does not, cover the vertical surface of the base with an underliner felt-type material. Dry fit the new cover to the base and check the fit.

Remove the excess material from the seam by trimming it as close to the stitching as possible without cutting into the thread. This will help the cover material lay smoother along the edge of the base. When you are satisfied with the fit, spray glue along the top edge of the base and onto the inside of the cover without getting glue onto the jute pad. When the glue becomes dry to the touch, apply the cover material and work the seam along the upper edge of the base. You want to remove as many of the wrinkles as possible during this operation.

Spray glue onto the outer edges along the backside of the base and onto the extended cover material. Pull down from the bottom of the cover and wrap it onto the backside of the base. You will need to make relief cuts into the inner points of the base to allow the cover to wrap over the base without wrinkling.

Apply glue to the backside of the armrest surface and extended cover material and allow the glue to get tacky. Pull the material taut as it is wrapped over the outer edge of the panel. Make some relief cuts along the inner arch of the base and finish applying the cover material to the base. Check for wrinkles and make any adjustments necessary by lifting and repositioning the cover material.

Wrapping the Armrest Base

1 *A simple and less-messy solution for the new armrest pad is to use jute carpet padding. To get a good fit, the top of the armrest makes a perfect template to trace for the new padding. The jute pad is also easy to cut and attach.*

2 *Before the new cover can be attached, the underlying padding must be secured to prevent the metal base from damaging the cover material. An even coat of contact cement is used to keep the jute pad in place on the armrest base.*

3 *Prefitting the new armrest cover is vital to getting a good finish. Attach the new cover in small increments to help get it positioned correctly and reduce the number of wrinkles that form by pulling it over the panel.*

4 *Securing the cover material to the metal base began by allowing the contact cement to set up before it was attached. Working the cover material in small sections and making the appropriate relief cuts reduces the chance for wrinkles to form.*

5 *Spray a thin, even coat of contact cement to the inner surfaces of the armrest to allow the new cover to bond nicely to the base. When the glue is dry to the touch, wrap the cover material around the edges of the base.*

6 *Fitting the stainless-steel trim molding onto a curved surface can be a little intimidating. Locating the mounting holes without breaking off the anchoring tabs can be a challenge if you do not prepunch the cover material. Fit the front first as you work toward the rear.*

7 *The ashtray has to have an opening cut into the new cover for it to be installed. To create the opening, make small cuts from the corners of the cutout in the base with a razor blade. This will also allow the trim bezel to be inserted.*

8 *When inserted properly, the ashtray bezel will cover the cuts made in the cover material. Use a small hammer to secure the bezel to the base by flattening the retainer tabs over the edge on the underside of the armrest base.*

Fitting the Trim

From the backside of the panel, use a regulator to locate the through holes for the trim molding. Turn the panel face up and begin installing the trim molding from the front pin to the rear, inserting the pins into the indicator holes you made. Secure the trim on the backside by tapping the pins over with a tack hammer.

You can also use your own judgment on what items you wish to add to the trim panel. Not all the trim accessories need to be installed. I try to inform my customers that the ashtrays are not practical. You most likely do not want anyone smoking in your car or filling the ashtrays with gum wrappers, so the ashtrays can be omitted. This can save you the cost of buying new ones. If you choose to install the ashtrays, they are easy enough to fit.

Feel for the ashtray opening through the cover material. Use a razor blade to make an inward cut in the cover material from each corner. Be careful when cutting the cover; you want the edges of the retainer bezel to cover the cuts of the opening. Insert the retainer bezel into the opening and turn the base over. From the backside, use a tack hammer to bend over the locking tabs of the retainer. Do not bend over the side tabs; these are used to secure the ashtray in the bezel.

Convertible Upper Panel

If you are working on a convertible, install the upper panel covers in the same manner as the lower covers. When the upper panels are covered, they can be reattached to the lower panel with flathead trim screws on the inside of the panel.

If your upper panel had boot retainer snap studs, reinstall them now. Feel for the cage nut in the panel and use the tip of your Phillips screwdriver to make a hole in the cover material to allow the treaded stud of the snap to be reinstalled.

Convertibles have a small trim piece that is fit inside of the upper panel. This piece helps conceal the lower part of the top frame and hydraulic cylinder. The trim piece is typically made of metal and can be wrapped in matching cover material, painted, or sometimes is a colored piece of panel board. Trim screws are used to hold it into the forward corner of the upper trim panel.

The upper cylinder is attached by adding small trim screws to the backside of the trim panel along the lower edge. Use a regulator to locate the anchor holes in the base panel, and install the flat-head screws with a screwdriver.

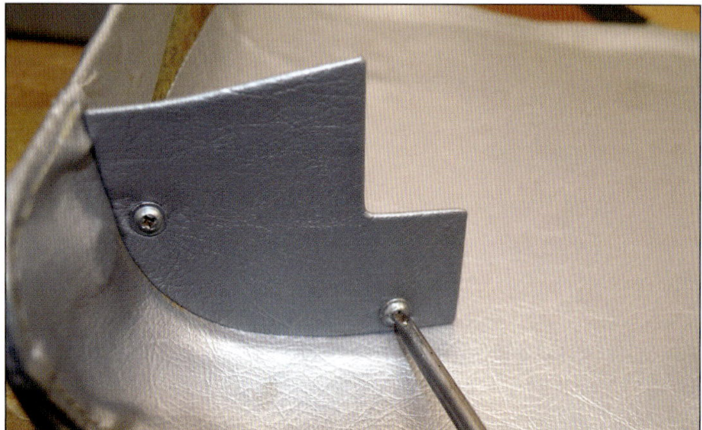

This small trim panel is located inside the front of the upper trim panel. The only practical use for the panel is to hide the mechanical works of the convertible top. Two small trim screws are used to hold the trim panel in place.

Installing the Rear Panels

1 The wind lace was intended to hide the gap between the body and the door opening. This wind lace is attached to the underlying tack strip material with staples. After the wind lace is secured to the car, the new rear quarter trim panel can be installed.

2 Small relief cuts in the selvedge of the foam core wind lace help it contour to the door opening profile. The extra piece of material sewn to the wind lace is pulled down to cover the staples and fill the gap between the armrest base and wind lace.

3 This quarter trim panel uses nail-type fasteners along the front edge to hold it in place. A soft-faced dead-blow hammer is used to set it into the tack strip below. When the quarter trim panel is correctly fit, the front edge will cover the stitches in the wind lace.

4 *Friction and pressure from raising the quarter window can cause the top of the trim panel to become displaced. By adding a small trim screw through the cap on the trim panel, it will stay in place and prevent damage to the trim panel.*

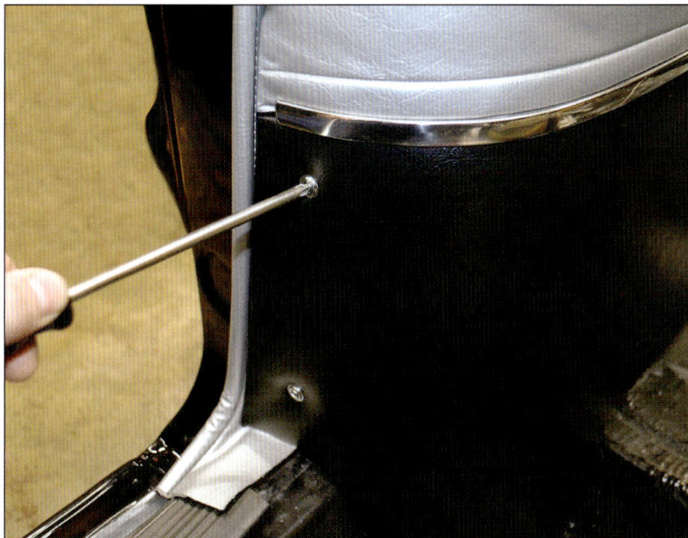

5 *Trim screws used to attach the armrest base have a special washer attached to make the highly visible fastener look more appealing. After the rear armrest is carefully aligned to the inner body of the car, the fasteners are tightened in place.*

6 *The installation of the rear armrest and quarter trim panel is now complete. If you take your time and pay attention to the little details, you can get results like this.*

A sewn foam core wind lace is first applied to the rear edge of the door opening to help conceal the gap between the car body and the door. Place the top edge of the wind lace at the upper edge of the rear pillar and line the seam up along the edge of the door opening. Begin to staple the selvedge of the wind lace to the underlying tack strip. The bottom of the door opening is curved, and to help the wind lace, make some small relief cuts in the selvedge to allow the wind lace to gradually follow the profile of the opening.

The quarter trim panel is fit over the top edge of the window opening and the leading edge is aligned to cover the wind lace seam. A slight downward pressure is put on the panel to settle it in place as the panel fastening nails are driven into the tack strip with a dead-blow hammer. The fasteners are set from the top of the panel downward to help keep the panel from raising up when completely fastened.

To prevent the panel from coming loose when the window is raised, a small trim screw is added through the cap of the panel and driven into the body panel. Another screw is used at the rear of the panel to secure it to the car. The manual window crank can then be installed.

Now, the lower armrest panel can be set in place. However, before the armrest is secured, connect the courtesy light and power window wires. The front edge of the armrest should butt up to the edge of the wind lace, and the top edge must conceal the lower edge of the quarter trim panel.

Use washer head trim screws to secure the armrest. Use a regulator to pierce the front of the armrest, and then locate the screw hole in the anchor tab. Insert the trim screws and tighten them with a Phillips-head screwdriver. If the armrest has an upper convertible trim panel, you will need to add two additional trim screws much the same as the lower panel was attached.

*H*EADLINERS

The correct installation of an auto headliner is considered to be one of the more difficult upholstery installations—second only to a convertible top. Because the roof of a car is curved, the difficulty associated with a headliner lies with getting the wrinkles out of the material.

The cost associated with a professional installation of the headliner is a big deterrent to a lot of car owners.

Since the headliner is often thought of as a project that is not to be taken on by the faint of heart, it may never get replaced. When the courage hits, the hobbyist will take on the task to save the budget. What happens next is probably why you bought this book: you bought a headliner and have no idea on how to install it.

Installation of a headliner may seem a little overwhelming at first, but if you take your time and work the process one step at a time you can get the job done without too much stress.

Glass Removal

You may have heard that the front and rear glass must be removed from the car prior to the installation of the new headliner. Not only is this an expensive and risky procedure, it is not necessary.

Some cars have glass that is set in rubber. As the rubber ages, it will crack and allow water to enter the car. Removing an old seal can cause damage to the hard rubber and may also break or crack the glass. If your rubber is already cracked or the glass has become delaminated, replace the failed components prior to fitting the new headliner.

The process of roping in a new rubber seal can cause damage to a new headliner by creating wrinkles in the headliner material as the new rubber is worked in. If the headliner fabric is wrapped over the window opening, it is prone to water wicking in from under the rubber seal and will cause rust and staining of the fabric.

Years of neglect took their toll on the headliner of this 1969 Chevelle. There is no way to clean or cover up the smell that is left behind by mold and mice on this original headliner. The only option that the owner has to regain the use of his or her car is to remove and replace the headliner.

You can see the deteriorated condition of this rubber seal and know that it is no longer flexible and viable. When the rubber reaches the point of visual cracks, it is best to remove the glass and replace the seal before the new headliner is installed.

Glass that is set with an adhesive sealer can also cause problems with a new headliner. Not all installers are careful, and it is easy to apply too much sealant to the window opening. The excess sealant can get onto the headliner and make a mess that cannot be removed.

I have installed hundreds of headliners in my career and have found that it is unnecessary to remove the glass from any vehicle. It may take extra effort to work the material into the back corners, but it can be done, and the end result will save you a lot of money.

Headliner Components

With the internet so accessible, you can find many sources to obtain the new replacement headliner parts for your car. There are several pieces that are needed for a headliner replacement, and many of the box houses offer reproduction headliners and most of the individual components needed to finish a project.

The main element of an auto headliner is the headliner itself. This is the large sewn piece that covers the inner surface of the roof and is made of a lightweight vinyl or fabric. The headliner is attached to the car along the perimeter of the roof line by glue, staples, or small tacks that hold it securely in place. Support for the headliner material comes from several arched rods or bows. The bow is run through a fabric channel or listing that is sewn along the inside of the seam line. This is what is called a suspended headliner. The bows are supported by friction from coming in contact with the insulation. Later-model cars used plastic clips that hold the bow in position. These clips often break and need to be replaced along with the new headliner.

Many premade headliners come with sail panels, or they include enough extra material to cover the sail panels and sun visors. Sail panels and sun visors are not always included with a headliner kit. Make sure to always ask what is included with the headliner that you are ordering so you do not come up short when you begin the installation.

Insulation

Insulation material is under the headliner. Original insulation materials were made of asphalt-coated paper, paper wadding, or fiberglass batting. The insulation helps with sound deadening and provides comfort to the passengers by acting as a buffer to hot and cold outside temperatures.

There are many supporting pieces that are associated with a headliner that get overlooked and are often not purchased. The first of these is the wind lace that encircles the door opening. This is a fabric- or vinyl-covered length of 1/2-inch foam core used to conceal the gap around

When the headliner was removed, it was discovered that the underlying insulation had dried up and started to delaminate from the inner roof of the car. It needs to be scraped off and replaced with new insulation before the new headliner is installed.

the door opening of many cars. This material often becomes frayed and torn as a passenger enters or exits the car. The wind lace is also the first element to be installed. Late-model headliners use a quick-edge covering that has a spring metal core that is vinyl coated.

Sail Panels

Sail panels, or ear muff boards, are the solid panels found near the rear of the car between the quarter glass and rear window. The sails are made of standard panel board and usually covered in the same material as the headliner. The sail panels help transition the lower curved portion of the headliner to the package tray.

These panels are not always included in a headliner kit. They can be purchased separately to replace damaged or missing panels and are available uncovered or covered in matching material. Many sail panels require small clips to attach them to the car. These clips are usually not included with the sail panels and need to be purchased separately.

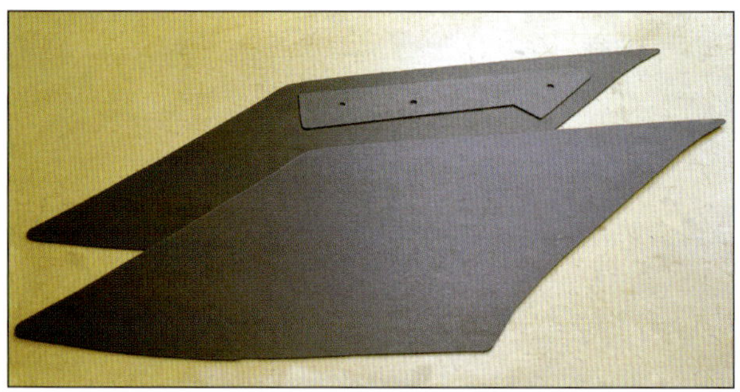

These replacement sail panels have not yet been covered with the matching headliner material included in the premade headliner kit. Glue will be sprayed onto the material and panels before they are installed in the car. Panel clips will be added to the retainer strip to hold the panels in place.

All that remains from this old headliner is a well-worn garment hook. Corrosion has damaged the finish on this metal part, and a new reproduction hook will be used to replace the old one and finish off the newly installed headliner.

Sun Visors

Sun visors are another trim panel that are upholstered in matching headliner material. It takes a special binding attachment to correctly sew the decorative trim to cover the outer edge of the visors, which makes restoring a sun visor very difficult even for the trained professional. Most car owners will choose to reuse the old visors instead of recovering or replacing them, although this is not always a good choice since the new headliner will not match the old sun visors. Fortunately, new sun visors can be purchased at a reasonable cost to replace the old, worn, faded, and dirty sun visors.

Garment Hooks

Another accessory that is often associated with a headliner are the garment hooks. These decorative and utilitarian devices are made of metal or plastic and located above the quarter window to provide a safe place to hang a dress or suit. Hanging helps prevent items from wrinkling instead of being stowed in the trunk of the car. Garment hooks are not a critical part of a headliner. Replacements are available, but they are only an accessory and can be omitted if you choose not to reinstall them.

Other Considerations

It is all the "while you're at it" and "might as well" items that blow a budget. If you actually think about the cost of having a project done for you, replacing individual pieces later will actually cost more than if it was completed altogether.

If you have to pay for a service and it involves labor charges, it makes sense to not pay for the removal of the same component two or three times. While the rear seat is removed, it makes sense from a labor standpoint to have the package tray and rear side panels repaired or replaced. Making these repairs later would involve paying to have the rear seat removed and reinstalled once again. You will save money by having more done at one time.

Replacing the Headliner

After evaluating the condition of the old headliner, create a list of replacement materials and order them. It is always best to have all

This original sun visor shows signs of wear and needs to be replaced with the headliner. While the sun visors are often overlooked, they are a vital piece of safety equipment. It is always best to replace the visors to ensure that they match the new headliner.

Personal art touches and audio modifications have dated this package tray and the choices made by the former owner. The decision to install an original-style package tray with a new headliner makes sense for this restoration.

the essential materials for a project at hand before starting the job. A stalled project will encounter problems with the reassembly due to misplaced pieces and forgetfulness.

What to Order

Before ordering any parts, you will need to know the exact make, model, and number of bows that your car has. The roof line of a hardtop, coupe, and sedan requires a specific headliner. Some models also had mid-year changes, so you must make sure that you order the correct headliner.

You will need the headliner that is made for your car along with headliner insulation, bow clips, and wind lace if the originals are no longer viable. Worn or damaged sun visors should be replaced as they will look out of place with the new headliner material. Dome light lenses may also need to be replaced as they tend to become fragile with age and use.

It is not a problem if your car is missing headliner bows. Replacement bows can be ordered or made. If the supplier does not have a bow set for your car, check with a local car club or parts yard to obtain a viable set.

Verify Parts Order

After the headliner is made, it is folded flat and stuffed into a small box. When your new headliner and replacement parts arrive from the supplier, they must be unpackaged and inspected to ensure they are the correct parts you need. Because the material was folded and not rolled onto a tube, it will develop wrinkles from being in the box. These wrinkles leave unsightly marks in the vinyl material, and depending on

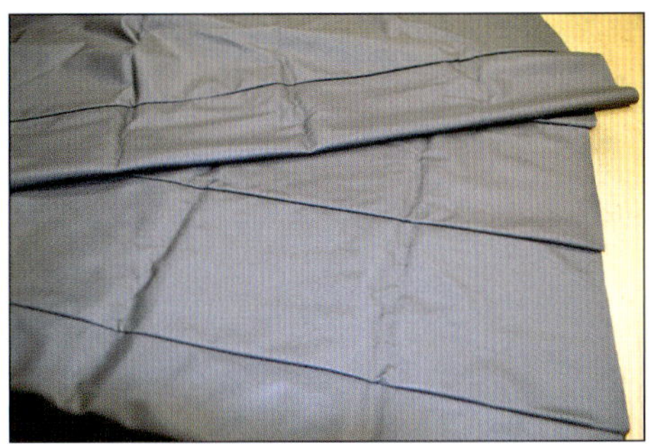

This is what happens to the headliner after the factory folds it and ships it to you. Nasty box wrinkles begin to form in the vinyl, and the longer the headliner stays folded, the worse these creases get. It is important to unfold the material and let it rest flat to help relax the wrinkles.

how long the headliner has been in the box, they may be difficult to remove.

The best way to relieve box wrinkles is to remove the headliner from the box then and lay it out flat to help relax the wrinkles that have formed in the material. Do not place the headliner in the sun or try to warm it up with a hair dryer as this can cause the material to shrink, which will make the headliner unusable. If you are not installing the headliner right away, it should be carefully rolled onto a tube for storage.

Headliner Removal

Removing a headliner is easy. It's the installation that will take some effort. Since the doors of the car will be open for extended periods of time, pull the fuse for the dome light to prevent it from overheating and draining the battery.

Some find that removing the front seat will make it simpler to get around inside the car, but it is not required. The rear seat may need to be removed to gain access to the sail

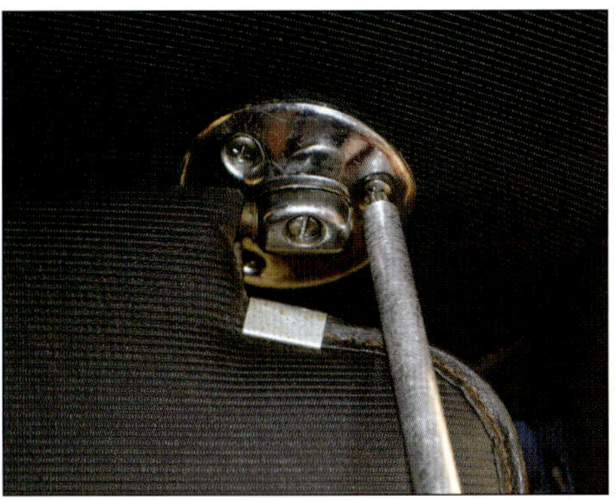

Three small oval-head trim screws hold the sun visor bracket to the inner roof line. Use a #2 Phillips screwdriver to remove the screws. Care is needed when removing the bracket to protect the soft pot metal from becoming damaged.

The boot of the rearview mirror bracket has been removed to gain access to the anchor screws. A Phillips screwdriver is used to remove the anchor screws. The bracket and boot will be cleaned and reinstalled after the new headliner has been hung.

panels and package tray. There may be a number of surprises lurking behind the headliner. Mouse nests, dirt, and falling debris can get into the upholstery and carpet, so it is a good idea to use a drop cloth to protect the interior from falling debris.

I like to start by taking out the sun visors. The brackets are held into the front corners of the inner roof with three screws. Support the sun visor bracket as you remove the screws to prevent the metal from breaking. Bag and tag the screws and set them aside so that they can be used later.

Attached to the center point of the windshield is the rearview mirror bracket. To remove the bracket, take out the screws holding it in place. If the bracket has a boot covering the base, it must be removed to access the mounting screws. Some boots are held in place with a screw, and others are held in place by small tabs. Be careful if you pry the boot off; you don't want to crack the plastic or tear the vinyl. If the boot becomes damaged, you may need to replace it.

Dome Light

Most cars have a dome light located in the center of the inner roof. Others may be above the rear window or in the sail panels. The location of the dome light will differ depending on the car and model you are working on, but what they all have in common is a thin opaque plastic lens. Removal of the lens can be achieved by carefully lifting the edge of the plastic from the casting with an upholsterer's regulator. Sometimes the lens is affixed into the outer cover of the light and the

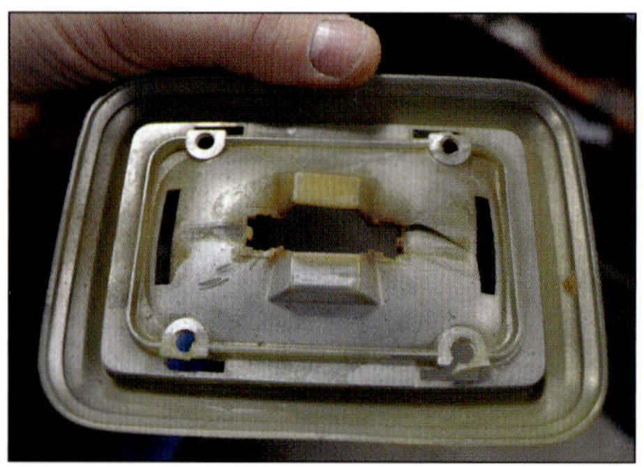

After the bulb terminals were removed from the dome light base, a close inspection revealed a lot of damage and wear. For less than $20, a new reproduction dome light and lens can replace this damaged piece.

cover can be popped off the base of the fixture.

After the lens has been taken off, the screws or metal tabs that hold the dome light base in place are exposed and can be removed. Disconnect the dome light base from the power wires. Some cars may have an inline connector that will separate, and others have bulb terminals that press through the base. Be careful as you separate the wires so that you do not damage the fixture or wiring. Bag and tag all the pieces and set them aside for the reassembly.

Optional Items

Not all cars are equipped with the same equipment. You may encounter some accessory items that will need to be removed from the inner roof line before the headliner can be removed. You may find a small garment hook just above the rear quarter window. Remove the screw securing the garment hook to the roof rail.

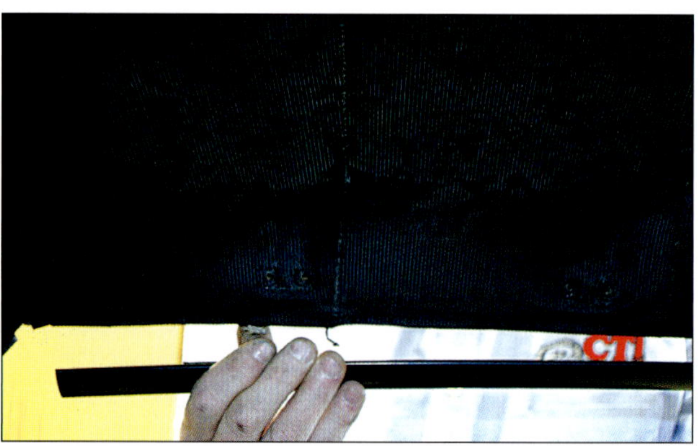

Shoulder restraint belt retainers are held in place with two small trim screws. Remove the screws and retainers and set them aside. To access the attachment bolts for the shoulder belt, use a flat-blade screwdriver to lift the lower edge of the retainer cover upward to expose the fasteners. A 1/2-inch wrench or socket can be used to remove the bolts and shoulder belt from the car.

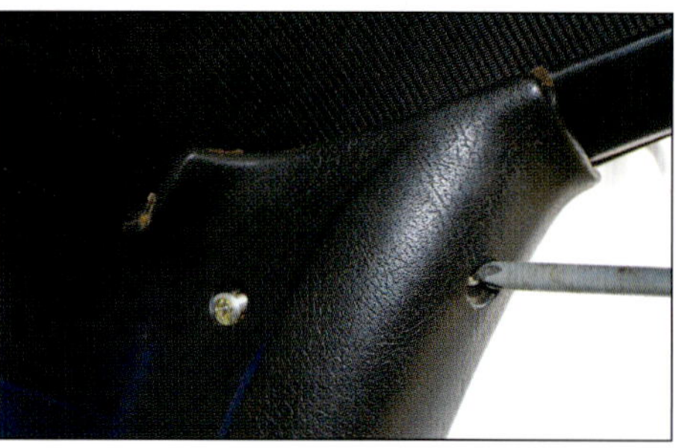

Special moldings are used to conceal the raw metal of the A-pillar and the ends of the headliner trim. Use a Phillips screwdriver to remove the small trim screws that secure the A-pillar molding to the car.

Remove the side trim molding by pulling downward to release the retaining clip from the pinch weld along the roof rail. Some cars secure the trim with screws and others use a color-coordinated, vinyl-coated, quick-edge molding.

This car has shoulder belts that are manually stacked along the roof rail when not in use. The retainer looms are held in with two small trim screws that will be removed and saved for the reinstallation.

An oval-head trim screw is removed from the rear retainer molding. This small piece of trim conceals the end of the rear window trim molding. New trim pieces are available to replace damaged moldings because the plastic is prone to sun damage.

Remove the rear window trim molding by pulling it free from the metal anchor strip. The molding helps hold the headliner material in position as it fills the gap between the glass and finished headliner.

A quick-edge-type header molding is pulled from the leading edge of the headliner. This molding also helps keeps the headliner material in place as it transitions the headliner to the glass windshield. Replacements for damaged or worn molding are available if needed.

finish the headliner. Quick-edge is a great name for the product because it is installed over the pinch weld by pressing it in place to finish the raw edge of the upholstery.

Rear Panels

After the trim moldings are removed, the sail panels can be detached from the rear quarter of the inner roof. Free the forward edge of the sail panel by lifting it from the vertical rise pinch weld along the roof line. The rear edge of the panel can then be removed from the outer vertical edge of the rear window

Moldings

Along the sides of the windshield are the A-pillar trim panels. These can be made of stamped metal or molded vinyl. Trim screws are used to hold them to the inner A-pillar. Remove the screws and lift off the cover.

Before the sail panels can be removed, the outer side garnish moldings need to be removed. Cars built before the mid-1960s had metal moldings to conceal the attached edge of the headliner. These moldings encircled the roof line of the car as well as all the windows. Small oval-head trim screws were used to attach the decorative metal mold-

ings. To save money on later models, manufacturers began to use vinyl-coated quick-edge moldings to

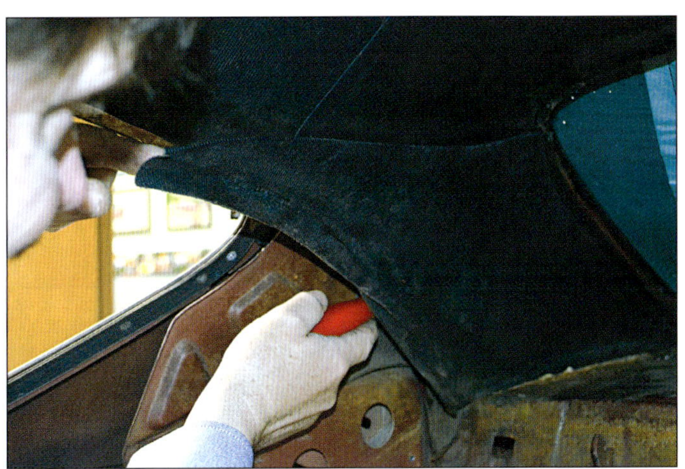

A panel clip lifting tool is placed behind the sail panel to help release the hidden retaining fasteners from the body of the car. After the sail panel is removed, inspect it to verify if the part can be recovered or needs to be replaced.

opening. Small panel clips are sometimes attached to the backside of the sail panel to hold it in place. These clips need to be pried from the inner structure with a panel-lifting tool before the sail panel can be removed from the car.

If the panels are in good condition, they can be rewrapped with new headliner material and used again. Usually the underlying panel board is warped and will need to be replaced with new sail panels.

Package Tray

The deck area below the back window is called a package tray. Some people refer to this space as a hat tray. Back in the day when gentlemen wore hats, this is where they would put them while they were driving. Today's audiophile has cut holes in the panel and fit speakers for the modern in-dash stereo system.

At this stage, you may opt to replace the package tray if it shows signs of sun damage or is warped due to water from a leaky window. In some cases, large holes may have been cut into the package tray to accommodate speakers.

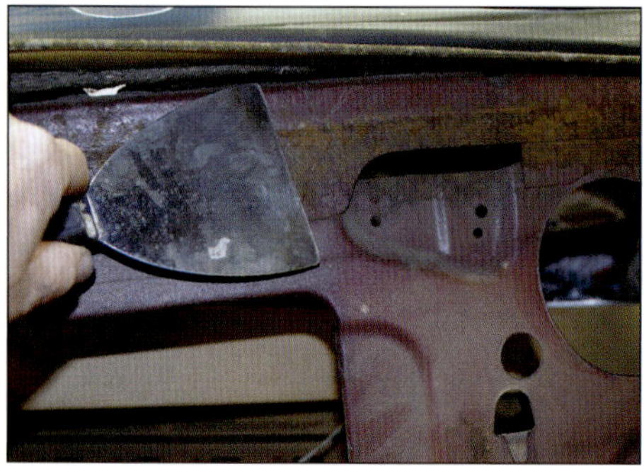

The package tray is held in position by friction and a padded gluing strip across the leading edge of the panel. To break the bond on the gluing strip, get under the vinyl with a broad knife to separate the panel from the rear seat support.

To remove the package tray, first remove the surface-mounted speaker grilles. The studs go through the deck and suspend the speakers from underneath. Small nuts and washers secure the speakers against the underside of the deck. Remove the nuts from the studs and lift the speaker grille from the top side of the package tray.

The leading edge of the package tray was glued to the top of the rear backrest support. This needs to be lifted before the package tray can be removed. A stiff-blade putty knife can be used to get under the glue strip to free it from the car. Now, slide the package tray forward to remove it from the rear deck.

Clean off any residual foam and glue that remains and dry fit the new package tray. Make any alterations necessary and the set the package tray aside so that it can be installed later.

Detaching the Headliner

At this point the only component left to remove is the headliner material. Before you start pulling at the material, you may want to get a vacuum cleaner to cut down on the falling debris. Wear protective eye wear and a respirator to protect your lungs from the fine dust particles that can be toxic if ingested.

If you start vacuuming at the hole made by the visor bracket before tearing the headliner fabric, you will avoid a lot of mess. Once you hear that the debris has cleared, tear a larger hole in the material and continue to evacuate the debris as you continue to work.

The edges of the headliner are either attached with small staples along the outer edges of the material, or they are glued to the inner roof

The front corner of the old headliner has been lifted away from the roof of the car, and it appears that a lot of mouse activity has been going on overhead. It will be necessary to use proper safety equipment during the removal of this headliner.

Mouse nests are commonly found during the removal process of an old headliner. Always protect yourself from the toxic mouse dirt by wearing eye protection and an approved respirator. A vacuum cleaner can also help keep the mess to a minimum during the removal.

line of the car. Sometimes it is faster to cut or tear the material to free the headliner from the car and then go back and remove the remaining fragments.

Bows

A suspended headliner relies on bows to keep the material from sagging. A fabric sleeve, or listing, houses the bow, which is anchored to the side rails of the cab. These bows support or suspend the headliner across the inner roof of the car. The bows are connected to the side rails with small clips and a sheet-metal screw or the ends are slipped into a small hole to secure them to the side rails of the inner roof.

Later-model cars may have a metal or plastic bow clip that holds the bow in a vertical position along the inner roof. Cut away the listing and leave the bow in place as you remove the headliner material.

Many GM cars that were made prior to the late 1950s used these small metal clips to secure the headliner bow to the side roof rail. A small pan-head sheet-metal screw is used to hold the clip to the car. These clips are getting harder to acquire, and if you lose or break any, they can be fabricated from sheet metal.

As you peel back the headliner fabric, you will encounter bows that are concealed inside of the listing sleeves. The bows can remain in position as the listing is torn from the bow as the headliner is peeled back and removed.

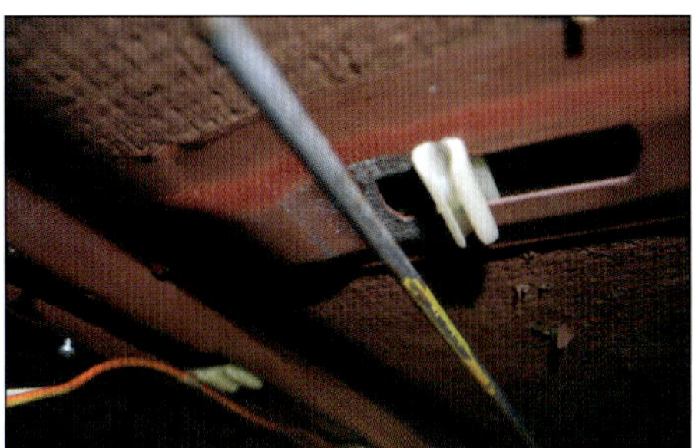

The vertical position of the bow is maintained by these small plastic clips fitted into the ribs of the inner roof. Pull down on the bow to release it from the clip. Damaged and missing clips can be replaced with reproduction pieces that are available from supply houses.

The bow needs to be released from the fastener before it can be removed. This can be done with a panel-lifting tool, or grab the bow on both sides of the plastic fastener and pull straight down. If the bow is retained by a metal clip, rotate the bow to clear the fastener.

Multiple mounting holes are provided to help with the tensioning of the headliner bows. Mark the anchor position of each bow end before it is removed from the side rail to help with the reassembly of the headliner.

To remove the bow from the car, rotate it to release the tension so that the end can be extracted from the side rail. If multiple fastening holes are available in the side rail, mark the bow position before it is removed. This way it can be reattached correctly when it comes time for reassembly.

This is the foundational or anchor bow from a 1956 Chevrolet headliner. With the headliner materials removed, you can see the small metal tabs that secure it to the inner roof cross brace. The cross brace also supports the dome light housing.

These bows have been correctly marked to ensure that they stay in the proper order for the new headliner. The right end of each bow is flagged with masking tape and numbered with a marker for positive identification and installation placement.

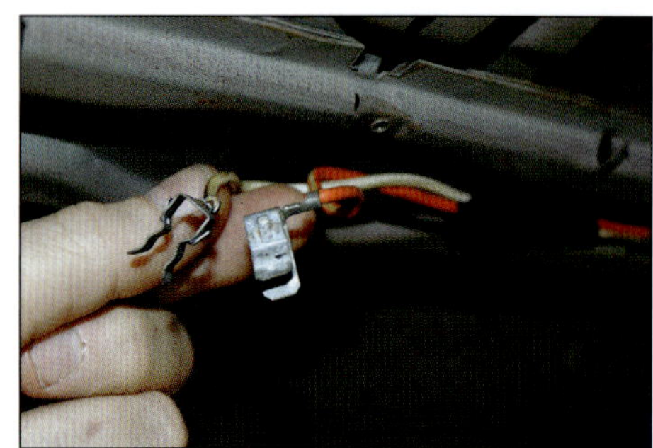

After the headliner has been removed, the wires that supply power to the dome light are now fully exposed, and they can be given a thorough inspection to ensure that they are not brittle and frayed. Damaged wires can short out and cause a fire.

Often the center bow is nothing more than a heavy wire that is anchored to the inner roof bracing with several metal pins. These pins can be bent outward to release the bow. Use care when you pry the pin away so that it is not broken off.

After the headliner is unfastened, take it out of the car. It is important to keep the bows in the proper order. To avoid confusion as to their placement, the bows should be numbered from front to rear. Use a piece of tape to mark the bows before they are removed from the old headliner. I like to place tape on the right end of the bow so that you can reinstall them just as they were.

You may notice that the bows may have different colors on the ends. You would think that the color would give you a clue as to the order they are placed in the car, but they have nothing to do with the bow order or placement. You may get conflicting theories on the paint colors, but what matters is the actual shape and fitment of the bow to the roof line.

Clean and Prep

Now is the time to remove all the old insulation material that remains attached to the inner roof and vacuum up all the fallen debris. The use

Perimeter tack strips were needed when the factory first installed the headliner. Small tacks and staples were used to fasten the edges of the headliner material to the car. The old fasteners will be removed, and the new headliner will be glued into place.

The heavy tack strip that surrounds the door opening is most likely damaged and will no longer hold a tack or staple, so it must be replaced to ensure that the new wind lace and interior trim panels have something to be secured to.

of a putty knife will help speed up the removal of the remaining roof liner pad. Wear a dust mask and eye protection during the clean-up process.

Headliner Bows

The headliner bows should be cleaned with a wire brush to remove any corrosion and scale on the surface of the metal. After they are clean, paint the bows to prevent any further corrosion. The smooth, painted surface will help the bows slide through the headliner listings with less friction.

Perimeter Tack Strips

Headliners on cars with perimeter tack strips should be checked for any remaining staples. Remove the staples but do not be concerned about missing pieces of tack strip. The new headliner will be glued in place along the edges so the tack strip will not need to be replaced, but the surface needs to be clean so that the contact adhesive can take hold.

Dome Light Wiring

Now is a good time to check and secure the dome light wiring. Frayed

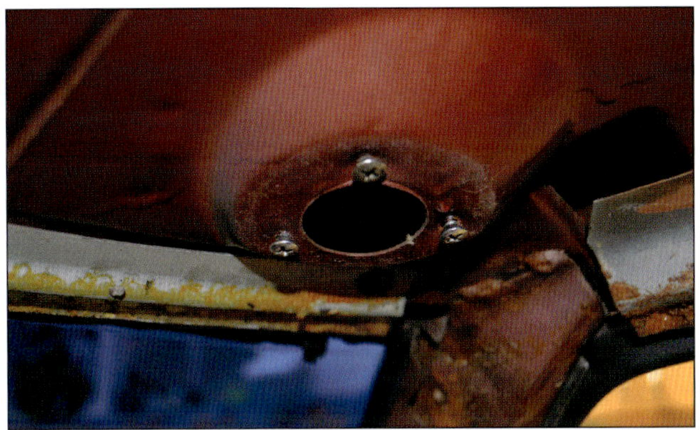

or damaged wires and connectors must be properly repaired before the new headliner can be installed. Failure to make proper electrical repairs can lead to a possible fire.

To make the location and installation of the dome light and sun visors easier, install just the retaining screws of these devices into their appropriate holes before hanging the headliner. When it comes time to finish the project, the screws can be easily located under the headliner material and removed. This will help you locate the correct mounting place of the device without cutting an oversized hole that could ruin the headliner.

Now that all the disassembly and preparation work has been completed, the installation and reassembly of the new headliner can begin.

Insulation

Before the headliner is installed, apply a layer of insulation to the inside of the roof to help repel heat and noise. It is not practical to use the original fiberglass matting that was installed by the factory. The fiberglass material is delicate and sometimes difficult to install without getting the fibers all over yourself. Dacron batting is used as a modern substitute for the fiberglass insulation blanket and insulates much better. Dacron is also lighter in weight and will not sag or deteriorate with age like fiberglass.

Spray contact adhesive to the inner roof and onto one side of the Dacron batting before it is set in place. Once the batting is applied, it can then be trimmed to fit if necessary.

Wind Lace

Cars that require an applied wind lace around the door openings need to have any damaged or missing tack strip material replaced. This is usually a heavy paper material measuring a 1/2 inch wide. Small metal retainer tabs are used to hold the tack strip material in position.

Up to the mid-1960s, a decorative foam-core wind lace was used to conceal the space between the body and door of the car. This style of trim was applied around the inner door opening with tacks or staples.

The wind lace is fit to the body by placing the sew line tightly along the edge of the metal and stapling the flat seam allowance onto the tack strip. Ford used metal retainer clips along the perimeter of the opening to secure the wind lace. The front edge of the wind lace on a GM car is held in place by sliding the small welt keeper into the channel on the metal kick panel retainer. Work the wind lace up and around the door

Most wind lace has a 1/2-inch foam rubber core that is wrapped with a decorative woven material. Presewn wind lace comes in a variety of colors and materials. Raw materials are also available for those that want to make a custom application.

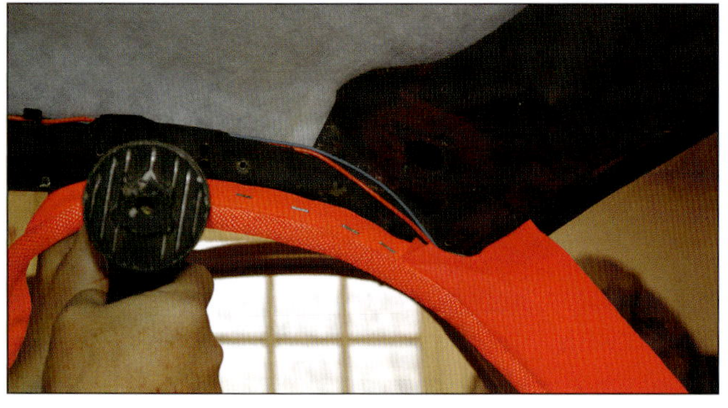

Before the headliner is installed, a new piece of wind lace is applied to conceal the gap on the inside of the door jamb. Staples are used to attach the wind lace to the tack strip that runs around the inner edge of the opening.

opening. Keep the material taut and staple as you go. End the application with about 2 inches of material along the bottom. The excess can be trimmed to length later on when the sill plates are applied.

Valance Retainers

Before the headliner on a GM sedan can be installed, the over-door valance needs to be installed. The valance is a metal piece with triangular fingers that holds the headliner material snugly along the roof line over the top of the door. Small sheet-metal screws are used to hold the metal retainer in position.

The valance needs a good cleaning and reconditioning before installation. Rust can form on the metal due to mice building nests in the headliner. Bead blasting the valance will remove the corrosion before it is primed and painted. The metal fingers must be reset to a 45-degree angle to properly and securely hold the headliner material.

To install the valance, place the retainer into position with the triangle fingers pointing inward with the lower edge of the retainer just touching the wind lace. Attach the retainer to the inner structure of the car with the small pan-head sheet-metal screws.

Prepping the Headliner

There is not a lot of extra material to work with on a premade headliner, so it is important that the material is centered properly to avoid fitment errors. Reference marks need to be added to the backside of the material to indicate the front and center line.

Do not place the old headliner on top of the new material. Premarking the placement for external components is not a good idea since the old headliner has shrunk. Doing this will only get the new headliner dirty. Keep the old headliner and use it as a reference guide to remind you of where to feel for the mounting places for trim items.

Start by laying the headliner face up on the workbench. Fold the headliner in half and use chalk or a pencil to mark along the crease to create the center reference line on the backside of the new headliner material. This will aid in positioning the headliner. To prevent an orientation error, mark the forward panel to indicate the front of the headliner.

This retainer valance is in poor shape because of rodent damage and age. It needs to be sanded to remove the rust and scale before a protective coat of paint can be applied. All this reconditioning work is necessary to make the valance useable.

To ensure the proper alignment of the headliner, draw a reference line down the center of the headliner material. After the headliner is folded in half, mark the crease so that the material will line up in the proper position.

Inserting the Bows

After the reference marks have been made on the headliner, the bows can be added. Each bow will be inserted into its corresponding listing and centered. This will make the process of hanging the new headliner much easier.

Begin by measuring the length of each bow and divide that distance

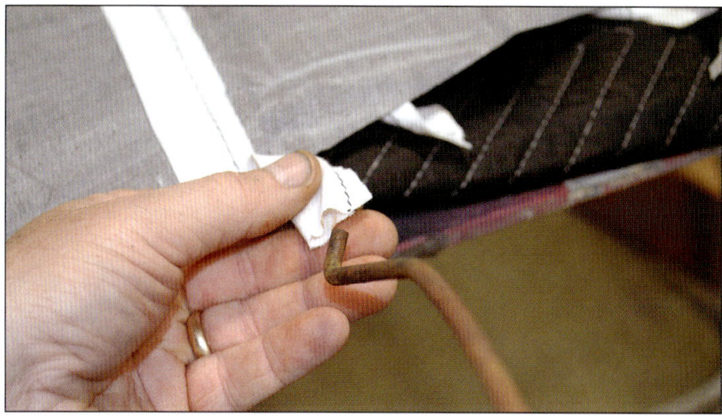

The whole concept of a suspended headliner begins with the bows that hold it in place. After the bows have been cleaned, insert them into the listing on the backside of the headliner. Insertion may be difficult depending on the curvature of the bow.

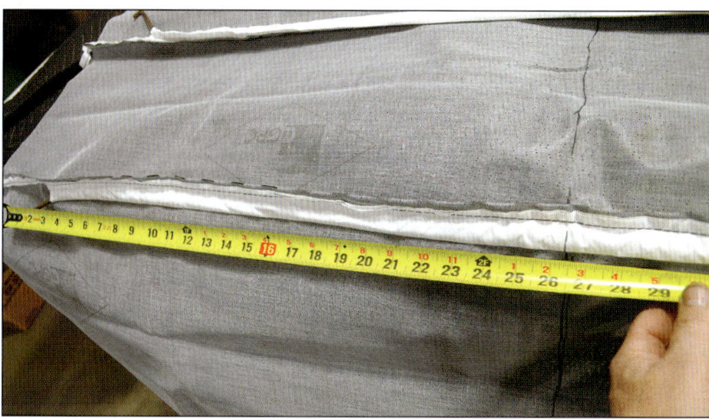

Centering of the headliner bows in the listings helps with positioning during the installation. Measure the length of the bow and then divide it in half to guide you to where the listing material needs to be trimmed to reveal the ends of the bows.

in half. Transfer the bow dimensions to the corresponding listing fabric and carefully trim the material to the bow length. Do not cut any of the stitches that hold the listing fabric to the headliner material.

Start adding the bows from the front of the headliner. Slide each bow into its corresponding listing and check the fit and position of the bows. After all the bows have been inserted into the listings, the headliner is now ready to be hung in the car.

Hanging the Headliner

Before the headliner can be fit to the roofline, determine where to

begin setting the bows. If you have a headliner with a fixed or set center bow, the thin wire-type bow needs to be anchored in place first. If you do not pin the wire bow before setting the others, you will not be able to bend over the anchor pins that hold the bow in place.

Headliners without a fixed center bow can be started from either end. The only thing to remember is that each bow must then be set in progression from the last one set.

Setting the Bows

If you are working with a center fixed bow headliner, begin by aligning the center line of the headliner

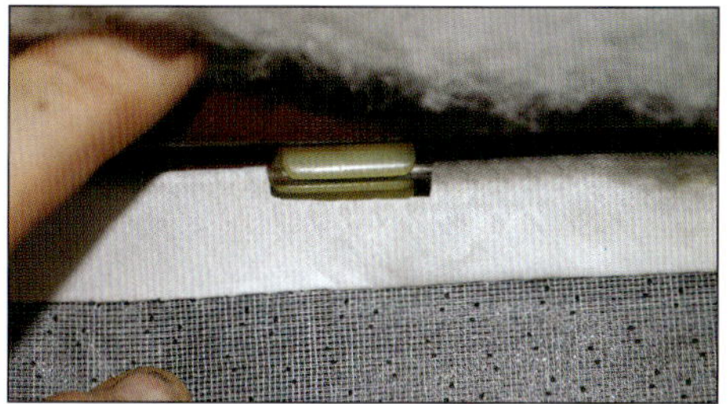

The thinner third bow of this 1969 Chevelle is set into a series of plastic retainer clips affixed across the center structural rib in the inner roof of the car. Before the bow is snapped into the retainer clip, a small amount of the listing fabric is removed to allow the headliner to move without binding.

with the center point of the roofline. Allow the headliner to drape from the listing and then pierce the fabric with the metal pins found along the inner bracing of the roof, but do not bend the pins over at this time.

After you have the fixed bow in position, remove the bow and cut away a very small amount of the listing fabric to expose the bow. Be careful when cutting the fabric so that you do not cut into the stitches of the listing. By exposing the bow, the bow can be anchored securely without causing the listing material

Before the headliner can be installed in the car, carefully cut back the fabric listing sleeve to reveal about 2 inches of the suspension bow. Removing the excess material along the seam allows the headliner to lay smoothly along the roof rail.

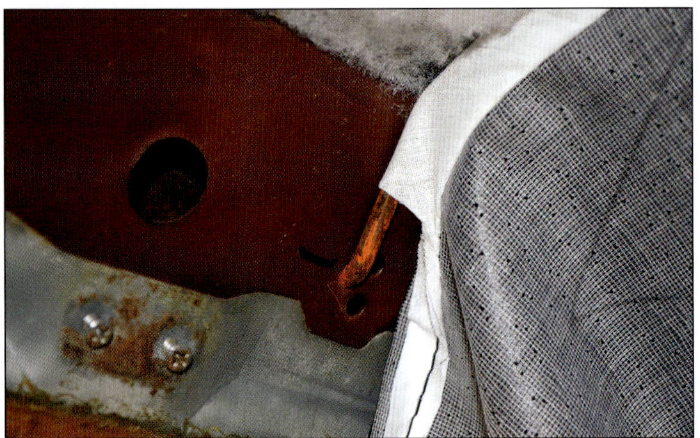

Hanging the headliner requires the exposed ends of the bows to be inserted into the anchor holes of the side rail. With the ends of the bows secured, they can be set in the vertical position with slight tension to expand the panel of the headliner material.

Most headliners rely on the insulation material to provide enough tension to keep them in place. Plastic bow clips are also used on some models to lock the bow in its vertical position. Removal of the listing fabric allows the headliner material to move without binding in the clip.

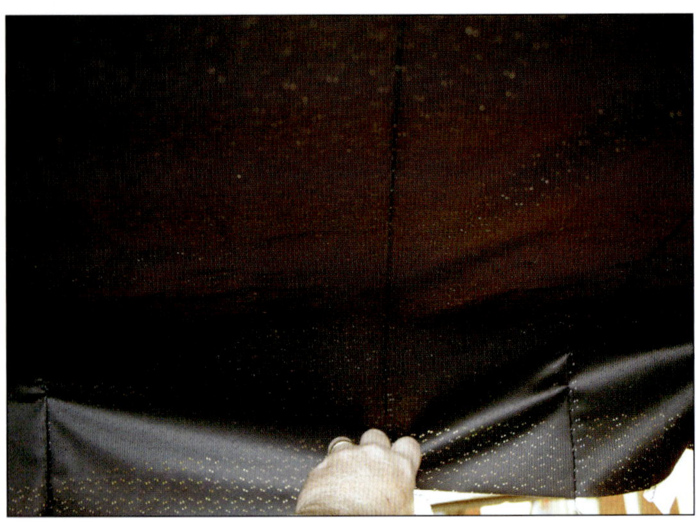

Wrinkles are worked out of the headliner material by pulling down at the seams. This pulling action helps the material lay smooth and yield a better fit when the headliner is attached to the perimeter roof rail of the car.

After the headliner has been hung, adjustments can be made to help position the material for optimum fitment. At this stage, a majority of the wrinkles that were caused by sewing can be worked out of the material before it is attached along the perimeter of the inner roof line.

to stress or pucker the headliner as it is attached. Work the headliner material from the center point outward as you hammer the pins over the listing wire. This same procedure works with later-model headliners that have plastic retainer clips along the roof line.

Work forward and insert the end of the next bow into the anchor hole along the outer roof rail. Insert the other end of the bow into its corresponding anchor point and rotate the bow forward until it is in a vertical position. The insulation should provide enough tension on the bow to keep it in place. Smooth the headliner material from the center line outward to relieve tension in the fabric. This will relieve wrinkles and make finishing easier.

Continue with the bow installation all the way to the front of the car. Keep a slight amount of forward tension on the headliner as you go. Always work the material from the center line outward to minimize wrinkles.

If the headliner has bow clips to hold it in place along the roof line, the listing fabric should be trimmed away from the clips to prevent any unnecessary binding or wrinkles in the headliner.

The rear bows are installed in the same manner as the forward bows. After all the bows have been set in place, check the overall fit of the headliner and make any adjustments to ensure that an even amount of material is around the perimeter for attaching.

Attaching the Headliner

The factory originally attached the headliner to the car with small staples. Workers stood on each side of the car and fit the headliner. They pulled and tacked the material in unison to install a headliner within minutes. It will take a little longer to do the job yourself, and securing the fabric to the car is best done by applying contact adhesive to the metal body and the backside of the headliner.

The headliner is best installed by anchoring the front and then the rear. Once the front-to-rear stretch has been established, the sides can be attached and worked to relieve wrinkles in the headliner material.

Gluing

I like to use a small 1-inch chip brush to spread the contact cement onto the headliner material and roof line of the car. The glue can be sprayed, but the spraying process is messy. Spreading glue with a brush gives you more control over how much glue is applied and where it ends up. Working from a small glue pot is less cumbersome than trying to wrestle with air hoses.

Apply about a 3-inch-wide swath of glue along the center point of the front roof line and a matching amount of glue on the backside of the headliner material. Wait a minute for the glue to tack to ensure that a good bond will be made before pressing the material into position.

Align the headliner with the header panel and pull gently on the material to remove the slack in the headliner. Press or tuck the material into the glue. Working outward from the center point, apply more glue to the roofline and material and continue to attach as before. Work one side at a time along the front until you have the full length attached. Do not trim off any of the extra material at this stage of the installation. Trimming can be done after the final adjustments have been made.

With the forward section in place, move to the rear and apply glue from the center point outward. Pull gently on the headliner and check that the bows are in their correct vertical position as you press the headliner into the glue. Work the rear the same as you did for the front. If the rear edge of the headliner tucks under the rubber window molding, use a tuck tool and pry the molding down just enough to apply the glue in the same way.

When the front and rear have been set, look at the headliner and make any adjustments necessary to minimize wrinkles in the material. Adjustments are made by carefully lifting the glued edge from the roof line and repositioning the material until it looks good. You may need to reapply glue to reactivate the old glue when repositioning the material.

Make Small Corrections

Do not overstretch the headliner material. Overstretching will cause excessive wrinkles that may not be able to be worked out. Work the material with small corrections until you get the proper result. ■

Gluing the Headliner in Place

1 Before the headliner can be attached to the car, contact cement is applied to the perimeter attachment strips with a small chip brush. An ample amount of the adhesive can be applied to the attaching surfaces with a lot less mess than spraying the glue.

2 *Preparing the headliner for attachment is done by spreading contact cement on the backside of the headliner with a small chip brush. Contact cement works best when both mating surfaces are coated with the glue. After the glue has flashed, the surfaces can be pressed together.*

3 *Forward tension is put on the headliner material before it is pressed into the glue on the center portion of the front rail of the car. Additional glue is applied to the back of the headliner and attachment rail as the material is worked from the center point outward.*

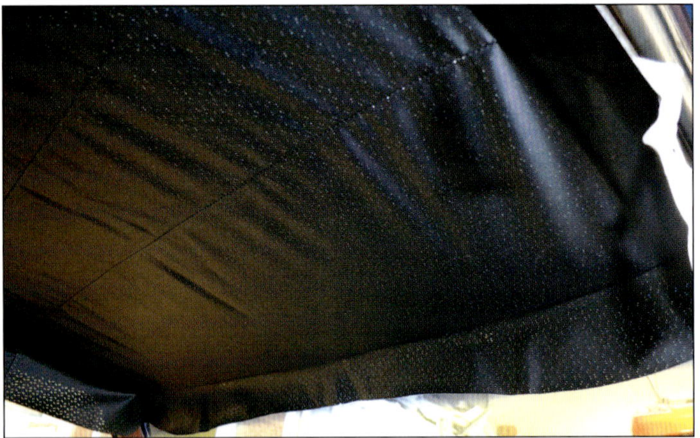

4 *The initial stretch of the headliner may need to be adjusted and re-tensioned to minimize the number of wrinkles before proceeding to the rear. It is not uncommon for adjustments to be made throughout the installation process, so wait to trim until you have a wrinkle-free fit.*

5 *The rear of the headliner has been glued and set in place across the rear window. Even tension has been applied to the headliner material to ensure that the cross bows are in proper vertical alignment. At this stage, all the adjustments have been made to the material to prevent any defects.*

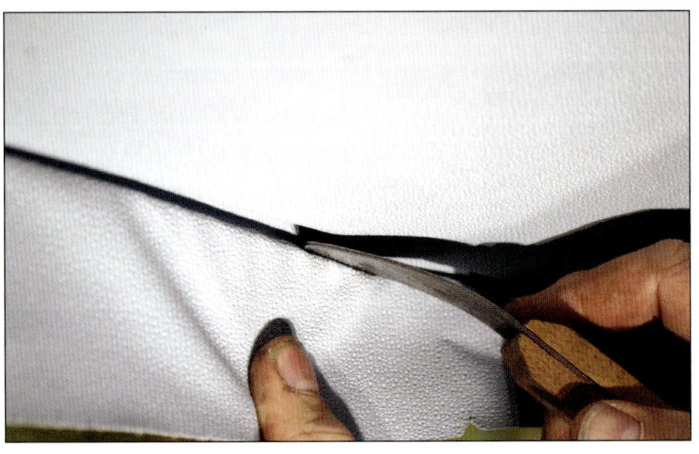

6 *Glue has already been applied to the metal roof line on the underside of the rubber window gasket and the backside of the headliner. A tuck tool is used to push the headliner material into place under the rubber gasket. After the glue has set, the material can be trimmed.*

No Glass Removal

Many trimmers will tell you that the glass needs to be removed on Ford and Chrysler models before the headliner can be installed. I have never felt the need for this added work or expense. It may make the task easier, but the risk of breaking the glass is too great, and customers are not happy when you ask them for more money to remove and reinstall their glass.

If you use a tuck tool to pry the rubber glass seal from the inner body, spread glue under the seal and tuck the headliner material into the opening. This method takes a little more time and effort, but it works, and you can achieve the same results without any of the risks.

The key here is to make sure the metal surface is clean, dry, and rust-free. Otherwise, you will not get a good bond from the contact adhesive. Once all of the adjustments have been made, the headliner material is in place, and the glue has set, the excess material is trimmed to 1/16 inch from the edge of the rubber seal. The remainder of the headliner material can now be carefully tucked under the seal to conceal the cut edge. Excessive amounts of material will cause a bulge in the rubber and become wavy, spoking the finished look of the installation.

Working the Sides

Attaching the outer edges of the headliner is similar to what you just did. Be careful that you do not pull too hard and distort the material. Only pull on the seams to tension the material. Pulling between the seams will cause the headliner to pucker. The goal here is to get the material to lay smoothly between the seams.

In preparation for the side of the headliner to be attached, glue has been spread on the roof rail and headliner material. The material will be anchored from the center seam forward to prevent excessive amounts of wrinkling from occurring as the material stretches.

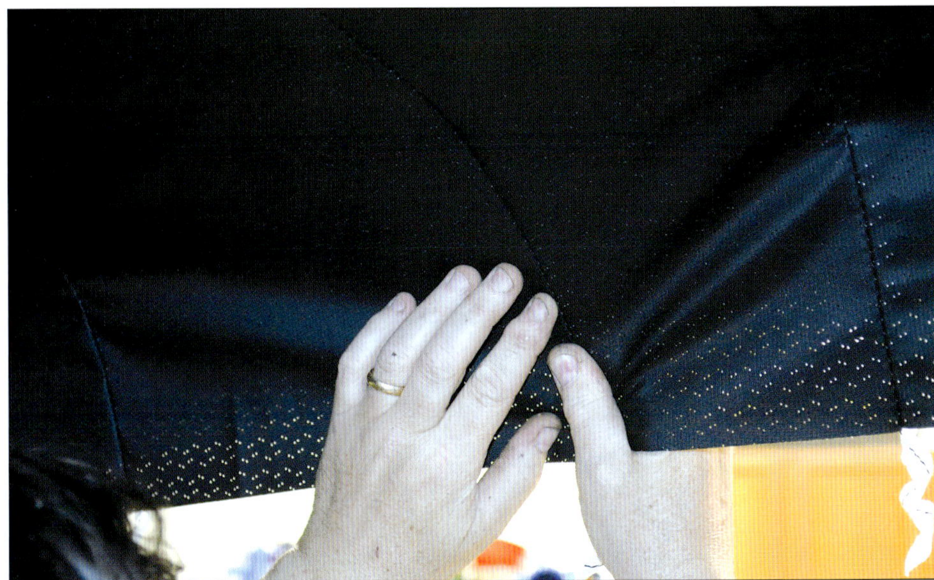

Smoothing the seam on the headliner before it is anchored will keep the material wrinkle-free. Take the time to remove wrinkles as you go. It will make the headliner not only look better but also it will help minimize adjustments later on. Adding heat now can cause problems with the final fit.

If you work each side from the center anchor bow forward and then from the center to the rear, you will achieve a better fit and eliminate most of the wrinkles without using any steam or heat. Apply glue to the roof line and material as before and work the seam from the center line of the roof to the outer roof rail. This will help remove the wrinkles as you lightly pull down on the seam. If you also pull slightly in the direction you are working, the tension will eliminate wrinkles as you press the material into the glue to anchor the headliner. Continue to add more glue along the roof rail and fabric as you move forward. Use your hand to smooth the material as it is kept taut. Anchor the second seam and continue forward to the windshield. Do not pull on the material between the seams. The

With a little extra effort, the front half of the headliner has been installed, and it turned out virtually wrinkle-free. Any remaining box wrinkles will be easy to remove with some heat or steam after the rear section and trim items are installed.

material should lay naturally between the seams without any wrinkles.

Tucking the Material

Headliners in cars equipped with metal retainers over the door can also be glued and tucked to secure the material. It is preferred to work the material along the retainer without glue to allow for adjustments. Begin by tucking the seam to anchor the material. The material between the seams can then be tucked to finish the area. Tucking is done with a thin flexible tuck tool to push the material up and behind the retainer.

To properly use the tuck tool, rest the blade on top of the material about a 1/4 inch below the lower edge of the retainer. Hold onto the extra material that is under the blade of the tool and gently push the headliner fabric behind the retainer strip. The triangular fingers will grab and keep the material from coming out of the retainer. When using the tuck tool, there must be a little slack in the material before it can be stuffed under the retainer. Without the slack, the material can tear because it will become too tight. You will eventually get a feel for this.

Adjusting

If you need to remove the material from under the retainer, do not pull on the fabric as it will tear. To safely extract the fabric, insert the tuck tool under the retainer and tilt the blade forward to dislodge the material from the metal fingers and apply a slight downward pressure on the excess material. As the headliner is pulled, it should draw out the material and tool to release the fabric from the retainer.

As you reach the windshield, you may notice that an adjustment may need to be made to relieve the extra material that has accumulated. To fix this, peel back the front of the headliner and work out the excess material from the center to the outside corner.

After you are satisfied with the

The seams of this older bow-type headliner are attached to the side rail by using a thin-blade tuck tool to force the material under the valance retainer. Small metal fingers physically hold the material in place to keep the headliner wrinkle-free.

A pair of scissors is used to trim the bulk of the excess headliner material to within a 1/2 inch from the edge of the metal retainer. The remaining amount of fabric is tucked up behind the retainer to conceal the cut edge from view.

front quarter, repeat the procedure with the other side and move toward the rear quarters. Always check for wrinkles and remember to have enough tension on the material without overtightening it. The overall goal is to get the headliner material as wrinkle-free as possible.

Finishing

If you have wrinkles that still remain, loosen the headliner and pull the material until the wrinkles come out. If the headliner is made of vinyl, apply a little heat from a heat gun to help relax the material as you reposition it. Do not overheat the vinyl as it will scorch and get shiny. Cloth headliner material can be steamed to help it relax.

If the material is lifted from the roofline, reapply contact cement to the material before it is reattached. When the headliner is virtually wrinkle-free and you are satisfied with its appearance, the excess material can then be trimmed.

Trimming

You must use your own judgement as to how much of the material can be trimmed. Cars with metal garnish moldings can be trimmed within 1/4 inch from the attachment point. This small amount of excess material will be covered by the molding and allow enough material to tweak the headliner if necessary. Older-model cars that have a decorative wire-on welt trim along the finished edge will need to be trimmed closer to allow the applied cover material to hide the raw edge of the headliner.

If your car has the metal valances over the door, trim the excess to

Speakers have been flush-mounted into the rear deck prior to the installation of the insulation pad. Speaker holes were cut into the pad before it was glued into place. A new package tray will cover the pad to give the car that factory look.

1/2 inch below the finished edge. Use your tuck tool to gently push the remaining material under the retainer. If you have too much material under the retainer, you may experience a bulge in the molding and need to readjust the material to eliminate the excess material.

Cars that have a pinch weld molding should be trimmed within 1/8 inch on the outside of the pinch weld. Make sure that you have glued the material securely to the roof line before trimming. The push-on pinch weld molding or quick-edge trim will cover the small amount of material that remains. If extra material still is visible, carefully remove the molding and re-trim the material until it is no longer visible.

Package Tray

With the main headliner in place, all the finish details can be addressed. Before the sail panels are installed, the package tray can be installed and finished. Some cars use a thin insulation pad under the package tray to help reduce road noise. If you are going to add rear speakers, precut the speaker holes into the insulation pad prior to fitting the speakers.

Speakers can be either flush or surface mounted. The option is yours, but consider the look of modern speaker grilles made of plastic that can warp and pop off, or the clean look of the flush-mount speaker.

Set the package tray panel on top of the insulation pad and push the panel into position along the rear of the shelf. The leading edge of the panel should lay flush with the front edge of the rear seat support. Apply contact cement along the upper edge of the seat support and to the backside of the vinyl retainer flap that is sewn to the package tray. Do not apply glue to the foam filler on the panel. When the glue has flashed, press the flap evenly along the seat back support to secure the package tray into position.

Installing the Package Tray

1 After the package tray has been seated into position along the rear window, glue is applied to the backside of the flap and onto the surface of the rear seat support. Glue is not applied to the foam pad because it will cause dimples in the foam.

2 The package tray is held in place by gluing the vinyl strip across the front of the panel to the rear seat support. The vinyl trim strip is pulled over the foam to give the package tray a finished appearance and keep it from moving out of place.

3 Our finished package tray has the deluxe mesh finish with blind speaker grilles just like the factory would have installed. If you have surface-mounted speakers, holes need to be cut into the package tray before the speakers are installed.

Sail Panel Installation

Fitting the sail panel is pretty straightforward. Set the panel in position and line up the panel clips with the corresponding mounting holes located in the body. Use a soft mallet to tap the panel clips into the body. Apply glue to the flap of material along the front and rear of the sail panel and along the corresponding metal edge of the car. Allow the glue to tack and then wrap the flap of material over the edge of the body to secure the sail panel in place.

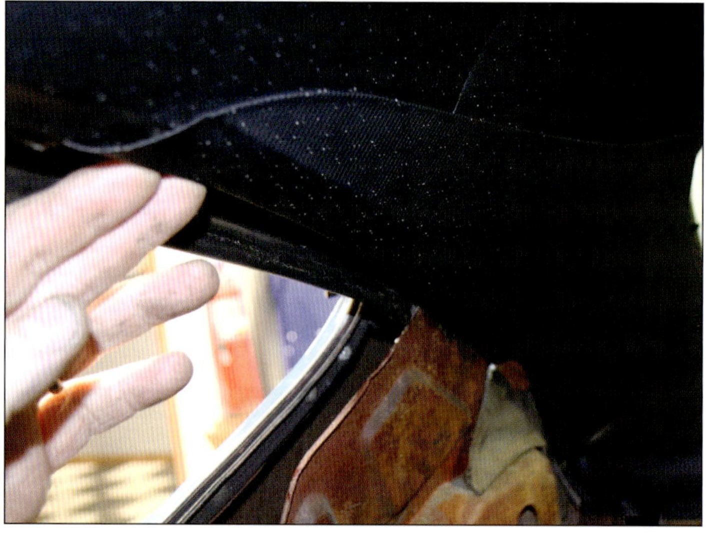

The purpose of the sail panel is to make a smooth transition from roof line to the package tray. Wrapping the glued front and rear edges of sail panel around the trim rails keeps it from shifting position before the trim is installed.

A decorative pinch weld molding is tapped into place with a small rubber mallet. The metal clips inside the rubber molding work well to hold the headliner material tight to the metal ridge and the trim securely along the roof line.

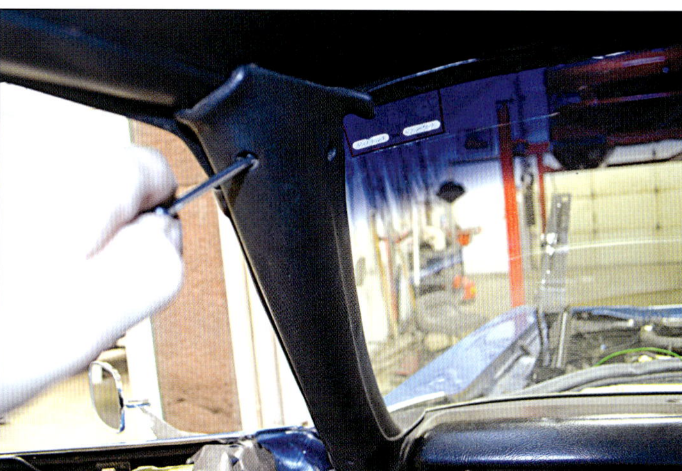

Small oval-head trim screws are tightened to retain the decorative moldings that are used to cover the front A-pillar. The moldings also conceal the ends of the front and side trim moldings to give the headliner a smooth appearance.

Moldings and Accessories

To finish and conceal the stapled or glued raw edges of the headliner, many manufacturers used elaborately crafted metal moldings around the perimeter of the cab and window openings. The moldings were either painted to match the theme of the upholstery or chrome plated to set off the luxury interior.

These moldings were held in place with oval-head trim screws. After the molding is fitted into position, an upholsterer's regulator can be used to help locate the underlying screw hole. Once the piece is lined up, the proper length trim screw is inserted and tightened down without distorting the molding.

Cars produced after the mid-1960s began to use a simpler and less costly pinch weld molding to finish the edges of the headliner. These moldings had a spring steel core imbedded in a textured vinyl jacket that allowed the moldings to grip the perimeter of the headliner to hold it in place. The pinch weld molding is installed by placing it over the extended body seam and tapping it into position. The vinyl covering of the moldings are color matched to the interior which helps them blend in with the upholstery.

After the trim moldings have been installed, the A-pillar moldings can be fit and secured with the correct trim screws. The rear window corner moldings are installed next. These pieces are used to conceal the raw ends of the window and side trim moldings.

Garment Hook

Replacing the garment hooks is an option that is entirely up to you. If the old hardware is rusty and hard to locate, you may opt to omit them from your new headliner installation. Reproduction garment hooks are available for most manufacturers and are generally very good for a reproduction part.

To install the hook, feel through the headliner for the raised metal mounting base and pierce the headliner material with a regulator to mark the location of the mounting screw hole. Align the hook into position and insert the trim screw to secure it into the side of the car.

Late-model garment hooks are made of plastic and have a vinyl cover that is most likely color-matched to the headliner. These garment hooks have a mounting hole that accommodates a screw and locating pin used to index the position of the hook. After locating the mounting position, the base plastic is attached

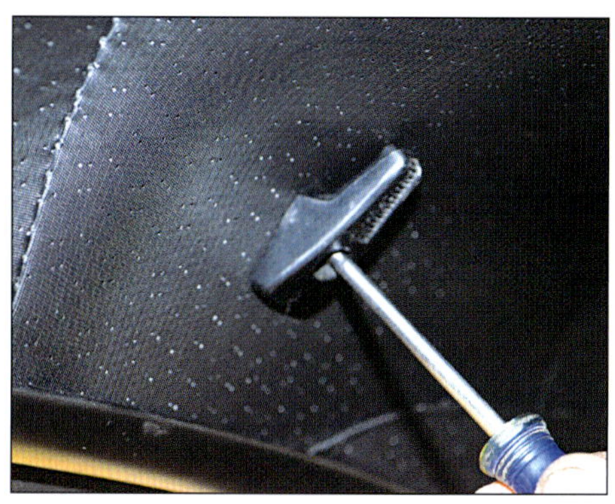

This small device is utilitarian by design and is used to prevent wrinkles in an article of clothing as it is suspended from a hanger. A Phillips screwdriver is used to tighten the mounting screw as the garment hook is set in place just above the roof line.

with a small pan-head screw and the vinyl cover is slid over the base to complete the installation.

Dome Light

Fitting the dome light requires feeling through the headliner material to locate the mounting holes. If you replaced the dome light screws prior to installing the new headliner, they should be easy to locate.

Press the headliner material tight to the head of the screw to make a very small slit in the material and extract the screw with a screwdriver. When all the screws have been removed, the wires for the dome light can be exposed.

Cut a small opening in the headliner material at the center point of the dome light. The base of the dome light must conceal the hole you make, so start with the small-est opening possible. Pull the wires through the opening and connect them to the dome light base.

Position the dome light and locate the screw holes with a regulator. Insert the screws and tighten them to secure the dome light in place. Install the dome light bulb and then the dome light lens. Re-install the fuse for the dome light and check that the light functions properly with the door and dash switches.

Dome Light Installation

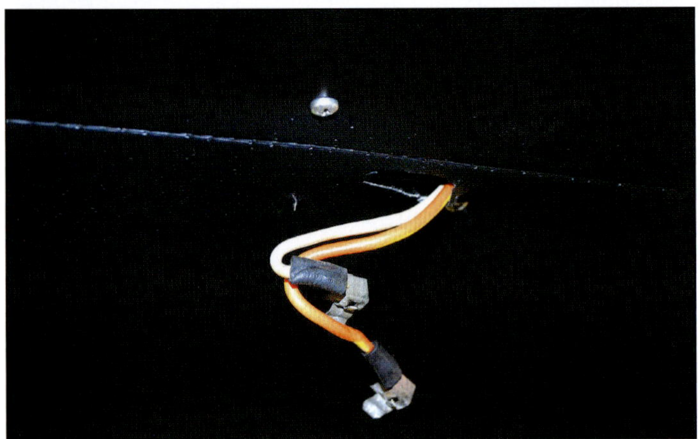

1 *A small opening in the headliner is made to extract the dome light wires. Once exposed, the wires can be inserted into the base of the dome light before it is attached to the roof of the car to conceal the hole and wires.*

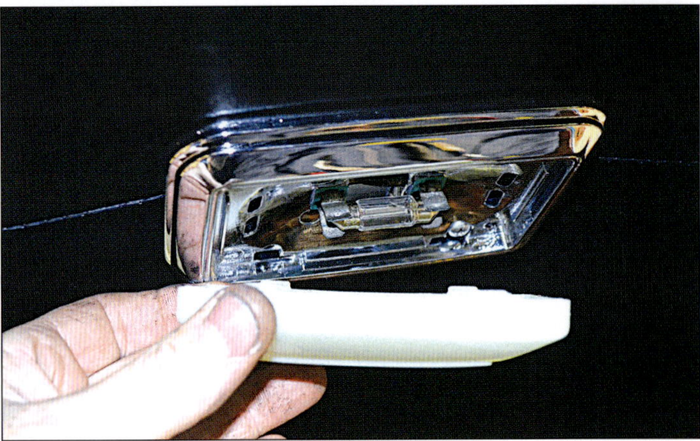

2 *After the dome light has been properly positioned, the retaining screws are replaced and tightened. A new light bulb is inserted into the fixture before the dome light lens is snapped into place to complete the installation.*

Restraint Belts

If your car is equipped with retainer loops and shoulder belt restraints, they can now be reinstalled to the inner side rail of the roof line. Feel for the retainer screws and extract them as you did for the dome light. Line up the restraint retainers and securely fasten them to the car.

Feel through the headliner material to locate the anchor bolt holes for the shoulder belt. Use the tip of a pair of scissors or a Phillips-head screwdriver to open the material

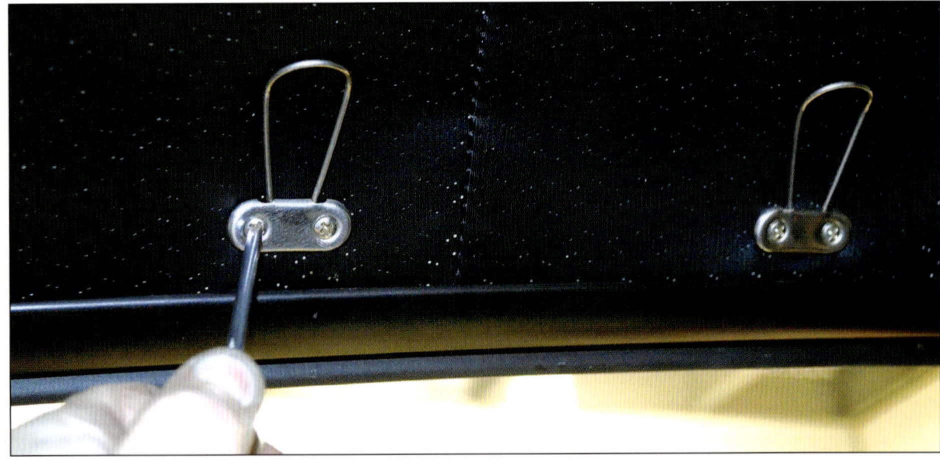

Screws are tightened with a screwdriver to hold the retainer loops of the shoulder restraint belts to the roof rail. The retainers are aligned with the small holes made in the headliner fabric when the screws were removed.

INSTALLING AUTOMOTIVE INTERIOR KITS

Two small bolts are used to secure the shoulder restraint to the roof rail. The bolts go through the base plate of the belt and are tightened to keep the restraint in place. A decorative cover is snapped over the baseplate to conceal the bolts.

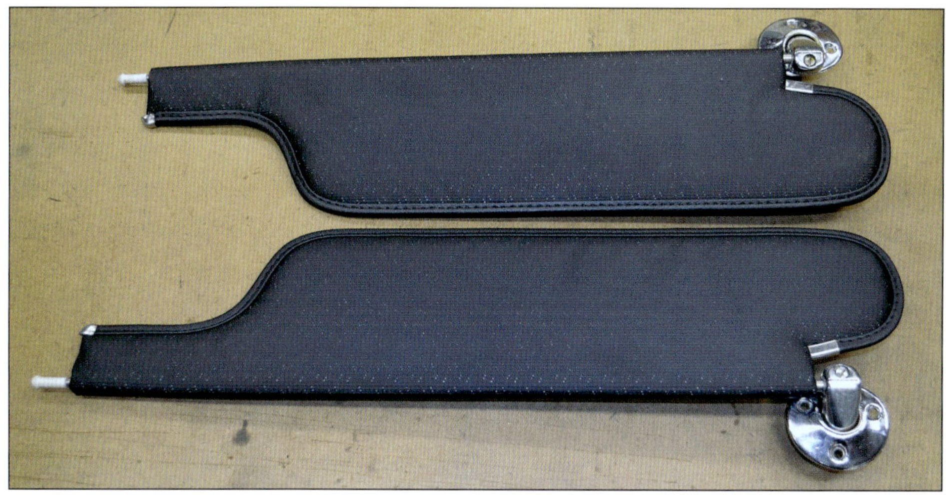

Nothing spoils the look of a new headliner installation more than damaged and dirty sun visors. New sun visors will match perfectly with the newly installed headliner and are the finishing touch needed to tie the headliner project together.

for the anchor bolts. Place the anchor plate in position with the open side of the cover downward and tighten the mounting bolts. Snap the cover closed and secure the restraint to the roof rail.

Sun Visors

The last pieces to be installed are the sun visors. Do not skimp on the installation now. Your old sun visors are worn, dirty, and will not match the look of your newly installed headliner. New sun visors should have been ordered along with the headliner kit to make the project complete.

Your old visor brackets are most likely very dirty, but with a little cleaning they can look as good as new. If the old support brackets are broken or badly pitted, they should be replaced with new reproduction pieces.

Removing the Bracket

Removing the old sun visors is not a difficult process, but it does take a little fineness to get them off without damaging the delicate pot metal of the old brackets. Your first instinct is to take a screwdriver to the bracket and twist the clamping part of the bracket open to release the sun visor. The bracket will break if you do that. The pot metal is brittle and cannot withstand the pressure of being forced open.

The proper way to separate the sun visor from the bracket is to remove the adjustment screw in the bracket. Next, take a thin, flat-blade screwdriver and place it along side of the sun visor with the tip of the screwdriver blade aligned with the split in the bracket. Use a small hammer to lightly tap the screwdriver into the slot which will drive the bracket off

of the sun visor shaft. As you gently tap the screwdriver, it will spread the bracket open just enough to release it from the visor. Carefully remove the screwdriver blade from the bracket without twisting the screwdriver.

If the original bracket is not pitted, it can be reconditioned and used. Clean the bracket with 0000 steel wool and use a good chrome polish to protect the metal surface before re-fitting it to the sun visor.

Many cars have a thin plastic bushing or sleeve that fits over the visor shaft to help tension the visor so that it can rotate in the bracket as needed for the passenger's driving comfort. Insert the bushing into the bracket, align the visor shaft to the opening, and slide it into the bracket. Replace the tensioning screw and tighten it just enough to hold the sun visor without slipping. Install new rubber visor tips at the front of the visor if required. The visor tip will fit snugly into the rearview mirror bracket retainer to hold the sun visor firmly in place along the windshield of the car.

Reconditioning the Sun Visor Bracket

1 *A flat blade is used to drive the bracket off the end shaft of the old sun visor. Only a small portion of the screwdriver's tip will enter the clamp allowing it to come off. If you twist the visor bracket open, the force will cause the pot metal to crack.*

2 *These mounting brackets came off the same car. They look bad, but no pitting was found on the chrome plating. With a little elbow grease applied to bracket on the left, it shined right up and looks almost as good as new.*

3 *These small plastic bushings slide into the bracket to help the tension of the visor shaft. When properly adjusted, the visor will be able to rotate in the bracket clamp and stay in position without flopping loosely in the bracket.*

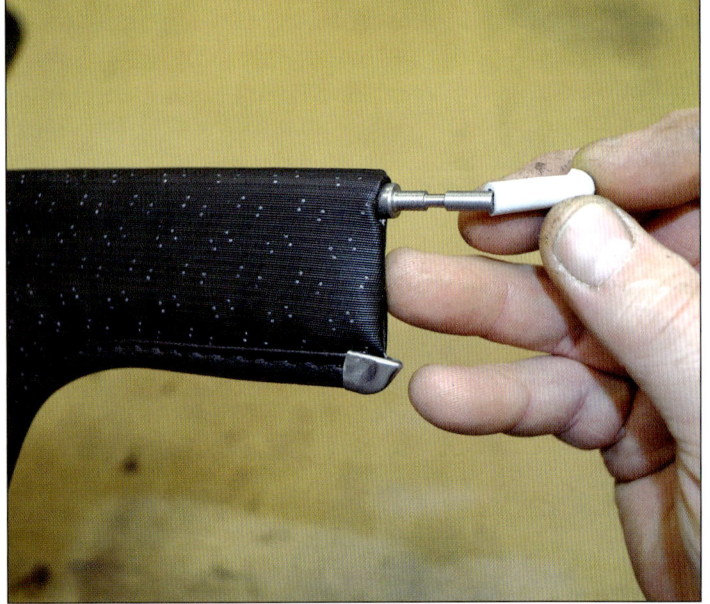

4 *A new rubber visor tip will help lock the sun visor into the windshield retainer to support the visor and prevent it from bouncing when the car is in motion. The tip is installed by pushing it onto the small rod on the front of the visor.*

Installation

The sun visors are positioned in the front outer corners on the inside of the car. If you feel through the headliner material, there are large holes in the underlying metal that give a place for the spring in the base of the bracket to go. There are also three screw holes for the fastening screws.

Cut an access slit in the top material to expose the large hole and allow the insertion of the bracket. Align the bracket to the roof of the car by locating the screw holes with the help of a regulator. Support the bracket while you insert the mounting screws to prevent the any damage to the soft metal. Snug up the screws to secure the sun visor into position. Repeat the process to install the other sun visor.

Position the rearview mirror to the center of the windshield and secure the bracket with the correct screws. Fit the rubber boot over the base plate of the mirror to conceal the bracket hardware. Fasten the boot in place with the correct trim screws. The sun visors can be moved into position and the tips can be fit into the boot retainers.

Finishing

Inspect your work for irregularities and apply a little heat to help relax any wrinkles in the material. Clean up any fingerprints or smudges left behind from the headliner installation. Now, the rear seat can be reinstalled and the dome light fuse returned to the fuse block. Be confident in the work you have done. Installing a headliner is something to take pride in.

Correcting Sail Panel Issues

Depending on how you ordered the sail panels, they may either be already wrapped or they need to be. I

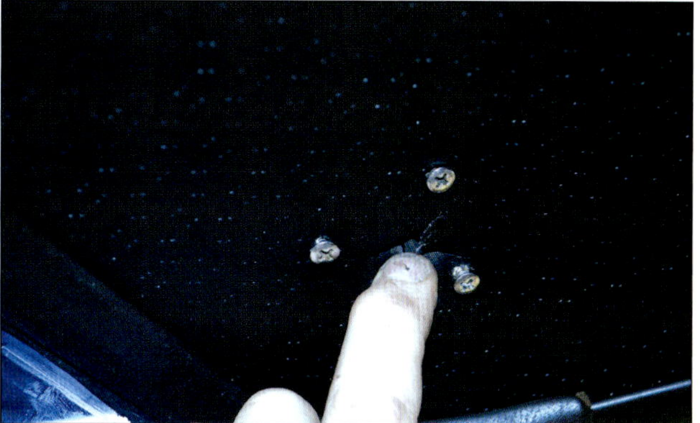

After locating the large retainer relief hole, small pie cuts are made in the headliner material to allow the bracket to sit flush against the underlying metal support. Use an upholsterer's regulator to locate the screw holes for the bracket.

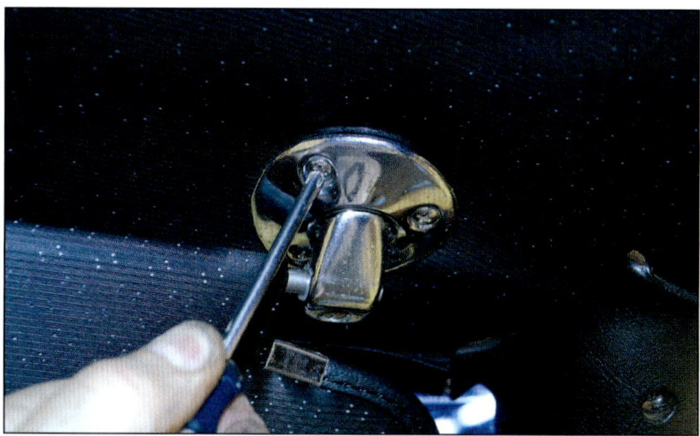

The sun visor bracket will only fit in one position. If the base of the bracket is clocked incorrectly, the visor will not swing correctly and the screws will not line up. Support the sun visor when tightening the screws to prevent damage to the bracket.

This decorative cover serves multiple purposes. It not only covers the base plate and screws used to secure the rear-view mirror to the roof of the car but it also grips the rubber tips on the sun visors to prevent them from bouncing.

Before this project began, it may have been a little intimidating and perhaps something that you wished that you did not start. It took some time to get to the finish line on this project, but the result is something that you can feel good about.

It is to your advantage to test fit the sail panels before you begin working on the project. Overcoming any fitment issues early on will be less discouraging than when you are about to finish the project and run into problems.

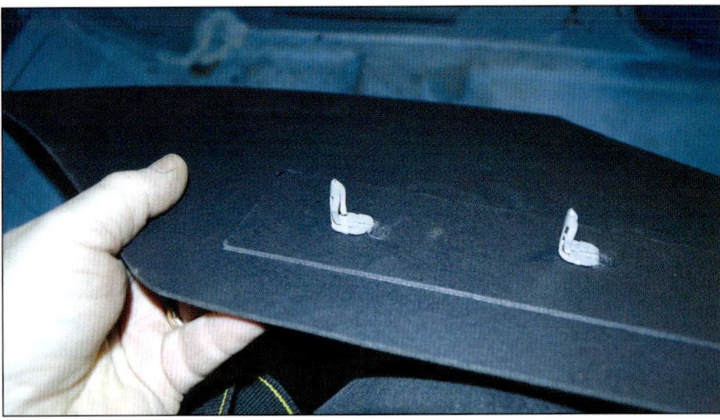

Proper orientation of the panel clips ensure that they line up correctly with the anchor holes located in the rear quarter roof section of the car. Presetting the clips will make installation of the sail panel much quicker.

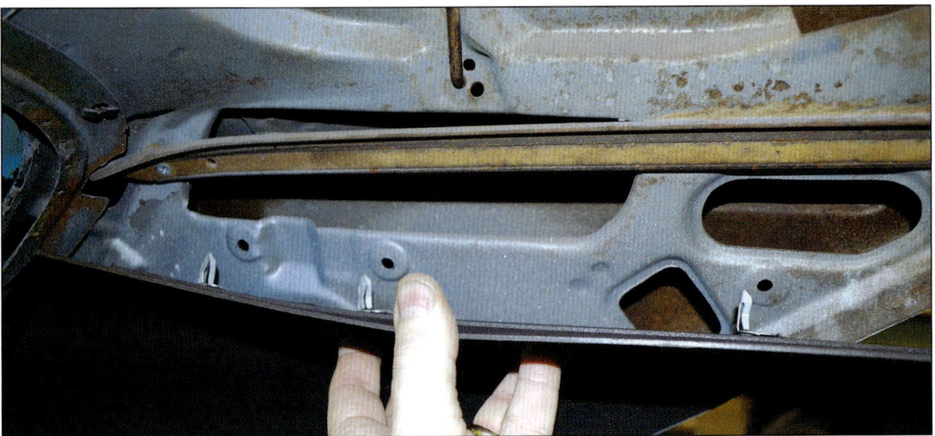

During the prefit of the sail panel, it was determined that the clips were not lining up properly with the anchor holes. An adjustment of 1/2 inch needs to be made to the retainer strip before the sail panel will fit in the correct position.

prefer to order the sail panels for my projects unwrapped because sometimes they do not fit correctly or the glue used by some manufacturers to attach the headliner material is not as good as it could be and the panels will develop bubbles or wrinkles.

Before the project is started, dry fit the sail panels by setting them into place. Check the height of the panel to ensure that it will cover the raw edge of the headliner and extend to the front and rear with enough material to allow for the attachment. If the panel fills the sail area properly, check to see if the attachment clips on the backside of the panel are positioned correctly to mate with the anchor holes on the body.

To verify the fit, install the panel clips. To do this, place the panel face down on the workbench and use a screwdriver or upholsterer's regulator to clear the attachment hole for the panel clip. Install the clips into the retainer holes and fit the panel to the car. You may need to curl the top of the sail panel down to be able verify the correct positioning of the panel clips. If the panel fits and the clips line up with the attachment holes, cover the panel and install it. If you have a fitment issue, the clip positions can be corrected before you are ready for the sail panel to be installed.

Covering and Fitting

When the clips are offset and do not align correctly, the clip retainer must be repositioned to allow the sail panel to fit. To fix this condition, measure the distance of the offset and remove the clip retainer so that it can be adjusted.

Remove the retainer by placing the panel face down on the workbench and then trace around the retainer to mark its current position. Next, remove the retainer by sliding a stiff-blade broad knife under the applied panel to free it from the backside of the larger panel. Measure the panel clip to determine the distance from the center point of the prong to the throat of the clip. This will let you know how much you must reposition the retainer on the panel to correct the offset. Reposition the retainer on the panel and trace the new position of the retainer to the larger panel, and then remove the retainer for gluing. Apply contact cement to the backside of the retainer

A pencil is used to mark the original location of the clip retainer on the backside of the sail panel before it is removed. This line is a reference guide to help with the repositioning of the inner panel.

The clip retainer is carefully removed from the sail panel with the help of a wide-blade scraper. The heavy flat blade works well to prevent damage to the panel board as it is used to separate the panels. Once removed, the retainer will be reused.

This panel clip measures a 1/2 inch from the center of the prong to the throat of the clip. An accurate measurement of the panel clip is needed to calculate the amount of adjustment required to make the sail panel fit correctly. It may be fussy, but getting the panel to fit will be worth the effort.

Our panel clips were only a 1/2 inch offset from the anchor holes, which meant that the retainer needed to be adjusted a 1/2 inch to make it fit correctly. A measurement was made from the original position of the retainer, and the edge of the panel will be repositioned so that the clips will line up with the anchor holes in the car.

An adequate amount of glue is applied with a small chip brush to both mating surfaces of the sail panel and retainer to ensure that they will stay bonded. After the pieces are assembled, the sail panel will be ready for the new headliner cover material to be applied.

and to the inside area of newly traced location on the panel. Allow the glue to tack before it is assembled.

Reassembly

After the glue has set and the retainer is anchored to the panel, the panel is ready to be covered with headliner material. At this point, the surface of the panel board may have some creases in it. These imperfections will show through the thin cover material and spoil the look of the finished panel. To remedy this, the surface of the sail panel should be covered with a felt underlining material prior to attaching the headliner material.

Apply contact cement to the face of the sail panel and the backside of the felt underliner. When the glue has tacked up, press the material together and smooth out any wrinkles in the felt. The surface of the panel has to be smooth or the imperfections will show. When the glue has set, the felt underliner will need to be trimmed flush to the edge of the panel board.

Lay out the sail panel material face down on the workbench and then place the sail panel face down on the material to size it before cutting. You should have at least 1½ inches of material extending beyond the front and rear edges of the panel for attachment to the car. Make sure that the pattern in the headliner material is aligned correctly before setting the panel into the fabric. Apply glue to the felt and the backside of the headliner material.

Assemble the panel and work out any wrinkles in the face of the material with your hand. Once the material is set, turn the panel over and apply glue to the upper and lower edges along the backside of the panel. Trim the material to 3/4 inch along the top and bottom only, and then fold the glued material over the edge. Insert the panel clips into the retainer. The panel is now ready to be installed into the car.

Reassembling the Panels

1 Contact cement is sprayed onto a felt underliner to cover the creases that formed in the panel board. After the felt has been applied to the face of the sail panel, it will then be trimmed to the edge of the panel before the final headliner cover material is applied.

2 The sail panel has been turned over and the headliner material is smoothed out across the surface to prevent wrinkles from forming. An even pressure is needed when setting the material to prevent dimples from forming in the surface of fabric before the glue dries.

3 The excess material along front and rear sections is left longer, and it is used to secure the sail panel to the inner fastening rails of the car. The panel clips can be inserted into the retainer and then the sail panel will be ready to be installed in the car.

4 Adjusting the fitment of the sail panels was worth the extra time and effort to correct the poor positioning of the panel. Without the correction, the outer trim pieces would not fit properly. This now looks how a sail panel should look.

Sail Panel Resurfacing

The sail panels are often shipped precovered and ready to install. Occasionally, you receive a set that has already started to form air bubbles and is unusable due to the failure of the factory adhesive. When a sail panel has a delamination issue, it will not get better on its own—trust me. So, you need to repair the panels before they are installed in the car.

If you tell the manufacturer about the issue, you will most likely receive another set. This process takes time and you may end up with another pair that has the same problem. The best solution is to strip the panels and use a better adhesive to secure the cover material to the panel board.

This repair is very simple to perform. Place the sail panel face down on your workbench and start to lift the turned edges of the cover material from the backside of the panel. If you use a stiff-blade broad knife to lift the material, it will help prevent the paper from tearing away with the headliner material. Work slowly and carefully to prevent tearing or cutting the headliner material.

After the edges are free, turn the panel face up and continue to remove the headliner material from the face of the sail panel. The goal is to remove the cover material without damaging the surface of the panel board. If the panel board begins to lift, stop pulling and use the broad knife to separate the materials. Do not pull so hard that it will stretch or distort the cover material. You can also apply a little heat with a steamer or heat gun to help soften the glue, but do not overheat and damage the cover material.

Clean the Surface

When the cover material has been separated from the panel board, remove any residual glue from the surface of the materials. If you do not clean off the old glue, there will be lumps in the panel and the new adhesive will fail. The best cleaner to remove the old adhesive is lacquer thinner. It will evaporate fast and soften the glue so that it can be wiped away without destroying the panel board. You can also use it to clean the backside of the headliner material. Remember that too much lacquer thinner can cause damage to vinyl.

You need to work in a well-ventilated area without any flames when using lacquer thinner. Use a clean, soft cotton cloth and wet it with the lacquer thinner. Wipe the surface of the panel board with the cloth until the glue is removed and let it air dry. If your headliner kit came with extra material to cover the sail panels, you will not need to reuse the old material. Otherwise, do the same for the backside of the headliner material. Do not over-wet the headliner material as it may bleed through to the front side. Use short, fast strokes to soften and remove the glue. After the material is clean, let it air dry before applying any new adhesive to the surface.

Gluing

Place the cover material and panel board on a piece of cardboard to prevent the overspray of glue onto your work surface. Apply an even coat of contact adhesive to both surfaces and allow the glue to tack before you assemble the pieces.

Position the panel board over the headliner material. Make sure the pattern in the material is in the correct orientation to the headliner. Press the panel board onto the headliner material and flip the piece over to work out any bubbles or wrinkles that may be visible on the surface of the panel. After the material has been secured in the correct position, flip the panel over so that the backside faces upward on the workbench.

Spray an additional coat of glue along the outer edge of the panel board and excess headliner material. These are the areas that need to be turned and secured to the backside of the panel. When the glue has flashed, the headliner material can be pressed onto the panel board. Pull on the material just enough to make it follow close to the edge of the panel without tearing it, and smooth it into place on the back of the panel.

Ready to Install

Turn the panel face up and check for any flaws in the surface of the sail panel. Panel clips can be inserted into the clip retainers on the backside, and the sail panel can be installed in the car.

Reconditioning the Sail Panels

1 *These sail panels are just not going to make this car look good. Right out of the box, it's obvious that the adhesive the manufacturer used has failed. The outer covering on the sail panel has started to separate, creating bubbles in the surface of the material.*

2 *As the headliner material is pulled back, it shows that there is very little glue on the surfaces to keep the material secured to the panel board. This lack of glue will make the cleanup and repair of the sail panel much faster and easier.*

3 To prevent the cover material from bubbling again, the sail panel components have been cleaned and sprayed with an even coat of contact cement. The even coverage of the adhesive ensures a good bond and eliminates lumps in the surface from clumps of glue.

4 Finishing the sail panel requires turning the edges of the cover material and securing them to the backside of the panel board with more glue. An even coat of glue is used on the mating surfaces to ensure a good bond will be made and the panel will not come apart.

5 With very little effort, the sail panel has been reconditioned and it looks great. Before the sail panel can be installed, small panel clips can now be added to the backside of the panel to retain it in the proper position.

Rework

Fixing poorly made upholstery has been a big part of my job and that has kept me busy my entire career. When customers supply their own products, it makes my task to install them even more challenging. I have preferred vendors that I work with, and I seldom have issues. However, when I do, they take care of it immediately.

This Camaro headliner was difficult enough because I had to work around the roll cage that was already welded into the car. After the work was done, I received a call the next day about the sail panels coming down. I went back to the customer's shop and encountered a flaw that I was able to correct. This is what I did.

I first removed the sail panel and discovered that the base material was made of embossing panel board. This material has a plastic coating on it that allows a dielectric machine to emboss patterns to the panel board. It works great for that purpose, but it is not intended to be glued together

The day after installing this customer-supplied headliner, I received this image of the sail panel lying down inside the car. When the panel was assembled at the factory, the manufacturer used a plastic-coated panel, and the glue failed to keep the retainers in place.

like it was.

To repair the clip retainers, I removed the plastic coating on the mating surfaces with a small 3-inch die grinder pad. Contact cement was applied to the cleaned surfaces with a chip brush and held the retainers in place without any further complications.

I contacted the manufacturer about the design flaw of its sail panels and included photos of the product and how I repaired it. When they followed up and contacted me, I was informed that no one ever had this issue before. This is why I am so busy, and now you are able see the solution to a common problem.

A small power sander was used to remove the plastic coating from the mating surfaces of the panels and clip retainers. The bare panel board will now be able to accept the adhesive and a proper bond can be achieved to hold the parts in place.

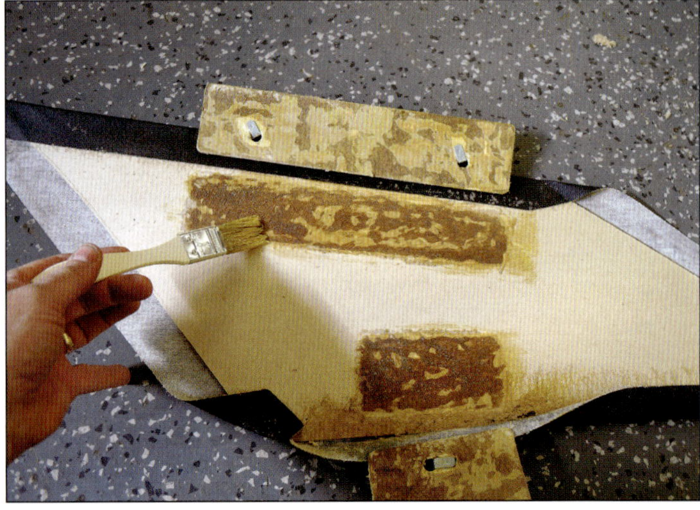

Contact adhesive has been brushed onto the panel board and retainer pieces. The glue will set up before the parts are assembled. This will ensure that the pieces will not come apart after they are reinstalled in the car.

CARPET

Automobile floor coverings have evolved over the years from simple, natural-fiber woolen rugs resting on wood floorboards to the modern, custom-formed carpets made of synthetic fibers. There are many options available today that can be used to cover the floor of your car. There are also several ways the floor coverings are installed. Some choices are better than others, and we will explore the good and bad options available.

The simplest way to get factory results is to purchase a premolded carpet set. These carpets are as close to original as you can get and are not difficult to install. Having a good experience with the simplicity of a carpet installation will give the DIYer the confidence to take on more advanced interior installations.

Composition

Modern auto carpet is made of woven synthetic fibers. Nylon, polyester, and rayon yarns are the most

Early classic cars had carpet that was cut and sewn to fit the contours of the floor. The raw edges of the tailored carpet were either finished by a contrasting binding or surged with an overlocking yarn to keep the carpet edges from fraying. A color-matched heel pad was also sewn in to protect the carpet from wear.

Stains, wear, and fading are the most common reasons to replace the carpeting in your classic car. Ordering a preformed carpet set is not only fast but also the easiest and the least-expensive way to restore the flooring in your car.

commonly used materials in the auto carpet restoration industry because they cost far less than wool.

Large tufting machines are used to insert the yarn into a woven polypropylene backing material. Hundreds of needles penetrate the backer, just like a large sewing machine, inserting the yarn and create the loop pile. The width of the carpet will vary depending on the type of carpet being made. After the fibers are set, the carpet is dyed and finished with a latex coating on the backside to lock the tufts in place.

Cut Pile

One variation during the tufting process is to have the loops of yarns cut by a knife to create what is known as cut pile. The exposed ends of the yarn fibers stand up and become the pile height. Durability is determined by the length of the cut. Short pile is more durable. The more tufts per inch will make the carpet more dense, which will wear better.

Molded Set

A tailored carpet is cut and sewn to fit the contours of the floor pan. These carpet sets look great and give a car that vintage look and feel. Modern stamping equipment can transform flat pieces of carpet into seamless contoured floor coverings that form-fit the car.

To prevent the carpet from wearing through under the driver's feet, a heavy rubber or vinyl pad was incorporated into the floor pan area. The added protection extended the life of the carpet and became a stylish addition to complement the upholstery.

You might count it as a blessing or as a curse, but the carpet padding has already been attached to the backside of this carpet section. Flaws in the pad require extra work to make it look right, and alterations are needed before installation.

Many color choices and styles of carpet are available for restoring your car. The more durable loop carpet of the 1950s and 1960s gave way to the plush cut pile carpet of the mid-1970s. The modern look of the carpet enhanced the plush modern car interiors.

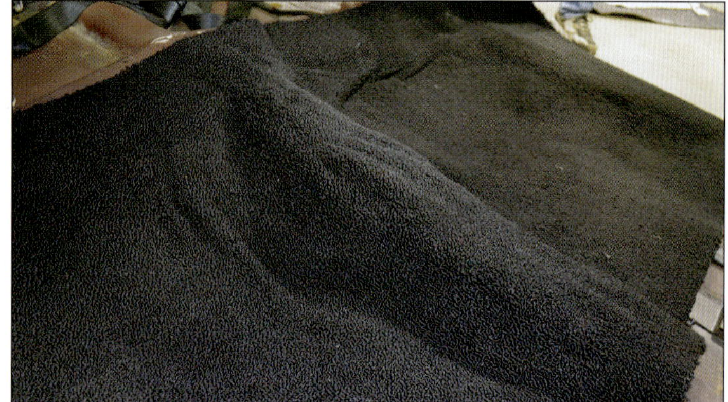

After dry fitting the rear carpet section in the car, we can immediately see many wrinkles in the carpet. To correct this condition, the preattached pad will need to be carefully trimmed to relieve the wrinkles.

Heel Pad

During the manufacturing process, a factory-style heel pad can be set into the carpet during the molding stage. The heavy vinyl or rubber pad adds another level of protection to help extend the life of the carpet and brings a level of authenticity to a restoration.

Jute Padding

Another feature that is common with premolded carpet sets is that they come with an attached jute padding. This makes the installation process much quicker, but sometimes it creates more problems. When the carpet pad is not attached perfectly, it can form unwanted wrinkles in the surface appearance of the carpet. If this occurs, the carpet will not lay correctly, and you will have trouble with lumps and irregularities when installing the carpet.

Correcting a wrinkly pad is often difficult. If you pull on the pad to loosen it, it can tear the yarn loose and ruin the carpet. The best solution when ordering a premolded carpet set is to ask for the padding to be loose. Fitting the carpet padding yourself is not a difficult task and will give a better final result.

Pad Options

An essential component to prolong the life of auto flooring is a quality pad. Without an underliner, the carpet will be subject to the sharp edges of the floor pan, which can cut through the backing and leave an unsightly hole.

Properly installed padding can enhance the overall look and comfort of the carpet while preventing the carpet from damage. Most tradi-tional padding is made of jute fiber. Modern padding contains recycled materials and other synthetic fibers.

Sound Deadener

The sole purpose of a sound deadener is to make the cab of the car quieter. There are many brands of auto sound and heat suppressors on the market today, and they all have different purposes and compositions. Premium products cost more because they are better suited for use in a car.

Vibrations created from the rotating tires and outside activities tend to multiply as the car moves down the road. The empty space inside of the cab can amplify these vibrations and create a very unpleasant environment. Applying a dampening material to the inner metal panels of the car will help absorb or muffle this unwanted noise.

Butyl Rubber

This product is best used for acoustic and heat suppression. The product is made with a foil backing, which makes for easy installation, and it is available in different thicknesses to meet the specific requirements of the project. The stable nature of the butyl rubber makes it a good choice for any restoration.

Asphalt-Based Products

Those who want to save a few dollars might go to the home-improvement store and pick up a roll of roofing material as an alternative to the superior butyl product.

The disadvantage of using asphalt-based products in an automotive application is due to the unstable nature of the material when exposed to extreme temperatures. High heat will cause the material to melt and create a smeary mess under the carpet. When applied to the inner roof, it can drip onto the headliner and stain the lightweight fabric.

When exposed to cold climates, an asphalt product will become fragile and can crack. In some cases, it will

Before the carpet pad is installed, apply a layer of Dynamat to the bare floor of the car. This is one of the many popular butyl sound-deadener products used by car enthusiasts to soundproof the car's interior. The results obtained by this easy-to-install product are well worth the investment.

Saving money is always a concern when restoring a car, but cutting corners on the foundational materials is not advised. This roofing material is designed to work well on your home, but it will create more problems than it is worth if it is installed in your car.

separate from the surface to which it was applied and create interference with other interior components.

Foil Bubble Wrap

Another product often used as an automotive insulation and padding material is foil-backed bubble wrap. This material is designed to be used as a heating and cooling duct insulation product for the home. Although the cost of the product is low, it is somewhat difficult to install in a car.

The plastic used in the product does not allow the material to lay smoothly over the contours of the floor in the car. When glued to the floor, the foil backing can separate from the product, which causes it to bunch up under the carpet. The thin profile of the bubble wrap does not provide very much padding to the carpet.

This 1957 Chevy rear floor has been padded with home heating duct insulation. The product has already failed and caused the carpet to bunch up. Placing the insulation under the lower rear seat has also made it difficult for the seat frame to stay in place.

Foam Padding

There are many different versions of foam-based carpet pads. They are generally used in house flooring and are not suitable for automotive use because the foam will absorb and

Re-bond foam is commonly used as a support for bedroom and living room carpeting. The foam will attract and hold water like a sponge, so it should not be used in a car because it will develop mold and cause the metal floor pan to rust.

hold water. Water will cause corrosion and mold to form in a car.

Preparation

Before the new carpet can be installed, all of the old floor coverings need to be removed from the car. It is obvious that the seats, seat belts, and sill plates need to be removed. If the car has a console, it may need to be removed to make the new flooring installation easier.

Care must be taken when unbolting the seats. Use a box-end wrench or a socket and ratchet to remove the bolts that secure the seats to the floor. After the bolts have been removed, disconnect any electrical connections that power the seat adjuster and seat heater. When the seat is lifted and removed from the car, be aware of the tracks so that they do not scratch the door panels or paint of the car.

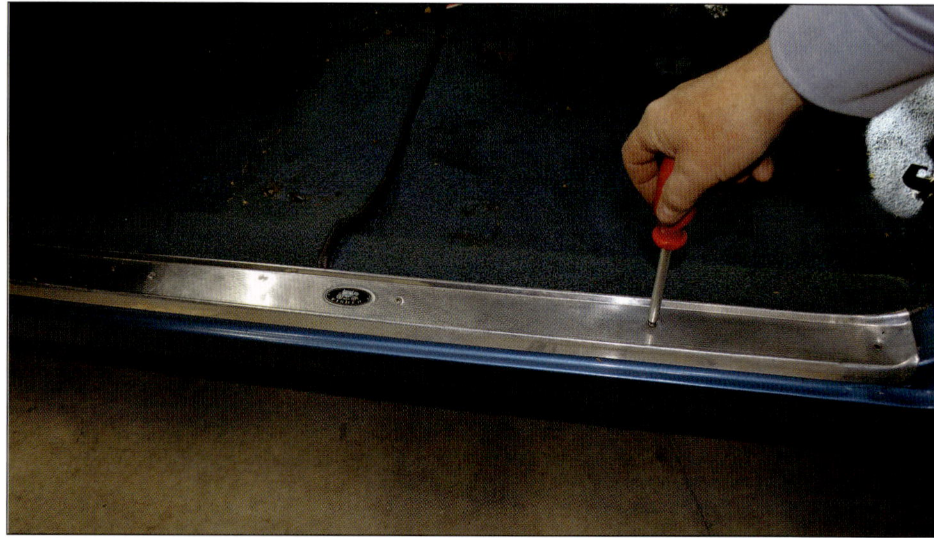

The first parts to be removed from the car are the sill plates. These decorative covers dress up the outer edge of the carpet along the bottom of the door opening. Removal of the sill plates requires the use of a screwdriver to loosen the fasteners holding it in place.

The seats, center console, and seat belts were removed from the car to allow the old carpet to be taken out with little effort. The carpet removal begins by lifting the corner of the front section and then peeling it back. After the carpet has been removed, repairs can be made to the floor.

Gas Pedal

There are generally three types of gas pedal configurations. The first type is the floater. This pedal has a bracket that is attached to the firewall and suspends the pedal so that it does not touch the floor. You do not need to remove this type of pedal to remove or install the carpet. Just be careful when spraying glue so that you don't get glue on the pedal. It is best to cover the pedal with masking tape before you spray the glue.

The two other types of pedals are attached to the floor. One uses ball studs that are threaded into the floor and the gas pedal snaps over the ball ends, and this allows the pedal to pivot forward. These studs may not easily come out of the floor. They tend to rust and are almost sure to break off during the extraction. If you break them off, the stud can

be drilled out and the anchor plate re-tapped for new studs. I prefer to leave them alone and install the carpet over the studs. Later I will expose the ball ends by melting the carpet away with a soldering iron.

Floor-mounted pedals attach two different ways. Some have studs in the floor that the base of the pedal is set over and secured with a locking nut, and the other models have studs that protrude from the bottom of the base of the pedal. The studs go through the floor and are secured underneath the pan area with lock nuts. These fasteners tend to break off when removed because of rust and damage from being exposed under the car.

It is best to remove the pedal to properly install the carpet. If the studs break during the removal process, you can either repair the broken stud or order a new pedal.

Sound Deadener Installation

After the cab has been emptied, a good cleaning is in order. Dirt, oil, and rusted metal should be taken care of while there is nothing in the way. Holes in the floor must be properly repaired, and bare metal needs to be primed and painted before the new materials are installed.

Having a bare floor gives you the option of adding more sound deadening to the car. Direct attachment of a foil-backed butyl rubber product can be applied at this time. Installing the sound deadener is nothing more than removing the protective backing from the sheets and aligning them onto the floor to cover the areas of the floor pans and transmission tunnel.

A small roller tool is useful in pressing the sheeting into the surface of the floor. The tool helps the material adhere better, and by turning the roller over and using the handle, you can get the material into tighter and deeper places.

It is not recommended to overlap the sound deadener, as this will create problems with the carpet installation. Use a stiff-blade utility knife to cut and trim the sound deadener. If you make a relief cut to allow the material to flow without bunching, the excess material that is removed can be reused by installing it into the corners and tiny voids that will occur during installation of the large sheets of sound deadener.

Be careful while handling the foil sheets. It is possible to get cut from the foil. If you ever had a paper cut, you do not want to experience a foil cut. It does happen, and you have been warned.

Installing the Sound Deadener

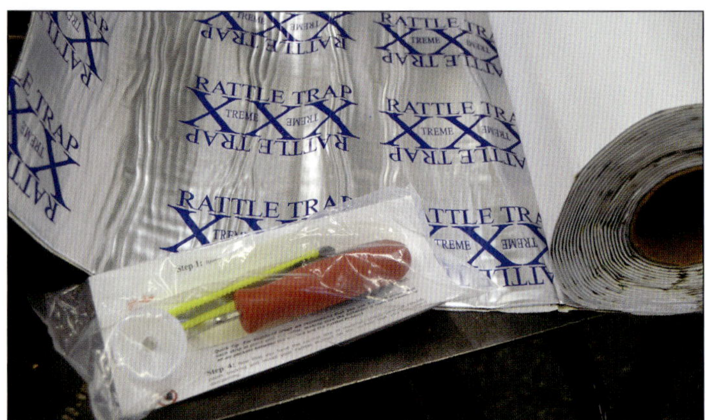

1 *Fresh out of the box, this Rattletrap sound proofing kit will help keep the interior of the car quieter. This product is heavier than the standard butyl rubber shielding made by FatMat Sound Control. A set of instructions, roller tool, and trim knife are included in the kit.*

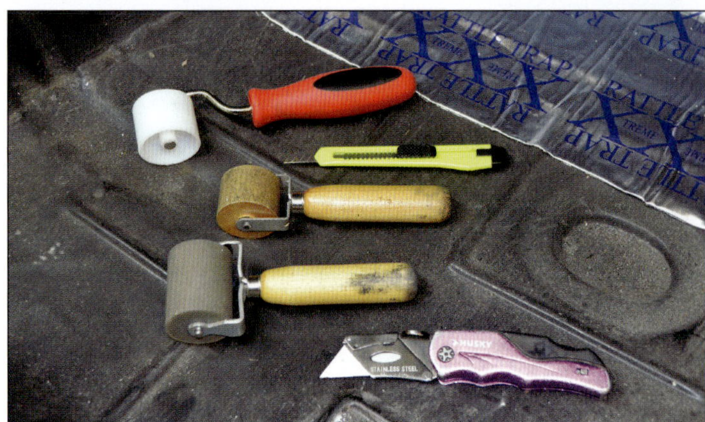

2 *Sound-deadening materials can be installed with simple tools. Your choice of application rollers varies (plastic, wood, or rubber) to help speed up the bonding process. The product can be cut with a snap blade or utility knife.*

3 *Before the sound-deadening product can be used, a protective paper liner is peeled away from the underside of the sheet. It works best to expose just enough adhesive as you work to prevent accidental placement of the product.*

4 *Adding sound-deadening to the floor pan will help limit unwanted heat and road noise. A roller is used to ensure good adherence of the material to the floor surface. The new carpet pad can then be directly applied over the sound barrier.*

5 *A relief cut has been made in the sound deadener along the contour of the floor and transmission tunnel. This will help the product lay flat and smooth. If the product is allowed to overlap, the carpet will not look nice when it is installed.*

6 *A trim knife is used to cut a pie-shaped section from the sound deadener. The cut line matches the edge of the previously secured section of the insulation to allow the material to butt together and form a smooth, non-overlapped seam. This extra material can be reused in other uncovered areas of the floor.*

7 *When the sound deadener is properly installed, it will lay flat and contour perfectly to the floor of the car. Be careful when working with the foil to prevent being cut by the sharp edges that occur when the product is trimmed.*

Carpet Padding

The next step is to cover the floor with a suitable jute carpet padding. The pad will help cut down on noise and insulate the car. Rolling out the jute pad and cutting it to conform to the contours of the floor will give support to the carpet and offer a layer of protection from wearing against the sharp metal.

How to keep the carpet pad in position is your choice. You may opt to allow gravity and friction to keep the padding from shifting under the carpeting, or the pad can be glued directly to the floor. If you choose to secure the carpet pad with glue, be aware of how much of the padding is glued to the floor of the car. Cars that require the flooring to be lifted to access a master brake cylinder cannot be sealed without causing damage to the floor covering.

Adding more wiring to the rear of the car can also be disruptive, so it is better to allow the outer edges of the padding to remain unglued. By detaching the sill plates and lifting the unglued edge of the flooring, more wires can be added without issue.

The carpet will fit better if the jute padding is installed before the carpet is laid down. When the pad is applied separately, it is much simpler to trim around objects like shifters and dimmer switches. Making a cutout for the seat belt and seat track bolt holes is a breeze, but not all carpet sets have a separate pad.

Before the carpet is installed, carefully trim the pad to fit around the floor shifter. Take the time required to get the pad to lay smooth. It will result in a nicer-looking finished carpet installation. After trimming, the pad is glued to the floor.

This carpet set was made with the jute padding already attached to the underside of the carpet. To make the installation of the seat belts and seats easier, the padding is marked with a Sharpie pen to indicate where the jute needs to be removed before it is anchored in place.

Less effort is required to trim away the unwanted areas of the pad when the carpet set is turned upside down to expose the markings. It is important that only the padding is cut and not the carpet. It is easier to access the mounting points when the pad is removed.

It doesn't matter if you use an aerosol spray glue or a commercial spray gun to apply the adhesive; just be sure to read the application and warning label on the product to avoid any personal harm or injury. Good ventilation and a respirator mask are recommended when spraying glue.

If your carpet set has a pre-attached pad, make note of the location of the seat belt and seat track mounting holes. Cutting away the small sections of the pad material from the attachment points during the installation process will make it easier to access these anchor points for the reinstallation of the anchor bolts.

Be very careful that you do not cut into the carpet when cutting through the jute pad to remove the unwanted areas when it is preattached to the carpet set. Pierce the jute with a pair of scissors and make small cuts in the pad to get under the pad and remove it from the carpet backing.

Gluing

Setting the carpet in position and having it stay where you place it requires the material to be fastened to the floor. Conventional attachment methods used nails or screws to hold the carpet in place. Because these fasteners ruined the look of the installed carpet, the adhesive alternative to keep the carpet in place is simple and effective.

There are several problems with glue. The first is that it is messy. Sprayed glue can end up on everything. Controlling the application takes a lot of practice and foresight. Another issue is if the glue will stick or not. The glue surface must be clean. Otherwise, the adhesive will let go. Also, if the glue is not applied correctly, it can dry too fast or too slow.

But the worst part of sprayed glue is the smell. The chemical composition can be hazardous, and once the glue is sprayed, it creates fumes that need to be vented out of your work area. Safety precautions must be taken when spraying glue. Whether you use a cup gun or aerosol can, the manufacturer's instructions must be followed for your own safety.

Fitting the Carpet Sections

Premolded carpet sets are typically made in two sections: a front and a rear. Other variations may be available, and it all depends on the model of your car and what choices the vendor has to offer.

In most applications, the rear section of the carpet is installed first. If the carpet section does not have a

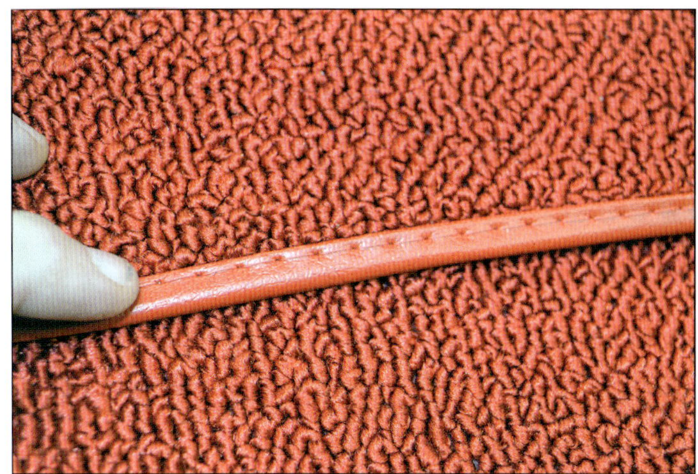

A bias binding is sewn onto the cut edge of the carpet to give it a finished and tailored appearance. The binding is not just a decorative element; it also helps keep the raw edge of the carpet from unraveling.

During the installation of the carpet sections, glue is first applied to the center line. Doing this will allow adjustments to be made to ensure that the proper alignment of the carpet is achieved as it is fit to the floor.

binding sewn along the front edge, it is installed first. To get the best fit, the carpet section is secured from the middle and worked outward toward the doors in both directions.

Begin by applying glue to the center line of the carpet and onto the top of the transmission tunnel. When the glue flashes and is no longer tacky, the carpet section is set in position and lined up with the contours of the floor. Work one side at a time and continue to glue and smooth the carpet to the floor. Watch the alignment, keep the section square with the floor, and work out any wrinkles that may form during the gluing process.

Trimming to Fit

Finishing the outer edges requires some cutting and trimming to get the carpet to fit correctly. Before trimming the carpet, check the alignment of the section to be fit and be conservative when making cuts in the carpet. You can always make the cut longer and wider if necessary.

The object here is to make the carpet lay flat around the obstacles in the way. Removing a small slice of carpet the width of a metal bracket can relieve the tension on the material so that it can tuck neatly into place. The result of trimming will give the carpet a tailored and professional appearance.

Removing bulk from the corners will also allow the interior trim panels to fit better. A direct or square cut in the carpet can actually make the carpet too small when it lays down. A diagonal cut into the protruding point of the door opening will leave enough carpet to cover the area behind the opening. Additional trimming can be made to the area as necessary. When the trimming is done properly, the carpet will fit better, and less steaming will be needed later to relax any wrinkles.

Trimming the Rear Carpet for Fitment

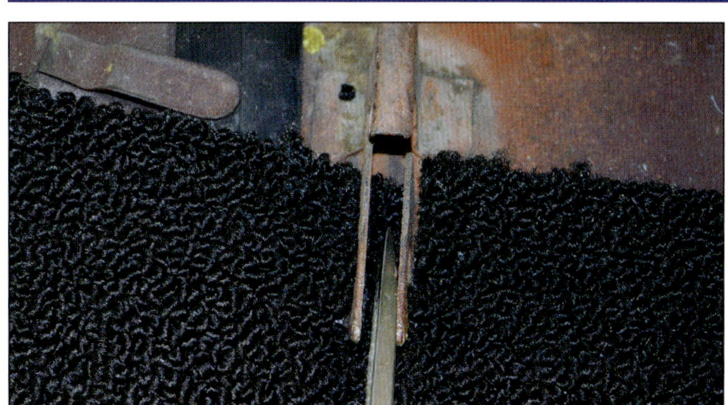

1 *The carpet has been trimmed to fit precisely around the rear seat anchor. With a pair of scissors turned on its edge, the carpet can be neatly tucked into the center section of the anchor with great ease. These are the little details that will give you the satisfaction of a job well done.*

2 *A diagonal cut has been made in the outer sill area to reduce the bulk in the rear corner of the carpet. This is necessary to prevent the side panel from bulging after it is installed. A straight cut here will not leave enough material to cover the floor.*

3 *This is the final result of trimming the rear corner of the carpet. You can clearly see that by making careful and deliberate cuts, the material will conform to the floor without any puckers. Since the carpet fits so well, the rear trim panel will look nice after it is installed.*

4 *After all of the trimming and finessing, the rear section of the carpet fits and looks great. Some of the small box wrinkles can be removed with a good steaming. Steam will not hurt the carpet; it will allow the carpet to relax and conform to the contours of the floor.*

Front Section

Dry fit the front section of the carpet and set it into position by squaring up the heel pad. Work the carpet so the inner edge of the heel pad is parallel with the transmission tunnel. Align the forward edge of the heel pad with the crease in the floor pan before it rises to the firewall. Check the position of the pad with the gas pedal to verify the correct alignment.

The front section of the carpet set is placed into position, and the fit is checked before it is cut and glued in place. Getting the placement of the heel pad takes some effort, but once it is correctly positioned, the installation can begin.

ensures that the position of the heal pad does not change after the carpet has been fit into the optimum visual placement.

Smooth the carpet over the transmission tunnel and onto the passenger-side floor and check the fit and position of the carpet. If the floor has a shifter, make relief cuts in the carpet to allow it to lay smoothly over the hump and give access to the shift lever. There should be enough carpet to cover up to the firewall and the outer sill area. Double check that the heel pad position is still correct, and if everything looks right, start gluing the carpet into place.

Anchoring the Heel Pad

Because the heel pad is a key visual to the front carpet, the position of the pad must look square. To ensure the proper position of the pad, lift the carpet and spray glue onto the floor and back of the carpet.

Allow the glue to flash before setting the carpet in place.

When the glue is ready, press the carpet into position and then re-check the heel pad for alignment. Correct the position if necessary, and now that the heel pad is stable, proceed with the rest of the installation.

Edging

To make the front carpet lay flat, a lot of fine trimming needs to happen to make it look right. It is not necessary to glue the edges of the front carpet for a couple of reasons. The first is that it is messy. Due to all the cutting and tucking, glue only makes it harder to work the carpet and keep it clean. The second is accessibility. Future repairs or additions to the wiring may require that the carpet is lifted to conceal the new wires. Finally, there are

Installing the front half of the carpet begins by gluing the driver's side first. This technique

many items along the outer perimeter of the carpet that will keep the edges from coming loose.

Dimmer Switch

Limited access space makes fitting the dimmer switch grommet more cumbersome than difficult. Cutting a round hole and lining it up with the floor switch is sometimes hit and miss. Try this: fold the carpet even with the edge of the switch. Use chalk to mark the position of the lower edge of the switch, and then measure and mark the width of the switch. This will give you an accurate guide for cutting.

Always cut as little as possible until you have the position perfected. If you make the hole too big or in the wrong place, patching the carpet will look bad, so take the time to get it right. Fold the carpet back over the switch to check the position of the hole. If you like how it looks without the grommet, leave it alone. To add the dimmer grommet, trim the hole an extra 1/8 inch larger and insert the grommet from the backside of the carpet and work the finished edge of the plastic over the top of the carpet. Lay the carpet back down with the grommet around the floor switch.

Fitting the Carpet Around the Dimmer Switch

1 A small hole has been initially cut in the carpet and then it will be test fit to verify its position. Adjustments can be made to a smaller hole to make the carpet fit without being distorted. After the fit has been adjusted, a decorative grommet can be installed.

2 With a little effort, we have achieved a perfect fit around the dimmer switch. Before the trim grommet can be installed, enlarge the hole by cutting away an extra 1/8 inch of material from the existing hole. The grommet is installed from the backside of the carpet and will cover the raw cut edge of the carpet.

Kick Panel

Before the carpet can be tucked under the kick panel, make a relief cut at the crease line in the floor. By cutting the carpet within a 1/2 inch of the bottom of the vertical kick panel wall, the carpet will keep from bunching up in the crease. If the kick panel is already installed, the carpet can be trimmed to 1 inch from the floor line. This will make it easier to tuck the carpet under the edge of the panel.

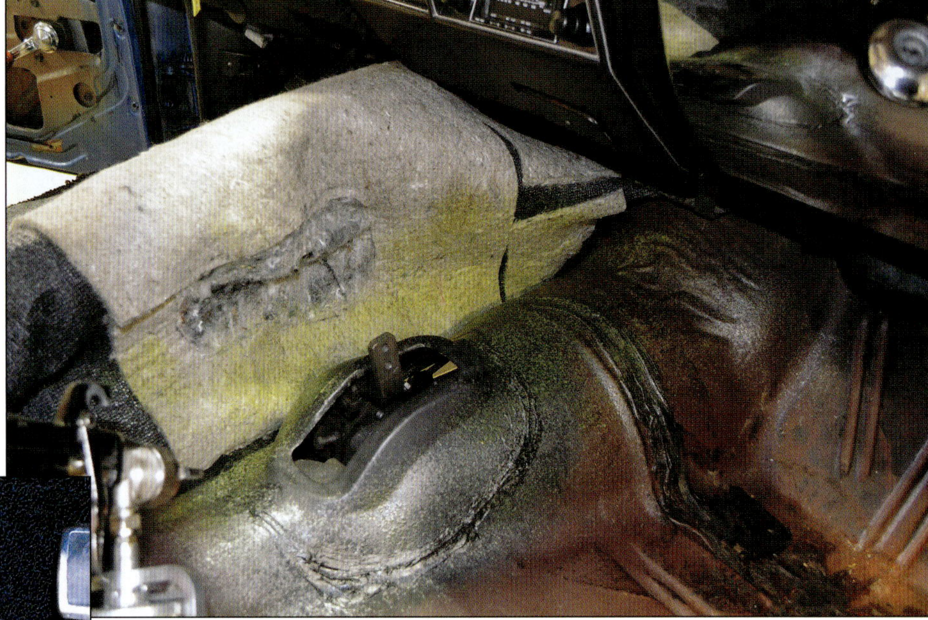

Glue has been applied to the carpet before it is worked over the transmission tunnel. When the carpet is secured in sections like this, not only will it take less effort to install but you also will have less chance of having any wrinkles in the carpet.

A cut has been made in the carpet at the crease in the floor to allow it to lay without buckling. Excess material can then be trimmed to about 1 inch along the lower edge of the kick panel before it is tucked under to hide the raw edge of the carpet.

Finishing

Working the rest of the front section of carpet from the anchored heel pad over the tunnel will keep wrinkles from forming as the carpet is smoothed back into place. Lift the carpet up so that glue can be applied to the floor and carpet. Press the carpet into the floor pan, paying attention to how the carpet lays along the contours of the metal.

To help eliminate bulk, any excess carpet material can be trimmed to 1

The outer edges of the passenger-side carpet have been trimmed to within 1 inch of the surrounding surfaces, and then glue was added to the underside of the material to keep it from moving. Tucking the edges under the trim panels gives the carpet a finished appearance.

inch from the bottom of the firewall insulation before tucking the forward edge under the vertical pad. The outer edges are trimmed and tucked under the kick panels the same way as the driver's side was finished.

Bolt Holes

Accessing the anchors for the seat belts and seat tracks can be a make-or-break task for most people. Cutting a nice hole in the carpet either with a pair of scissors or a razor blade is difficult and risky. The carpet is thick, and unless you have a very stiff-bladed pair of scissors, it is hard to neatly cut carpet. A razor blade is much sharper and can cut through the tough material, but it is hard to hold the blade and make a small round hole without cutting yourself. Try to imagine doing this with the carpet padding attached to the back of the carpet.

After the hole has been made, the edges are typically more on the square side than round, and when a bolt is run through, the chance of snagging a yarn fiber is good. If this happens, it will cause a run in the pile of the carpet. Repairing a run is difficult and sometimes impossible to hide.

Burning the hole through the carpet with a 40-watt soldering iron works best. By melting the fibers, it eliminates the possibility of snagging the carpet and takes a lot less effort to make a perfect hole in the carpet.

The process is done by locating the underlying anchor point with an upholsterer's regulator. Use a preheated soldering iron to pierce the carpet and slowly rotate the soldering iron to enlarge to hole. To prevent any binding of the anchor bolts when they are replaced, use a regulator to remove any melted carpet fiber that is trapped in the treads of the anchor.

Belts and Seats

Now, the seat belts can be installed. Use the correct bolts to secure the belt to the floor. Begin by tightening the bolt by hand to make sure that the bolt goes in straight without cross-threading the anchor. Use a 13/16-inch socket and torque wrench to further tighten them to

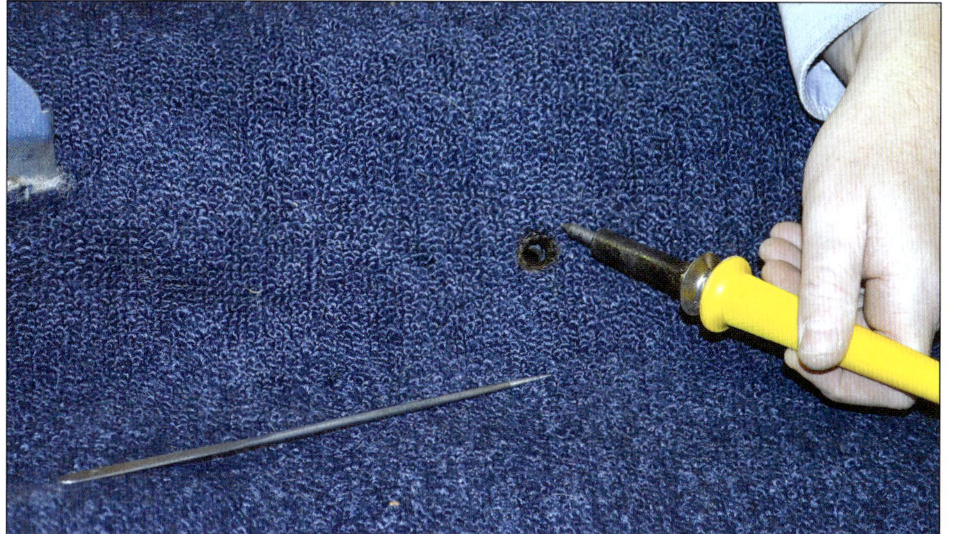

Making a clean hole in the carpet for the seat belt bolt is accomplished with a hot soldering iron. The seat belt anchor is located with an upholstery regulator and then enlarged to allow the bolt to pass through. By melting the edges of the hole, the bolt will not damage the carpet.

Installation of the seat belt is very easy with clean access to the anchor. After the anchor bolt has been hand-tightened, a socket wrench is used to fasten it in place. The seat belt bolt will be checked with a torque wrench to ensure the bolt is secured properly.

the recommended torque specifications, which is usually between 24 and 45 ft-lbs. For the actual specification, check the listing in the car's service manual.

Install the rear seat back and then the bottom cushion. The backrest usually hangs on hooks along the rear seat support and is anchored with sheet-metal screws or metal tabs that are threaded though the seat brackets and bent over to hold the seat in place. The lower cushion is then slid into position and locked into place by cleats on the floor.

Front seats are then placed in position and lined up with the anchor posts and bolt holes located in the floor. Apply the lock nuts and bolts and tighten them to prevent the seat from coming loose. Check the seat adjuster to ensure that it operates correctly and the seat moves freely.

Sill Plates

Installation of the sill plates should be the very last trim part installed. Due to their soft metal and delicate nature, I do not actually fit them to the car until the seats have been bolted in and all other work has been completed. This is done to prevent any accidental damage to them.

Preparing the sill area for installation of the trim panel can be done by dry fitting the panel to verify the fit in the door opening. The front and rear flares may need to be worked to allow the wind lace to fit under the soft aluminum panel. Chalk can also be used to mark the inside edge of the sill plate. This will give you an idea of how much area the sill plate covers so that you can prevent any cutting errors.

Remove the sill plate and fold back the carpet until you see the mounting holes in the sill of the door opening. Use a pair of scissors to cut the material so that it will just touch the screw holes. If the material is too wide, it will hang over the sill and the sill plate will not fit correctly. By cutting too much material, the sill plate will not cover the raw cut edge of the carpet and will look bad, so take your time when you make the cut.

When you do install the sill plates, position the trim panel over the sill and use a regulator to line up the screw holes. Do not use a power screwdriver to attach the sill plates because the screws can dimple the thin metal and ruin the look of the trim. Manually set the screws with a Phillips screwdriver to snug them up to keep the sill plate in position. The sill plates are the crowning jewel of a good carpet installation.

Shiny new sill plates are the first thing that will be seen when the door is opened, and you cannot change that first impression. Nothing beats the look of a well-tailored car interior, and you can take pride in knowing that you did it yourself.

Vinyl Top

From the mid-1960s to the late 1980s, many auto manufacturers applied a vinyl or textured covering to the outer metal roof of the car to simulate the look of a convertible top. The styling of the top was altered on some models by adding a fiberglass shell to emulate the profile of roof bows, which created the illusion that the car actually had a convertible top.

As the vinyl top gained popularity, other variations were made available to the consumer to give the car a specific appeal. One popular version was the landau or half top. This version gave the car a more sophisticated look with features of side-marker lights and thick padding. Simulated side irons were added to the sail panel of the top to give the retro appearance once found on horse-drawn carriages.

The biggest fault caused by a vinyl top is the damage that occurs to the metal understructure. Cars that were created with a factory-installed vinyl top often did not have the extensive metal finishing or protective paint that the rest of the car received. The reason for this lack of protection is strictly cost. The manufacturer felt that the added finishing expense was

This original 1963 Ford Thunderbird sports a classic cobra grain vinyl top. A stylish feature found on this model are the ornamental landau bars located on the sail area of the top. Back in the day, these side irons actually functioned on a carriage top.

Before a new vinyl top can be installed, the old top material must be removed so that repairs can be made to the underlying metal. The discovery of rust is common when the old vinyl top material is removed from the roof line of the car.

Poor surface preparation and years of exposure to the elements has caused extensive corrosion that has compromised the integrity of the underlying metal on the A-pillar. Proper repairs will be necessary to make the metal ready for a new vinyl top.

not necessary because the surface was covered with an applied vinyl fabric. The long-term effect was massive rust and deterioration of the unprotected metal.

As the original vinyl top material faded and dried out, it cracked, and water would wick into the material. The water would become trapped under the vinyl, which resulted in the metal rusting. When the top material was removed from the outer roof of the car, the damage was clearly visible. The underlying metal looked like Swiss cheese.

Before a new vinyl covering can be installed, extensive repairs must be made to the roof to eliminate all the rust, otherwise the new top will look bad and fail prematurely.

The glass will most likely need to be removed for these repairs. To ensure a good fit and seal, remove all of the window trim and moldings and install new molding clip retainer studs around the windows. These are needed to hold the new metal, nylon, or plastic retainer clips.

Replacing the Vinyl

During the repair process, order a new vinyl top for the car. When the new top arrives, remove it from the box and unfold it. Inspect the top for any defects in the seams. Lay the new top over the roof of the car and check that the material is wide and long enough to cover all the roof areas of the car.

Once the fit is determined to be correct for the car, remove the vinyl top and lay it out on a flat surface. You do not want to have any box wrinkles in the top material during the installation, so allow it to relax and let the wrinkles disappear. Do not use any heat or lay the new top in the sun because this these methods will cause it to shrink, and it will give you trouble during the installation. The top material can also be rolled onto a large tube if it needs to be stored during repairs.

To help relieve the wrinkles created by being folded, the top material is removed from the box in preparation for the installation. The new vinyl top is then carefully rolled onto a cardboard tube to help keep the material flat and allow the top fabric to relax.

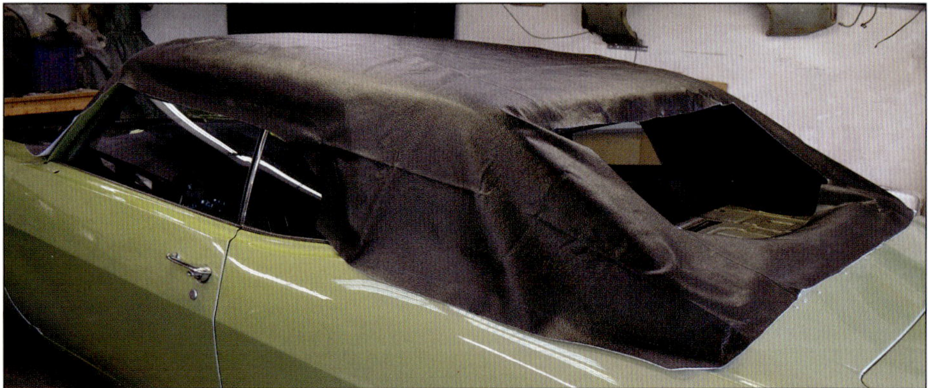

Before work begins, the new top is dry fit to the car. This is a sure way to determine that the new material is the right size and style for the project. If there is an issue with the top material, now is the time to get it resolved.

Reference Marks

It is critical to locate the center point of the roof to ensure that the position of the seams in the top run straight from front to rear. They also need to be an equal distance from the rain gutters.

To find the center point of the roof, measure the distance across the outer front edge of the windshield opening between the top inner A-pillars. Divide the measurement in half and mark the roof with a Sharpie pen. Do the same to the upper rear window opening and mark the center of the rear roof section. The roof line on this fastback has a lower valance section, and the center of the lower rear window needs to be measured and marked.

To make the reference line down the center of the entire roof, connect the front and rear reference marks. The best way to do this is by taping a string or tape measure to the front center point and running it to the rear center point with slight tension on the string. Connect the points with a Sharpie pen by drawing along the edge of the reference string.

Make a matching reference mark on the backside of the new vinyl top material by laying the top material on a work table, and fold the top in half. To get an accurate center line, use the seams in the top material as alignment marks. While the material is folded, use a Sharpie pen to make the reference line on the inside of the material.

Installation

Vinyl tops are glued directly to the metal roof of the car with contact cement. Vinyl top adhesive is formulated to withstand heat and provide excellent holding power. When you spray the glue, it tends to go everywhere, so drape the entire car in 1 mil poly sheeting to protect the paint from any accidental glue overspray. To prevent damage to the painted surfaces, use low-tack painter's tape to attach the plastic sheeting to the car. Taking the time now to cover the car will save you hours of cleanup. After the plastic is in place, the installation of the new top can begin.

A tape measure is used to make accurate measurements to determine absolute dead center on the roof of the car. Without taking the time to make these measurements, the new vinyl top will not fit correctly.

Reference marks are made directly on the roof of the car to ensure that the new vinyl top will be installed parallel to the roof rails. All measurements are cross-checked to ensure that the material will line up straight.

To help with the installation of the new vinyl top, a guide line is made on the underside of the material. This center mark will line up with and reference the line previously made on the top of the car to guarantee a good fit.

The new top will be glued directly to the metal roof of the car. A special vinyl top adhesive is needed to fasten the material to the car. The adhesive is applied with a spray gun to obtain an even and controlled pattern.

Before any work begins, the body of the car is covered in plastic sheeting to protect the paint from overspray. This preparation will prevent glue from damaging the painted surface of the car and save you a lot of cleanup time.

Refold the new vinyl top material so that the reference line is exposed face up on the top of the car. Adjust the spray pattern on your glue gun to a narrow pattern and spray a 3-inch-wide band of glue along the length of the top material and let it tack up, or flash.

While the glue on the top material gets tacky, spray a 3-inch band of glue along the center line on the roof of the car. Before the top material can be applied to the car, the contact adhesive must reach the stage that when it is touched, it will not stick to your fingers. At this point, the glue will stick to itself and create a strong bond. If the glue is too wet, the material will not hold, and the excess solvents will not be able to escape from under the vinyl top material, causing bubbles to form. This is a condition that is hard to correct and can lead to the top material coming loose.

Applying the Top

When the top material touches the glue on the surface of the car,

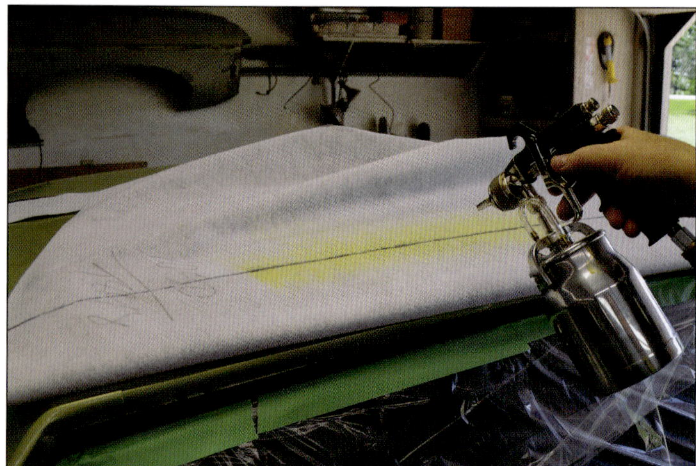

Only a small amount of glue needs to be applied to the top material at any given time. This allows the top to be anchored to the car without binding onto itself and makes it easier to reposition the material if necessary.

The mating surface of the roof is given a matching coat of contact cement. Contact cement works because both surfaces are coated. When the glue sets up and reaches the right amount of dryness, the pieces will bond instantly.

The initial positioning of the top material to the roof is done in small increments to ensure that the reference line is faultless. If the material is stretched or misaligned, it can cause a distortion in the top's appearance.

Anchoring the vinyl top to the roof is accomplished by doing one half at a time. Glue is applied to the roof in thin bands and then worked slowly to prevent bubbles and wrinkles. An extra set of hands can make the task easier.

the bond will be immediate. If you do not have the top lined up correctly, it will need to be pulled off and reapplied. You may elect to have a few extra people on hand to help suspend the top material so that it doesn't get tangled up.

At this point you may begin to press the top material into the glue on the car. Begin at the front of the top, allowing enough material to overhang the leading edge of the roof, and carefully line up the reference marks before pressing the top material onto the roof. Work toward the rear of the roof a couple of inches at a time. Keep the lines perfectly aligned as you press and smooth the material into the glue.

After the top has been anchored, step back and verify that the top is in the correct position. The next step is to secure the field of the top deck to the roof. Work on one side at a time by gluing the material in short drops of 3 inches at a time from the center outward to the drip rail. It is not necessary to work the top material all the way into the rain gutter at this stage. The last 2 inches of material will be finished by applying glue with a brush. This will ensure a better bond along the perimeter of the top.

Securing the Top

Pull the top material back against the previous glue edge to reveal about 1/2 inch of old glue and apply more glue to the top material and the metal roof. It is important to let the glue sit before applying the material in place. Buy working in small sections, or drops, you have less chance of creating wrinkles in the top material. Always work form a glued edge and avoid unglued metal and fabric. This will ensure the top material has a good bond to the roof of the car. If the top material has glue applied to only one surface, you will develop banding issues and the top material will not stay adhered to the roof.

Top Seams

Always be aware of how the vinyl top material is applied while positioning the fabric. Pay particular attention to how the seams are laying out, as it is easy to overstretch the material during installation. Some variation is acceptable, but you want the seams to be as straight as possible.

Continue the process of smoothing the top material onto the roof until you reach the outer edges, and then move on to the other side. Occasionally a bubble may occur under the new vinyl top material. This condition happens when the solvents in the glue have not had enough time to escape. Do not be alarmed as most bubbles will flatten out in a short period of time. If a bubble will not flatten, pierce the vinyl top material with a straight pin to release the trapped air and press down on the top material. When the entire deck area of the top has been attached, the sail areas can be applied.

Lower Valance

Some tops have vinyl below the rear window. This area of the top material is attached just like the main deck area. The center line of the top material is glued and aligned with the center reference mark on the lower edge of the rear window.

Once the center of the valance section is secured, each half of the valance is worked outward 3 inches at a time until you reach the seam line of the vinyl top. You may want to use a glue shield when spraying adhesive near the inner opening of the rear window. The flap from a cardboard box works well as a shield.

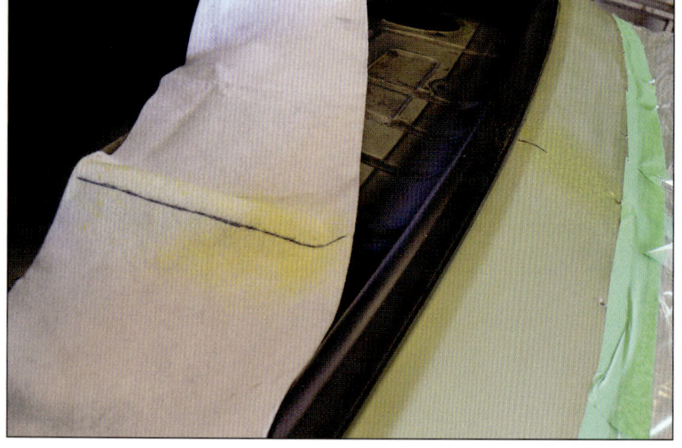

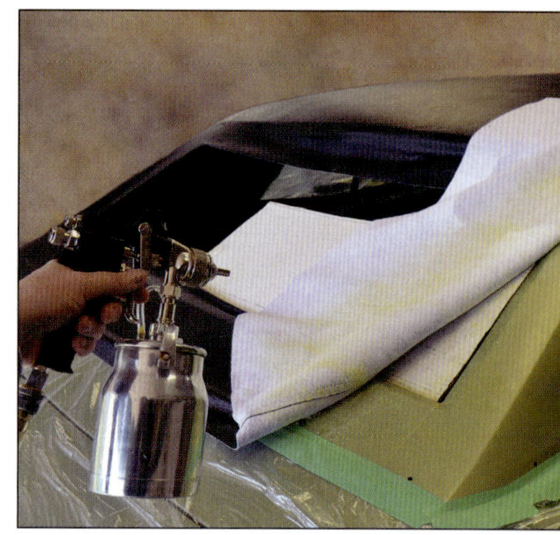

This project has an additional band of top material that runs below the rear window of the car. Although this valance section is smaller in area, the material is anchored by lining up the reference marks and smoothed out in the same manner as the main decking.

A piece of cardboard placed along the edge of the window opening on the inside of the car acts as a shield to prevent excess glue overspray from getting into the car. Now, the valance can be installed with less mess.

Glue is applied to the top material and around the rear window pillar, and it will be allowed to set up before the vinyl is smoothed into place. A glue shield has been placed in the window opening to prevent overspray from entering the car.

Sail Area

Essentially, the vinyl top material is a flat sheet and you need to make it follow the contours of the roof. To effectively make the top material wrinkle-free, it must be pulled and stretched to match the roof line of the car. The sail area is where the roof line dramatically changes and the new top material can bunch up and become problematic. To avoid major wrinkles, a prestretch of the top material must be made to guide you to the proper fitment of the sail area.

When the material is pulled down and away from the corner of the rear window, it will lay smoothly over the rear of the roof. When glued

Getting the rear corner and sail area of the vinyl top to be wrinkle-free requires a prestretch of the top material. This allows you to make any necessary adjustments to the rear valance material before the sail area is permanently glued into position.

To finish out the rear section, an even coat of glue is applied to the remaining field of the sail area. The top material is pulled down and stretched forward to remove any wrinkles in the sail before it is pressed into the glue.

     INSTALLING AUTOMOTIVE INTERIOR KITS

in place, the material can be worked forward and downward to eliminate wrinkles in the vinyl.

Spray glue onto the sail area and top material and allow the glue to flash before working it into position. The material is applied to the metal just like it looked during the prestretch. Smooth the material from the top downward to work out any wrinkles that may form in the sail area.

Edge Trim

As a precaution to avoid cutting the material too short, the trim molding can be dry fit into position along the lower edge of the top and carefully cut along the bottom edge of the molding to remove the excess material. Before the molding can be permanently attached, the profile can be marked with chalk to serve as a reference guide for final trimming.

To prevent the cut edge of the material from showing along the outside of the decorative molding, use a pair of scissors to trim the vinyl just above the chalk mark. Additional trimming is needed to reveal the molding clip studs. With the excess material removed, the molding fastener can be installed without causing a distortion in the trim molding. Brush additional glue under the trimmed edge to secure it to the car.

Finishing the Edges

Securing the last inches of the top material to the rain gutter is accomplished with glue and a brush. The unattached sides of the top are lifted to apply glue to the metal surface of the car and the underside of the top material. This technique ensures that the material will bond securely and prevent air from getting under the top and lifting it.

Work the top material into the

Before the sail area top material is trimmed, the lower trim molding is set in position and used as a cutting guide to keep from removing too much fabric. A pair of scissors is used to trim off the excess material by following close to the lower edge of the molding.

Concealing the edge of the top material under the trim molding will give a profession appearance to the finished vinyl top. Chalk is used to mark the lower edge of the trim molding to indicate how much material will need to be removed.

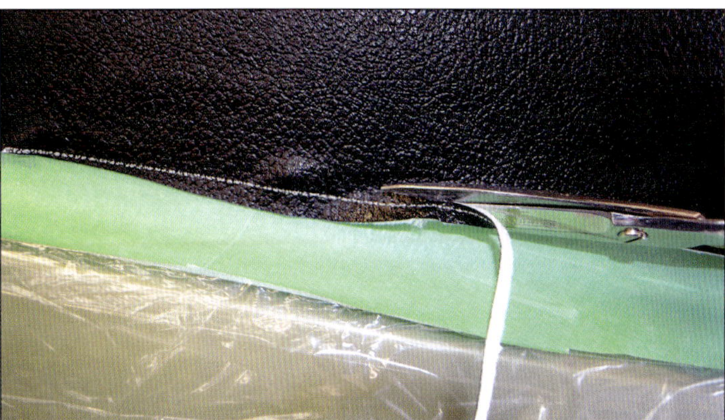

Use a pair of scissors to cut the vinyl top material flush with the bottom edge of the molding clip studs. Trim on the inside of the chalk mark to guarantee that the raw edge of the top material will be concealed under the trim molding when it is applied.

Before the molding clips can be installed, some fine cutting is required to remove the excess material surrounding the stud. The extra material can prevent the retainer clip from laying flat against the body, which will cause a bulge in the molding.

tight creases of the rain gutter to allow proper watershed from the roof of the car. A number of tools can be used to tuck the material in place, but be careful that the surface of the vinyl is not scratched or torn. If the surface is compromised, water can wick into the vinyl and cause rust to form under the vinyl top.

Spraying glue to bond the edges of the top to the car is messy and ineffective. Because the work area along the rain gutter is small and tight, use a brush to apply glue to the top material and metal when finishing the edges of the top.

A glass installer's plastic stick tool works well to tuck the top material into the tight recesses of the rain gutter. Without the use of the tool, the vinyl top material would take up more space in the gutter and prevent the proper flow of water from the surface of the top.

After the gutter material has been properly tucked into place, the excess can be trimmed flush with the top edge of the metal rain gutter. When the top installation is completed, the outer rain gutter stainless trim can be reinstalled.

A-Pillar

A-pillars flank each side of the windshield and are covered with vinyl top material. Application of the top vinyl is much the same as the rest of the car with the exception of how the contact adhesive is applied. Because the area is so small, it works best to use a brush to apply the glue needed to affix the top material to the car.

Glue is first applied at the top of the pillar and continued downward toward the fender. Glue is also applied to the underside of the top material and allowed to flash before the vinyl is smoothed into place on the A-pillar.

To gain access to the lower section of the A-pillar, open the car door and apply glue to the metal where it is needed. The top material can be

Seamed to the top are small strips of vinyl top material that are needed to cover the roof A-pillars. A brush is used to apply glue to the difficult-to-reach areas when the material is attached to the metal.

Because the A-pillar of the car gets the most exposure to wind, a good, even coat of vinyl top adhesive is applied by brush to make sure that all the surfaces are evenly coated to prevent the top material from lifting when the car is driven.

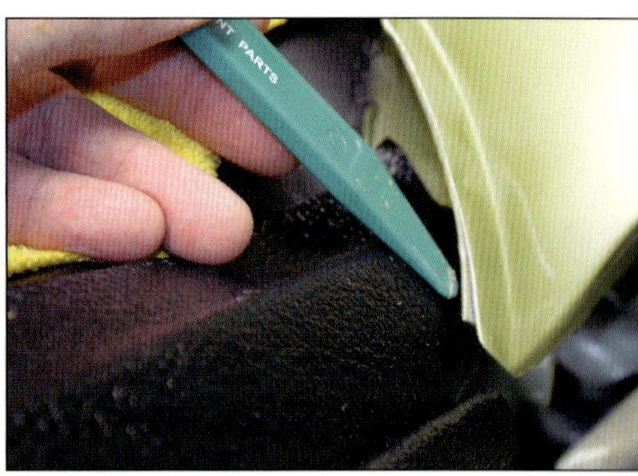

Smoothing the lower section of the A-pillar vinyl top material into place is possible with the help of a plastic stick tool. The tool can reach into the tight space without damaging the vinyl's surface.

worked into position with a tuck tool to ensure a good bond with the glue.

Trim the lower edge of the material to its correct length and apply ample glue to keep it from coming loose. The outer edge of the material can now be glued, worked into the rain gutter, and trimmed flush with the top edge of the gutter, just as we did with the main top.

Inside Edges

We are now at the stage of finishing the inner edges of the top, which will be somewhat of a tedious task. At this point, you will not pull or stretch the material. Just cut and glue. There are a lot of windshield clip posts that need to have the top material trimmed away while the edges are glued down. This is the final step in our project.

Lift up on the unfastened edge of the top and brush contact adhesive on the metal of the windshield opening and backside of the vinyl top material. When the glue has flashed, press the material into place. Use a pair of scissors to remove the small sliver of material from around the spring clip post. Do not cut too much of the material; just remove enough to allow the vinyl material to lay flat against the metal. The use of a plastic trim stick or upholsterer's regulator will help you get the material tightly in place around the post.

After the top material has been secured, it must be trimmed squarely with the bottom of the glass channel. You do not want any of the vinyl top material under the window glass. This will cause an unsafe condition that can create a leaky windshield or even lead to the glass improperly adhering to the body of the car.

To trim the material, run a razor blade or utility knife along the bottom edge of the channel to cleanly cut through the fabric. Remove the extra material and clean away any contact adhesive with a rag dampened with an appropriate adhesive remover. Repeat this procedure on the rear window opening.

Adding the Clips

Now is the time to install the window trim clips. These little spring clips are needed to hold the decorative window trim moldings in place after the glass has been installed. Replacing the clips now is safer and easier than after the glass has been set.

The spring clips snap in place over the clip stud. You can install them with a dedicated clip tool or use a door panel–lifting tool to set the clip in place.

Ready for Glass

Remove the plastic draping from the car and clean off any accidental glue overspray that may be on the top. The body trim molding can be installed along with the stainless-steel drip rail moldings.

Now that the top is finished, the new windshield and rear window glass can be installed and this car can get back on the road.

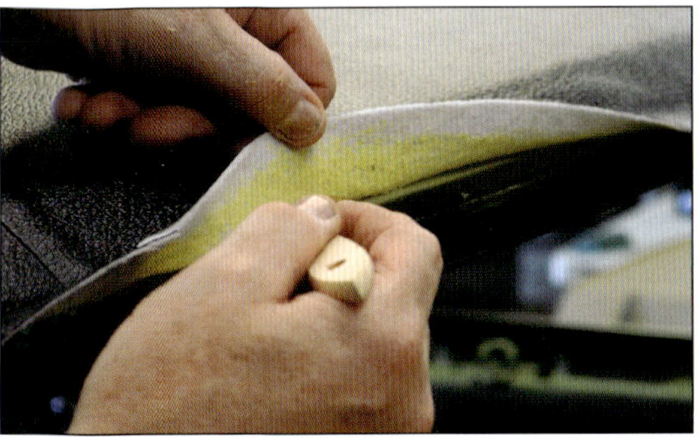

Glue is applied with a brush to the unfinished edge of the vinyl top material along the front of the car. After the material is pressed into place, it is trimmed to allow the proper installation of the windshield and trim molding.

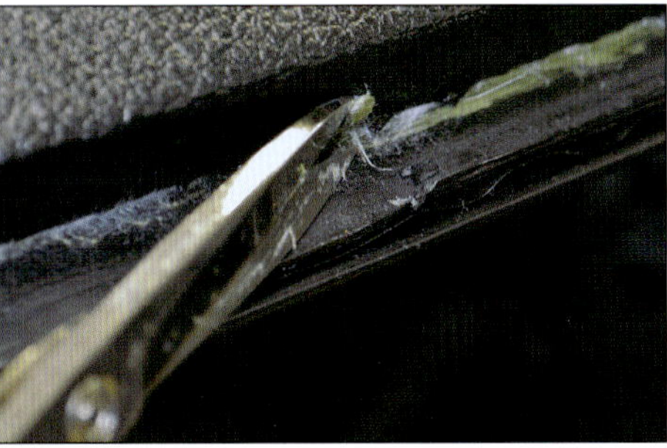

Preventative measures are taken to remove excessive bulk from around the barrel of the spring clip stud. Cut away a small amount of the top material to help the trim fastener fit better and allow the clip to work properly.

It may be the small things that make a big difference when working on a project. This small spring clip is used to attach the windshield trim molding. Install it before the glass is set to make finishing the trim a breeze.

The new vinyl top has given this 1969 Impala a sophisticated and stylish beauty. The formal look of a vinyl top can transform any car from a plain Jane to a Cinderella Classic in a matter of hours.

Auto Custom Carpets Inc.
P.O. Box 1350
1429 Noble St.
Anniston, AL 36202
800-325-8216
accmats.com

Al Knoch Interiors
9010 N. Desert Blvd.
Canutillo, TX 79835
800-880-8080
alknochinteriors.com

Berry's Staple Remover
Lubbock, TX 79423
806-799-5252
berrysstapleremover.com

CARS Inc.
2600 Bond St.
Rochester, MI 48309
248-853-8900
carsinc.com

Ciadella Interiors
3116 S. 52nd St.
Tempe, AZ 85282
800-875-8390
ciadellainteriors.com

Corvette Central
13550 Three Oaks Rd.
Sawyer, MI 49125
800 345-4122
corvettecentral.com

Corvette Pacifica
8981 La Lina Ave.
Atascadero, CA 93422
800-488-7671
corvettepacifica.com

C.S. Osborne & Co.
125 Jersey St.
Harrison, NJ 07029
973-483-3232
csosborne.com

Distinctive Industries
10618 Shoemaker Ave.
Santa Fe Springs, CA
    90670
800-421-9777
distinctiveindustries.com

Eckler's
7980 Grissom Pkwy.
Titusville, FL 32780
877-815-5799
ecklers.com

Electron Top
126-15 89th Ave.
Richmond Hill, NY 11418
800-221-4476
electrontop.com

Fabric Supply Inc.
3434 2nd St. N.
Minneapolis, MN 55412
800-645-9998
fabricsupply.com

Hydro-E-Lectric
5530 Independence Ct.
Punta Gorda, FL 33982
941-639-0437
hydroe.com

Jiffy Steamer Company,
    LLC
4462 Ken-Tenn Hwy.
Union City, TN 38261
800-525-4339
jiffysteamer.com

Legendary Auto Interiors
121 West Shore Blvd.
Newark, NJ 14513
800-363-8804
legendaryautointeriors,com

Master Appliance Corp.
2420 18th St.
Racine, WI 53403
800-558-9413
masterappliance.com

Metro Moulded Parts Inc.
11610 Jay St. NW
Coon Rapids, MN 55448
800-878-2237
metrommp.com

Milwaukee Tool
13135 West Lisbon Rd.
Brookfield, WI 53005
800-729-3878
milwaukeetool.com

Original Parts Group Inc.
1770 Saturn Way
Seal Beach, CA 90740
800-243-8355
opgi.com

PUI Interiors (Parts Unlim-
    ited Inc.)
2801 Interior Way
La Grange, KY 40031
800-342-0610
puiinteriors.com

Rochford Supply
7624 Boone Ave. N. Ste.
    200
Brooklyn Park, MN 55428
866-681-7401
rochfordsupply.com

Solderwld Inc.
2050 N. 300
Spanish Fork, UT 84660
info@solderweld.com

The Parts Place Inc.
630 Enterprise Ave.
Dekalb, IL 60115
630-365-1800
thepartsplaceinc.com

Top Flight Automotive
    (formerly Corvette
    America)
100 Classic Car Dr.
Reedsville, PA 17084
833-486-7354
topflightautomotive.com

Trim Parts
2175 Deerfield Rd.
Lebanon, OH 45036
513-934-0815
trimparts.com

Year One
P.O. Box 521
Braselton, GA 30517
800-932-7663
Year One.com

Wolfsteins Pro-Series
3040 Amwiler Rd. Ste. A
Atlanta, GA 30360
800-377-4700
wolfsteins.com